AF522552

History of English Language

HISTORY
of
English Language

Satish Malhotra

OMEGA PUBLICATIONS
NEW DELHI-110 002 (INDIA)

OMEGA PUBLICATIONS
4378/4B, G-4 JMD House
Murari Lal Street, Ansari Road
Daryaganj, New Delhi - 110 002
Phone : 011-23278062,9811787417
e-mail : omega_publications@yahoo.com

Edition : 2023

ISBN : 978-81-8455-141-9

Price : 1395/-

PRINTED IN INDIA

Published by Mahender Garg for Omega Publications, New Delhi- 110002
Printed at Tarun Offest Press-Delhi-110053

Preface

The present book of the English language really started with the arrival of three Germanic tribes who invaded Britain during the 5th century AD. Most of the Celtic speakers were pushed west and north by the invaders - mainly into what is now Wales, Scotland and Ireland. The Angles came from English and their language was called Englisc - from which the words England and English are derived.

English. Old English did not sound or look like English today. Native English speakers now would have great difficulty understanding Old English. Nevertheless, about half of the most commonly used words in Modern English have Old English roots. For a period there was a kind of linguistic class division, where the lower classes spoke English and the upper classes spoke French. In the 14th century English became dominant in Britain again, but with many French words added. This language is called Middle English.

The end of Middle English, a sudden and distinct change in pronunciation (the Great Vowel Shift) started, with vowels being pronounced shorter and shorter. From the 16th century the British had contact with many peoples from around the world. This, and the Renaissance of Classical learning, meant that many new words and phrases entered the language.

The main difference between Early Modern English and Late Modern English is vocabulary. Late Modern English has many more words, arising from two principal factors: firstly, the Industrial Revolution and technology created a need for new words; secondly, the British Empire at its height covered one quarter of the earth's surface, and the English language adopted foreign words from many countries.

Today, American English is particularly influential, due to the USA's dominance of cinema, television, popular music, trade and technology (including the Internet). But there are many other varieties of English around the world, including for example Australian English, New Zealand English, Canadian English, South African English, Indian English and Caribbean English.

Satish Malhotra

CONTENTS

	Preface	*v*
1.	Introduction	1
2.	Changing of Languages	21
3.	The Contact of English with Other Languages	52
4.	The Norman Conquest and the Subjection of English	94
5.	Language Changing after 1200–1500	118
6.	Middle English a Period of Great Change	156
7.	Changing Conditions in the Modern Age	206
8.	The Importanceof Language in the Ninteenth Century	269
	Bibliography	328

a Semitic people, the Phoenicians, who exerted a considerable influence upon the Hellenic world.

Into this mixture of often little-known populations and languages the Greeks penetrated from the north shortly after a date about 2000 B.C. The entrance of the Hellenes into the Aegean was a gradual one and proceeded in a series of movements by groups speaking different dialects of the common language. They spread not only through the mainland of Greece, absorbing the previous populations, but also into the islands of the Aegean and the coast of Asia Minor. The earliest great literary monuments of Greek are the Homeric poems the *Iliad* and the *Odyssey*, believed to date from the eighth century B.C. Of the Greek language we recognize five principal dialectal groups: the Ionic, of which Attic is a subdialect, found (except for Attic) in Asia Minor and the islands of the Aegean Sea; Aeolic in the north and northeast; Arcadian-Cyprian in the Peloponnesus and Cyprus; Doric, which later replaced Arcadian in the Peloponnesus; and Northwest Greek in the north central and western part of the Greek mainland. Of these, Attic, the dialect of the city of Athens, is by far the most studied. It owes its supremacy partly to the dominant political and commercial position attained by Athens in the fifth century, partly to the great civilization that grew up there. The achievements of the Athenians in architecture and sculpture, in science, philosophy, and literature in the great age of Pericles (495–429 B.C.) and in the century following were extremely important for subsequent civilization. In Athens were assembled the great writers of Greece—the dramatists Aeschylus, Euripides, and Sophocles in tragedy, Aristophanes in comedy, the historians Herodotus and Thucydides, the orator Demosthenes, the philosophers Plato and Aristotle. Largely because of the political and cultural prestige of Athens, the Attic dialect became the basis of a *koiné* or common Greek that from the fourth century superseded the other dialects, the conquests of Alexander (336–323 B.C.) established this language in Asia Minor and Syria, in Mesopotamia and Egypt, as the general language of the eastern Mediterranean for purposes of international communication. It is chiefly familiar to modern

1

Introduction

It was observed by that remarkable twelfth-century chronicler Henry of Huntington that an interest in the past was one of the distinguishing characteristics of humans as compared with the other animals. The medium by which speakers of a language communicate their thoughts and feelings to others, the tool with which they conduct their business or the government of millions of people, the vehicle by which has been transmitted the science, the philosophy, the poetry of the culture is surely worthy of study. It is not to be expected that everyone should be a philologist or should master the technicalities of linguistic science. But it is reasonable to assume that a liberally educated person should know something of the structure of his or her language, its position in the world and its relation to other tongues, the wealth of its vocabulary together with the sources from which that vocabulary has been and is being enriched, and the complex relationships among the many different varieties of speech that are gathered under the single name of the English language. The diversity of cultures that find expression in it is a reminder that the history of English is a story of cultures in contact during the past 1,500 years. It understates matters to say that political, economic, and social forces influence a language. These forces shape the language in every aspect, most obviously in the number and spread of its speakers, and in what is called "the sociology of language," but also in the meanings of words, in the accents of the spoken language, and even in the structures of the grammar. The history of a language is intimately bound up with the history of the peoples who speak it. The purpose of this book, then, is to treat the history of English not only as being of interest to the specialized student but also as a cultural subject within the view of all educated people, while including enough references to technical matters to make clear the scientific principles involved in linguistic evolution.

Foundations of Work on Language

The English language of today reflects many centuries of development. The political and social events that have in the course of English history so profoundly affected the English people in their national life have generally had a recognizable effect on their language. The Roman Christianizing of Britain in 597 brought England into contact with Latin civilization and made significant additions to our vocabulary. The Scandinavian invasions resulted in a considerable mixture of the two peoples and their languages. The Norman Conquest made English for two centuries the language mainly of the lower classes while the nobles and those associated with them used French on almost all occasions. And when English once more regained supremacy as the language of all elements of the population, it was an English greatly changed in both form and vocabulary from what it had been in 1066. In a similar way the Hundred Years' War, the rise of an important middle class, the Renaissance, the development of England as a maritime power, the expansion of the British Empire, and the growth of commerce and industry, of science and literature, have, each in their way, contributed to the development of the language. References in scholarly and popular works to "Indian English," "Caribbean English," "West African English," and other regional varieties point to the fact that the political and cultural history of the English language is not simply the history of the British Isles and of North America but a truly international history of quite divergent societies, which have caused the language to change and become enriched as it responds to their own special needs.

Growth and Decay

Moreover, English, like all other languages, is subject to that constant growth and decay that characterize all forms of life. It is a convenient figure of speech to speak of languages as living and as dead. Although we rarely think of language as something that possesses life apart from the people who speak it, as we can think of plants or of animals, we can observe in speech something like the process of change that characterizes the life of living things. When a language ceases to change, we call it a dead language. Classical Latin is a dead language because it has not changed for nearly 2,000 years. The change that is constantly going on in a living language can be most easily seen in the vocabulary. Old words die out, new words are added, and existing words change their meaning. Much of the vocabulary of Old English has been lost, and the development of new words to meet new conditions is one of the most familiar phenomena of our language. Change of meaning can be illustrated from any page of Shakespeare. *Nice* in Shakespeare's day meant *foolish; rheumatism* signified a cold in the head. Less familiar but no less real is the change of pronunciation. A slow but steady alteration, especially in the vowel sounds, has characterized English throughout its history. Old English *stân* has become our *stone; cû* has become *cow.* Most of these changes are so regular as to be capable of classification under what are called "sound laws." Changes likewise occur in the grammatical forms of a language. These may be the result of gradual phonetic modification, or they may result from the desire for uniformity commonly felt where similarity of function or use is involved. The person who says I*knowed* is only trying to form the past tense of this verb after the pattern of the past tense of so many verbs in English. This process is known as the operation of *analogy,* and it may affect the sound and meaning as well as the form of words. Thus it will be part of our task to trace the influences that are constantly at work, tending to alter a language from age to age as spoken and written, and that have brought about such an extensive alteration in English as to make the English language of 1000 quite unintelligible to English speakers of 2000.

The Importance of a Language

It is natural for people to view their own first language as having intrinsic advantages over languages that are foreign to them. However, a scientific approach to linguistic study combined with a consideration of history reminds us that no language acquires importance because of what are assumed to be purely internal advantages. Languages become important because of events that shape the balance of power among nations. These political, economic, technological, and military events may or may not reflect favorably, in a moral sense, on the peoples and states that are the participants; and certainly different parties to the events will have different interpretations of what is admirable or not. It is clear, however, that the language of a powerful nation will acquire importance as a direct reflection of political, economic, technological, and military strength; so also will the arts and sciences expressed in that language have advantages, including the opportunities for propagation. The spread of arts and sciences through the medium of a particular language in turn reinforces the prestige of that language. Internal deficits such as an inadequate vocabulary for the requirements at hand need not restrict the spread of a language. It is normal for a language to acquire through various means, including borrowing from other languages, the words that it needs. Thus, any language among the 4,000 languages of the world could have attained the position of importance that the half-dozen or so most widely spoken languages have attained if the external conditions had been right. English, French, German, and Spanish are important languages because of the history and influence of their populations in modern times; for this reason they are widely studied outside the country of their use. Sometimes the cultural importance of a nation has at some former time been so great that its language remains important long after it has ceased to represent political, commercial, or other greatness. Greek, for example, is studied in its classical form because of the great civilization preserved and recorded in its literature; but in its modern form as spoken in Greece today the Greek language does not serve as a language of wider communication.

The Importance of English

In numbers of speakers as well as in its uses for international communication and in other less quantifiable measures, English is one of the most important languages of the world. Spoken by more than 380 million people in the United Kingdom, the United States, and the former British Empire, it is the largest of the Western languages. English, however, is not the most widely used native language in the world. Chinese, in its eight spoken varieties, is known to 1.3 billion people in China alone. Some of the European languages are comparable to English in reflecting the forces of history, especially with regard to European expansion since the sixteenth century. Spanish, next in size to English, is spoken by about 330 million people, Portuguese by 180 million, Russian by 175 million, German by 110 million, French by 80 million native speakers (and a large number of second-language speakers), Italian by 65 million. A language may be important as a *lingua franca* in a country or region whose diverse populations would otherwise be unable to communicate. This is especially true in the former colonies of England and France whose colonial languages have remained indispensable even after independence and often in spite of outright hostility to the political and cultural values that the European languages represent.

French and English are both languages of wider communication, and yet the changing positions of the two languages in international affairs during the past century illustrate the extent to which the status of a language depends on extralinguistic factors. It has been said that English is recurringly associated with practical and powerful pursuits. Joshua A. Fishman writes: "In the Third World (excluding former anglophone and francophone colonies) French is considered *more suitable* than English for only one function: opera. It is considered *the equal of English* for reading good novels or poetry and for personal prayer (the local integrative language being widely viewed as superior to both English and French in this connection). But outside the realm of aesthetics, the Ugly Duckling reigns supreme."[1] The ascendancy of English as measured by numbers of speakers in various activities does not depend on nostalgic attitudes toward the originally English-speaking people or toward the language itself. Fishman makes the point that English is less loved but more used; French is more loved but less used. And in a world where "econo-technical superiority" is what counts, "the real 'powerhouse' is still English. It doesn't have to worry about being loved because, loved or not, it works. It makes the world go round, and few indeed can afford to 'knock it.'"[2]

If "econo-technical superiority" is what counts, we might wonder about the relative status of English and Japanese. Although spoken by 125 million people in Japan, a country that has risen to economic and technical dominance since World War II, the Japanese language has yet few of the roles in international affairs that are played by English or French. The reasons are rooted in the histories of these languages. Natural languages are not like programming languages such as Fortran or LISP, which have gained or lost international currency over a period of a decade or two. Japan went through a two-century period of isolation from the West (between 1640 and 1854) during which time several European languages were establishing the base of their subsequent expansion.

The Future of the English Language

The extent and importance of the English language today make it reasonable to ask whether we cannot speculate as to the probable position it will occupy in the future. It is admittedly hazardous to predict the future of nations; the changes during the present century in the politics and populations of the developing countries have confounded predictions of fifty years ago. Since growth in a language is primarily a matter of population, the most important question to ask is which populations of the world will increase most rapidly. Growth of population is determined by the difference between the birth rate and the death rate and by international migration. The single most important fact about current trends is that the Third World countries of Africa, Asia, and Latin America have experienced a sharp drop in mortality during the twentieth century without a corresponding drop in the birth rate. As a result, the population of these areas is younger and growing faster than the population of the industrialized countries of Europe and North America. The effect of economic development upon falling growth rates is especially clear in Asia, where Japan is growing at a rate only slightly higher than that of Europe, while southern Asia—India, Pakistan, Bangladesh—is growing at a rate more than twice as high. China is growing at a moderate rate, between that of Europe and southern Asia, but with a population in excess of one billion, the absolute increase will be very high. According to a recent United Nations analysis, by 2050 the United

States will be the only developed country among the world's twenty most populous nations, whereas in 1950 at least half of the top ten were industrial nations. The population of the less developed countries is expected to grow from 4.9 billion in 2000 to 8.2 billion in 2050, while the more developed countries will hold at 1.2 billion.[3] India is expected to replace China as the world's most populous nation in half a century, with a concomitant growth in Hindi and Bengali, already among the top five languages in the world. The one demographic fact that can be stated with certainty is that the proportion of the world's population in the economically developed countries will shrink during the next half century in comparison with the proportion in the presently developing countries. Since most of the native speakers of English live in the developed countries, it can be expected that this group will account for a progressively smaller proportion of the world's population. Counteracting the general trend somewhat is the exceptional situation in the United States, the only country among the more developed ones that is growing at slightly more than a replacement rate instead of actually declining.

If the future of a language were merely a matter of the number who speak it as a first language, English would appear to be entering a period of decline after four centuries of unprecedented expansion. What makes this prospect unlikely is the fact that English is widely used as a second language and as a foreign language throughout the world. The number of speakers who have acquired English as a second language with near native fluency is estimated to be between 350 and 400 million. If we add to first and second language speakers those who know enough English to use it more or less effectively as a foreign language, the estimates for the total number of speakers range between one and one and a half billion. In some of the developing countries that are experiencing the greatest growth, English is one of the official languages, as it is in India, Nigeria, and the Philippines. The situation is complex because of widely varying government policies that are subject to change and that often do not reflect the actual facts. Although there are concerted efforts to establish the vernaculars in a number of countries—Hindi in India, Swahili in Tanzania, Tagalog in the Philippines—considerable forces run counter to these efforts and impede the establishment of national languages. In some countries English is a neutral language among competing indigenous languages, the establishment of any one of which would arouse ethnic jealousies. In most developing countries communications in English are superior to those in the vernacular languages. The unavailability of textbooks in Swahili has slowed the effort to establish that language as the language of education in Tanzania. Yet textbooks and other publications are readily available in English, and they are produced by countries with the economic means to sustain their vast systems of communications.

The complex interaction of these forces defies general statements of the present situation or specific projections into the distant future. Among European languages it seems likely that English, German, and Spanish will benefit from various developments. The breakup of the Soviet Union and the increasing political and economic unification of Western Europe are already resulting in the shifting fortunes of Russian and German. The independent states of the former Soviet Union are unlikely to continue efforts to make Russian a common language throughout that vast region, and the presence of a unified Germany will reinforce the importance of the German language, which already figures prominently as a language of commerce in the countries of Eastern Europe. The growth of Spanish, as of Portuguese, will come mainly from the rapidly increasing population of Latin America, while the growth in English will be most notable in its use throughout the world as a second language. It is also likely that pidgin and creole varieties of English will become increasingly widespread in those areas where English is not a first language.

English as a World Language

That the world is fully alive to the need for an international language is evident from the number of attempts that have been made to supply that need artificially. Between 1880 and 1907 fifty-three universal languages were proposed. Some of these enjoyed an amazing, if temporary, vogue. In 1889 Volapük claimed nearly a million adherents. Today it is all but forgotten. A few years later Esperanto experienced a similar vogue, but interest in it now is kept alive largely by local groups and organizations. Apparently the need has not been filled by any of the laboratory products so far created to fill it. And it is doubtful if it ever can be filled in this way. An artificial language might serve some of the requirements of business and travel, but no one has proved willing to make it the medium of political, historical, or scientific thought, to say nothing of literature. The history of language policy in the twentieth century makes it unlikely that any government will turn its resources to an international linguistic solution that benefits the particular country only indirectly. Without the support of governments and the educational institutions that they control, the establishment of an artificial language for the world will be impossible. Recent history has shown language policy continuing to be a highly emotional issue, the language of a country often symbolizing its independence and nationalism.

The emotions that militate against the establishment of an artificial language work even more strongly against the establishment of a single foreign language for international communication. The official languages of the United Nations are English, French, Russian, Spanish, Chinese, and Arabic. Since it is not to be expected that the speakers of any of these six languages will be willing to subordinate their own language to any of the other five, the question is rather which languages will likely gain ascendancy in the natural course of events. Two centuries ago French would have appeared to have attained an undisputed claim to such ascendancy. It was then widely cultivated throughout Europe as the language of polite society, it was the diplomatic language of the world, and it enjoyed considerable popularity in literary and scientific circles. During the nineteenth century its prestige, though still great, gradually declined. The prominence of Germany in all fields of scientific and scholarly activity made German a serious competitor. Now more scientific research is probably published in English than in any other language, and the preeminence of English in commercial use is undoubted. The revolution in communications during the twentieth century has contributed to the spread of several European languages, but especially of English because of major broadcasting and motion picture industries in the United States and Great Britain. It will be the combined effect of economic and cultural forces such as these, rather than explicit legislation by national or international bodies, that will determine the world languages of the future.

Since World War II, English as an official language has claimed progressively less territory among the former colonies of the British Empire while its actual importance and number of speakers have increased rapidly. At the time of the first edition of this history (1935), English was the official language of one-fourth of the earth's surface, even if only a small fraction of the population in parts of that area actually knew English. As the colonies gained independence, English continued to be used alongside the vernaculars. In many of the new countries English is either the primary language or a necessary second language in the schools, the courts, and business. The extent of its use varies with regional history and current government policy, although stated policy often masks the actual complexities. In Uganda, for example, where no language is spoken as a first language by more than 16 percent of the population, English is the one official language; yet less than one percent of the population speaks it as a first language. In India, English was to serve transitional purposes only until 1965, but it continues to be used officially with Hindi and fourteen other national languages. In Tanzania, Swahili is the one official language, but English is still indispensable in the schools and the high courts. It is nowhere a question of substituting English for the native speech. Nothing is a matter of greater patriotic feeling than the mother tongue. The question simply concerns the use of English, or some other widely known idiom, for inter-national communication. Braj B.Kachru notes that it is a clear fact of history that English is in a position of unprecedented power: "Where over 650 artificial languages have failed, English has succeeded; where many other natural languages with political and economic power to back them up have failed, English has succeeded. One reason for this dominance of English is its propensity for acquiring new identities, its power of assimilation, its adaptability for 'decolonization' as a language, its manifestation in a range of varieties, and above all its suitability as a flexible medium for literary and other types of creativity across languages and cultures."[4] Kachru left open the question of whether the cultures and other languages of the world are richer or poorer because of "the global power and hegemony of English," and he called for a full discussion of the question.

Recent awareness of "endangered languages" and a new sensitivity to ecolinguistics have made clear that the success of English brings problems in its wake. The world is poorer when a language dies on average every two weeks. For native speakers of English as well, the status of the English language can be a mixed blessing, especially if the great majority of English speakers remain monolingual. Despite the dominance of English in the European Union, a British candidate for an international position may be at a disadvantage compared with a young EU citizen from Bonn or Milan or Lyon who is nearly fluent in English. Referring to International English as "Global," one observer writes: "The emergence of Global is not an unqualified bonus for the British... for while we have relatively easy access to Global, so too do well-educated mainland Europeans, who have other linguistic assets besides."[5]

A similarly mixed story complicates any assessment of English in the burgeoning field of information technology. During the 1990s the explosive growth of the Internet was extending English as a world language in ways that could not have been foreseen only a few years earlier. The development of the technology and software to run the Internet took place in the United States, originally as ARPANET (the Advanced Research Project Agency Network), a communication system begun in 1969 by the U.S. Department of Defense in conjunction with military contractors and universities. In 2000 English was the dominant language of the Internet, with more than half of the Internet hosts located in the United States and as many as three-fourths in the United States and other English-speaking countries. The protocols by which ASCII code was transmitted were developed for the English alphabet, and the writing systems for languages such as Japanese, Chinese, and Korean presented formidable problems for use on the World Wide Web. The technology that made knowledge of English essential also facilitated online English-language instruction in countries such as China, where demand for English exceeds the available teachers. However, changes in the Internet economy are so rapid that it is impossible to predict the future of English relative to other languages in this global system. It is increasingly clear that online shoppers around the world prefer to use the Internet in their own language and that English-language sites in the United States have lost market share to local sites in other countries. In September 2000 Bill Gates predicted that English would be the language of the Web for the next ten years because accurate computerized translation would be more than a decade away. Yet four months later China announced the world's first Chinese-English Internet browser with a reported translation accuracy of 80 percent.[6]

Assets and Liabilities

Because English occupies such a prominent place in international communication, it is worth pausing to consider some of the features that figure prominently in learning English as a foreign language. Depending on many variables in the background of the learner, some of these features may facilitate the learning of English, and others may make the effort more difficult. All languages are adequate for the needs of their culture, and we may assume without argument that English shares with the other major languages of Europe the ability to express the multiplicity of ideas and the refinements of thought that demand expression in our modern civilization. The question is rather one of simplicity. How readily can English be learned by the non-native speaker? Does it possess characteristics of vocabulary and grammar that render it easy or difftcult to acquire? To attain a completely objective view of one's own language is no simple matter. It is easy to assume that what we in infancy acquired without sensible difficulty will seem equally simple to those attempting to learn it in maturity. For most of us, learning any second language requires some effort, and some languages seem harder than others. The most obvious point to remember is that among the many variables in the difficulty of learning a language as an adult, perhaps the most important is the closeness of the speaker's native language to the language that is being learned. All else equal, including the linguistic skill of the individual learner, English will seem easier to a native speaker of Dutch than to a native speaker of Korean.

Linguists are far from certain how to measure complexity in a language. Even after individual features have been recognized as relatively easy or difficult to learn, the weighting of these features within a single language varies according to the theoretical framework assumed. In an influential modern theory of language, the determination of the difficulty of specific linguistic structures falls within the study of "markedness," which in turn is an important part of "universal grammar," the abstract linguistic principles that are innate for all humans. By this view, the grammar of a language consists of a "core," the general principles of the grammar, and a "periphery," the more marked structures that result from historical development, borrowing, and other processes that produce "parameters" with different values in different languages.[7]

One may think that the loss of many inflections in English, as discussed in § 10, simplifies the language and makes it easier for the learner. However, if a result of the loss of inflections is an increase in the markedness of larger syntactic structures, then it is uncertain whether the net result increases or decreases complexity.

It is important to emphasize that none of the features that we are considering here has had anything to do with bringing about the prominence of English as a global language. The ethnographic, political, economic, technological, scientific, and cultural forces discussed above have determined the international status of English, which would be the same even if the language had had a much smaller lexicon and eight inflectional cases for nouns, as Indo-European did. The inflections of Latin did nothing to slow its spread when the Roman legions made it the world language that it was for several centuries.

Cosmopolitan Vocabulary

One of the most obvious characteristics of Present-day English is the size and mixed character of its vocabulary. English is classified as a Germanic language. That is to say, it belongs to the group of languages to which German, Dutch, Flemish, Danish, Swedish, and Norwegian also belong. It shares with these languages similar grammatical structure and many common words. On the other hand, more than half of its vocabulary is derived from Latin. Some of these borrowings have been direct, a great many through French, some through the other Romance languages. As a result, English also shares a great number of words with those languages of Europe that are derived from Latin, notably French, Italian, Spanish, and Portuguese. All of this means that English presents a somewhat familiar appearance to anyone who speaks either a Germanic or a Romance language. There are parts of the language which one feels one does not have to learn, or learns with little effort. To a lesser extent the English vocabulary contains borrowings from many other languages. Instead of making new words chiefly by the combination of existing elements, as German does, English has shown a marked tendency to go outside its own linguistic resources and borrow from other languages. In the course of centuries of this practice English has built up an unusual capacity for assimilating outside elements. We do not feel that there is anything "foreign" about the words *chipmunk, hominy, moose, raccoon,* and *skunk,* all of which we have borrowed from the Native American. We are not conscious that the words *brandy, cruller, landscape, measles, uproar,* and *wagon* are from Dutch. And so with many other words in daily use. From Italian come *balcony, canto, duet, granite, opera, piano, umbrella, volcano;* from Spanish, *alligator, cargo, contraband, cork, hammock, mosquito, sherry, stampede, tornado, vanilla;* from Greek, directly or indirectly, *acme, acrobat, anthology, barometer, catarrh, catastrophe, chronology, elastic, magic, tactics, tantalize,* and a host of others; from Russian, *steppe, vodka, ruble, troika, glasnost, perestroika;* from Persian, *caravan, dervish, divan, khaki, mogul, shawl, sherbet,* and ultimately from Persian *jasmine, paradise, check, chess, lemon, lilac, turban, borax,* and possibly *spinach.* A few minutes spent in the examination of any good etymological dictionary will show that English has borrowed from Hebrew and Arabic, Hungarian, Hindi-Urdu, Bengali, Malay, Chinese, the languages of Java, Australia, Tahiti, Polynesia, West Africa, and from one of the aboriginal languages of Brazil. And it has assimilated these heterogeneous elements so successfully that only the professional student of language is aware of their origin. Studies of vocabulary acquisition in second language learning support the impression that many students have had in studying a foreign language: Despite problems with *faux amis*—those words that have different meanings in two different languages—cognates generally are learned more rapidly and retained longer than words that are unrelated to words in the native language lexicon.[8] The cosmopolitan vocabulary of English with its cognates in many languages is an undoubted asset.

Inflectional Simplicity

A second feature that English possesses to a preeminent degree is inflectional simplicity. Within the Indo-European family of languages, it happens that the oldest, classical languages—

Sanskrit, Greek, and Latin—have inflections of the noun, the adjective, the verb, and to some extent the pronoun that are no longer found in modern languages such as Russian or French or German. In this process of simplifying inflections English has gone further than any other language in Europe. Inflections in the noun as spoken have been reduced to a sign of the plural and a form for the possessive case. The elaborate Germanic inflection of the adjective has been completely eliminated except for the simple indication of the comparative and the superlative degrees. The verb has been simplified by the loss of practically all the personal endings, the almost complete abandonment of any distinction between the singular and the plural, and the gradual discard of the subjunctive mood. The complicated agreements that make German difficult for the non-native speaker are absent from English.

It must not be thought that these developments represent a decay of grammar on the one hand or a Darwinian evolution toward progress, simplicity, and efficiency on the other. From the view of a child learning a first language, these apparent differences in complexity seem to matter not at all. As Hans H. Hock and Brian D.Joseph put it, "the speakers of languages such as English are quite happy without all those case endings, while speakers of modern 'case-rich' language such as Finnish or Turkish are just as happy with them."[9] However, it is worth trying to specify, as ongoing research in second language acquisition is doing, those features that facilitate or complicate the learning of English by adult speakers of various languages. To the extent that the simplification of English inflections does not cause complications elsewhere in the syntax, it makes the task easier for those learning English as a foreign language.

Natural Gender

English differs from all other major European languages in having adopted natural (rather than grammatical) gender. In studying other European languages the student must learn both the meaning of every noun and also its gender. In the Romance languages, for example, there are only two genders, and all nouns that would be neuter in English are there either masculine or feminine. Some help in these languages is afforded by distinctive endings that at times characterize the two classes. But even this aid is lacking in the Germanic languages, where the distribution of the three genders appears to the English student to be quite arbitrary. Thus in German *sonne* (sun) is feminine, *mond* (moon) is masculine, but *kind* (child), *mädchen* (maiden), and *weib* (wife) are neuter. The distinction must be constantly kept in mind, since it not only affects the reference of pronouns but also determines the form of inflection and the agreement of adjectives. In the English language all this was stripped away during the Middle English period, and today the gender of every noun in the dictionary is known instantly. Gender in

English is determined by meaning. All nouns naming living creatures are masculine or feminine according to the sex of the individual, and all other nouns are neuter.

Liabilities

The three features just described are undoubtedly of great advantage in facilitating the acquisition of English by non-native speakers. On the other hand, it is equally important to recognize the difficulties that the foreign student encounters in learning our language. One of these difficulties is the result of that very simplification of inflections which we have considered among the assets of English. It is the difficulty, of which foreigners often complain, of expressing themselves not only logically, but also idiomatically. An idiom is a form of expression peculiar to one language, and English is not alone in possessing such individual forms of expression. All languages have their special ways of saying things. Thus a German says *was für ein Mann* (what for a man) whereas in English we say *what kind of man;* the French say *il fait froid* (it makes cold) whereas we say *it is cold.* The mastery of idioms depends largely on memory. The distinction between *My husband isn 't up yet* and *My husband isn 't down yet* or the quite contradictory use of the word *fast* in *go fast* and *stand fast* seems to the foreigner to be without reasonable justification. It is doubtful whether such idiomatic expressions are so much more common in English than in other languages—for example, French—as those learning English believe, but they undoubtedly loom large in the minds of nonnative speakers.

A more serious criticism of English by those attempting to master it is the chaotic character of its spelling and the frequent lack of correlation between spelling and pronunciation. Writing is merely a mechanical means of recording speech. And theoretically the most adequate system of spelling is that which best combines simplicity with consistency. In alphabetic writing an ideal system would be one in which the same sound was regularly represented by the same character and a given character always represented the same sound. None of the European languages fully attains this high ideal, although many of them, such as Italian or German, come far nearer to it than English. In English the vowel sound in *believe, receive, leave, machine, be, see,* is in each case represented by a different spelling. Conversely the symbol *a* in *father, hate, hat,* and many other words has nearly a score of values. The situation is even more confusing in our treatment of the consonants. We have a dozen spellings for the sound of *sh: shoe, sugar, issue, nation, suspicion, ocean, nauseous, conscious, chaperon, schist, fuchsia, pshaw.* This is an extreme case, but there are many others only less disturbing, and it serves to show how far we are at times from approaching the ideal of simplicity and consistency.

We shall consider in another place the causes that have brought about this diversity. We are concerned here only with the fact that one cannot tell how to spell an English word by its pronunciation or how to pronounce it by its spelling. English-speaking children undoubtedly waste much valuable time during the early years of their education in learning to spell their own language, and to the foreigner our spelling is appallingly difficult. To be sure, it is not without its defenders. There are those who emphasize the useful way in which the spelling of an English word often indicates its etymology. Again, a distinguished French scholar has urged that since we have preserved in thousands of borrowed words the spelling that those words have in their original language, the foreigner is thereby enabled more easily to recognize the word. It has been further suggested that the very looseness of our orthography makes less noticeable in the written language the dialectal differences that would be revealed if the various parts of the English-speaking world attempted a more phonetic notation on the basis of their local pronunciation. And some phonologists have argued that this looseness permits an economy in representing words that contain predictable phonological alternants of the same morphemes (e.g., *divine~divinity, crime~criminal).* But in spite of these considerations, each of which is open to serious criticism, it seems as though some improvement might be effected without sacrificing completely the advantages claimed. That such improvement has often been felt to be desirable is evident from the number of occasions on which attempts at reform have been made. In the early part of the twentieth century a movement was launched, later supported by Theodore Roosevelt and other influential people, to bring about a moderate degree of simplification (see § 231). It was suggested that since we wrote *has* and *had* we could just as well write *hav* instead of *have,* and in the same way *ar* and *wer* since we wrote *is* and *was.* But though logically sound, these spellings seemed strange to the eye, and the advantage to be gained from the proposed simplifications was not sufficient to overcome human conservatism or indifference or force of habit. It remains to be seen whether the extension of English in the future will some day compel us to consider the reform of our spelling from an impersonal and, indeed, international point of view. For the present, at least, we do not seem to be ready for simplified spelling.

REFERENCES

1. Joshua A.Fishman, "Sociology of English as an Additional Language," in *The Other Tongue: English across Cultures,* ed. Braj B.Kachru (2nd ed., Urbana, IL, 1992), p. 23.
2. Fishman, p. 24.
3. Barbara Crossette, "Against a Trend, U.S. Population Will Bloom, U.N. Says," *New York Times* (February 28, 2001), Section A, p. 6.

4. Braj B.Kachru, "The Sacred Cows of English," *English Today,* 16 (1988), 8.
5. Michael Toolan, "Linguistic Assets," *English Today,* 15.2 (April 1999), 29.
6. AP Online, 12 September 2000; Xinhua News Agency, 15 January 2001.
7. See Vivian J.Cook, "Chomsky's Universal Grammar and Second Language Learning," *Applied Linguistics,* 6 (1985), 2-18, and her *Second Language Learning and Language Teaching (2nd* ed., London, 1996).
8. See Gunilla M.Andeman and Margaret A.Rogers, *Words, Words, Words: The Translator and the Language Learner,* especially Paul Meara, "The Classical Research in L2 Vocabulary Acquisition," pp. 27-40, and Peter Newmark, "Looking at English Words in Translation," pp. 56-62 (Clevedon, UK, 1996). See also John Holmes and Rosinda G.Ramos, "False Friends and Reckless Guessers: Observing Cognate Recognition Strategies," in *Second Language Reading and Vocabulary Learning,* ed. Thomas Huckin, Margot Haynes, and James Coady (Norwood, NY, 1993), pp. 86-108.
9. *Language History, Language Change, and Language Relationship* (Berlin, 1996), p. 144.

2

Changing of Languages

In the mind of the average person language is associated with writing and calls up a picture of the printed page. From Latin or French as we meet it in literature we get an impression of something uniform and relatively fixed. We are likely to forget that writing is only a conventional device for recording sounds and that language is primarily speech. Even more important, we tend to forget that the Latin of Cicero or the French of Voltaire is the product of centuries of development and that language as long as it lives and is in actual use is in a constant state of change.

Speech is the product of certain muscular movements. The sounds of language are produced by the passage of a current of air through cavities of the throat and face controlled by the muscles of these regions. Any voluntary muscular movement when constantly repeated is subject to gradual alteration. This is as true of the movements of the organs of speech as of any other parts of the body, and the fact that this alteration takes place largely without our being conscious of it does not change the fact or lessen its effects. Now any alteration in the position or action of the organs of speech results in a difference in the sound produced. Thus each individual is constantly and quite unconsciously introducing slight changes in his or her speech. There is no such thing as uniformity in language. Not only does the speech of one community differ from that of another, but the speech of different individuals of a single community, even different members of the same family, also is marked by individual peculiarities. Members of a group, however, are influenced by one another, and there is a general similarity in the speech of a given community at any particular time. The language of any district or even country is only the sum total of the individual speech habits of those composing it and is subject to such changes as occur in the speech of its members, so far as the changes become general or at least common to a large part of it.

Although the alteration that is constantly going on in language is for the most part gradual and of such nature as often to escape the notice of those in whose speech it is taking place, after a period of time the differences that grow up become appreciable. If we go back to the eighteenth century we find Alexander Pope writing

Good-nature and good-sense must even join;

To err is human, to forgive, divine..

where it is apparent that he pronounced *join as jine.* Again he writes.

Here thou, great Anna! whom three realms obey,

Dost sometimes counsel take—and sometimes Tea.

It is demonstrable that he pronounced *tea* as *tay.* Elsewhere he rhymes *full—rule; give-believe; glass—place; ear—repair; lost—boast; thought—fault; obliged—besieged; reserve—starve.* Since Pope's time the pronunciation of at least one in each of these pairs has changed so that they are no longer considered good rhymes. If we go back to Chaucer, or still further, to King Alfred (871-899), we find still greater differences. King Alfred said *bân* (bone), *hû* (how), *hç ah* (high); in fact all the long vowels of his pronunciation have undergone such change as to make the words in which they occur scarcely recognizable to the typical English-speaking person today.

Dialectal Differentiation

As previously remarked, where constant communication takes place among the people speaking a language, individual differences become merged in the general speech of the community, and a certain conformity prevails. But if any separation of one community from another takes place and lasts for a considerable length of time, differences grow up between them. The differences may be slight if the separation is slight, and we have merely local dialects. On the other hand, they may become so considerable as to render the language of one district unintelligible to the speakers of another. In this case we generally have the development of separate languages. Even where the differentiation has gone so far, however, it is usually possible to recognize a sufficient number of features which the resulting languages still retain in common to indicate that at one time they were one. It is easy to perceive a close kinship between English and German. *Milch* and *milk, brot* and *bread, fleisch* and *flesh, wasser* and *water* are obviously only words that have diverged from a common form. In the same way a connection between Latin and English is indicated by such correspondences as *pater* with English *father,* or frâter with *brother,* although the difference in the initial consonants tends somewhat to obscure the relationship. When we notice that *father* corresponds to Dutch *vader,* Gothic *fadar,* Old Norse *faðir,* German *vater,* Greek *patçr,* Sanskrit *pitar-*, and Old Irish *athir* (with loss of the initial consonant), or that English *brother* corresponds to Dutch *broeder,* German *bruder,* Greek *phrâtçr,* Sanskrit *bhrâtar-,* Old Slavic *bratm,* Irish *brathair,* we are led to the hypothesis that the languages of a large part of Europe and part of Asia were at one time identical.

The Discovery of Sanskrit

The most important discovery leading to this hypothesis was the recognition that Sanskrit, a language of ancient India, was one of the languages of the group. This was first suggested in the latter part of the eighteenth century and fully established by the beginning of the nineteenth.[1] The extensive literature of India, reaching back further than that of any of the European languages, preserves features of the common language much older than most of those of Greek or Latin or German. It is easier, for example, to see the resemblance between the English word *brother* and the

Sanskrit *bhrâtar-than* between *brother* and *frâter.* But what is even more important, Sanskrit preserves an unusually full system of declensions and conjugations by which it became clear that the inflections of these languages could likewise be traced to a common origin. Compare the following forms of the verb *to be:*

Old English	*Gothic*	*Latin*	*Greek*	*Sanskrit*	
eom	*(am)*	im	sum	eimi	asmi
eart	*(art)*	is	es	ei	asi
is	*(is)*	ist	est	esti	asti
sindon	*(are)*	sijum	sum us	esmen	smas
sindon	*(are)*	sijuþ	estis	este	stha
sindon	*(are)*	sind	sunt	eisi	santi

The Sanskrit forms particularly permit us to see that at one time this verb had the same endings ***(mi, si, ti, mas, tha, nti)*** as were employed in the present tense of other verbs, for example:

Sanskrit	*Greek*	
dádâmi	dídômi	*(I give)*
dádâsi	dídôs	
dádâti	dídôsi	
dadmás	dídomen	*dial.* didomes)
datthá	dídote	
dáda(n)ti	didóâsi	*dial.* dídonti)

The material offered by Sanskrit for comparison with the other languages of the group, both in matters of vocabulary and inflection, was thus of the greatest importance. When we add that Hindu grammarians had already gone far in the analysis of the language, had recognized the roots, classified the formative elements, and worked out the rules according to which certain sound-changes occurred, we shall appreciate the extent to which the discovery of Sanskrit contributed to the recognition and determination of the relation that exists among the languages to which it was allied.

Grimm's Law

A further important step was taken when in 1822 a German philologist, Jacob Grimm, following up a suggestion of a Danish contemporary, Rasmus Rask, formulated an explanation that systematically accounted for the correspondences between certain consonants in the Germanic languages and those found for example in Sanskrit, Greek, and Latin. His explanation, although subsequently modified and in some of the details of its operation still a subject of dispute, is easily illustrated. According to Grimm, a *p* in Indo-European, preserved as such in Latin and Greek, was changed to an f in the Germanic languages. Thus we should look for the English equivalent of Latin *piscis* or *pçs* to begin with an *f,* and this is what we actually find, in *fish* and *foot* respectively. What is true of *p* is true also of t and *k:* in other words, the original voiceless stops *(p, t, k)* were changed to fricatives *(f, þ, h)*. So Latin trçs=English *three,* Latin centum=English *hundred.* A similar correspondence can be shown for certain other groups of consonants,[2]

and the Consequently Sanskrit *bhárâmi* (Greek φερω)=English *bear,* Sanskrit dhâ=English *do,* Latin *hostis* (from **ghostis)*=English *guest.* And the original voiced stops *(b, d, g)* changed to voiceless ones in the Germanic languages, so that Latin *cannabis=English hemp* (showing also the shift of initial *k* to *h),* Latin decem=English *ten,* Latin genu=English *knee.* In High German some of these consonants underwent a further change, known as the Second or High German Sound-Shift. It accounts for such differences as we see in English *open* and German *offen,* English *eat* and German essen.formulation of these correspondences is known as Grimm's Law. The cause of the change is not known. It must have taken place sometime after the segregation of the Germanic from neighboring dialects of the parent language. There are words in Finnish borrowed from Germanic that do not show the change and that therefore must have resulted from a contact between Germanic and Finnish before the change occurred. There is also evidence that the shifting was still occurring as late as about the fifth century B.C. It is often assumed that the change was due to contact with a non-Germanic population. The contact could have resulted from the migration of the Germanic tribes or from the penetration of a foreign population into Germanic territory. Whatever its cause, the Germanic sound-shift is the most distinctive feature marking off the Germanic languages from the languages to which they are related.

Certain apparent exceptions to Grimm's Law were subsequently explained by Karl Verner and others. It was noted that between such a pair of words as Latin *centum* and English *hundred the* correspondence between the c and h was according to rule, but that between the *t* and *d* was not. The *d* in the English word should have been a voiceless fricative, that is, a *þ*. In 1875 Verner showed that when the Indo-European accent was not on the vowel immediately preceding, such voiceless fricatives became voiced in Germanic. In West Germanic the resulting *ð* became a *d,* and the word *hundred* is therefore quite regular in its correspondence with *centum.* The explanation was of importance in accounting for the forms of the preterite tense in many strong verbs. Thus in Old English the preterite singular of *cweþan* (to say) is *ic cwæþ* but the plural is *we*

In the latter word the accent was originally on the ending, as it was in the past participle *(cweden),* where we also have a d.[3] The formulation of this explanation is known as Verner's Law, and it was of great significance in vindicating the claim of regularity for the sound-changes that Grimm's Law had attempted to define.

The Indo-European

The languages thus brought into relationship by descent or progressive differentiation from a parent speech are conveniently called a family of languages. Various names have been used to designate this family. In books written a century ago the term

Aryan was commonly employed. It has now been generally abandoned and when found today is used in a more restricted sense to designate the languages of the family located in India and the plateau of Iran. A more common term is *Indo-Germanic,* which is the most usual designation among German philologists, but it is open to the objection of giving undue emphasis to the Germanic languages. The term now most widely employed is *Indo-European,* suggesting more clearly the geographical extent of the family. The parent tongue from which the Indo-European languages have sprung had already become divided and scattered before the dawn of history. When we meet with the various peoples by whom these languages are spoken they have lost all knowledge of their former association. Consequently we have no written record of the common Indo-European language. By a comparison of its descendants, however, it is possible to form a fair idea of it and to make plausible reconstructions of its lexicon and inflections.

The surviving languages show various degrees of similarity to one another, the similarity bearing a more or less direct relationship to their geographical distribution. They accordingly fall into eleven principal groups: Indian, Iranian, Armenian, Hellenic, Albanian, Italic, Balto-Slavic, Germanic, Celtic, Hittite, and Tocharian. These are the branches of the Indo-European family tree, and we shall look briefly at each.[4]

Indian

The oldest literary texts preserved in any Indo-European language are the Vedas or sacred books of India. These fall into four groups, the earliest of which, the *Rig-veda,* is a collection of about a thousand hymns, and the latest, the *Atharva-veda,* a body of incantations and ritual formulas connected with many kinds of current religious practice. These books form the basis of Brahman philosophy and for a long time were preserved by oral transmission by the priests before being committed to writing. It is therefore difftcult to assign definite dates to them, but the oldest apparently go back to nearly 1500 B.C. The language in which they are written is known as Sanskrit, or to distinguish it from a later form of the language, Vedic Sanskrit. This language is also found in certain prose writings containing directions for the ritual, theological commentary, and the like (the *Brahmanas),* meditations for the use of recluses (the *Aranyakas),* philosophical speculations (the *Upanishads),* and rules concerning various aspects of religious and private life (the *Sutras).*

The use of Sanskrit was later extended to various writings outside the sphere of religion, and under the influence of native grammarians, the most important of whom was Panini in the fourth century B.C., it was given a fixed, literary form. In this form it is known as Classical Sanskrit. Classical Sanskrit is the medium of an extensive Indian literature including the two great national epics the *Mahabharata* and the *Ramayana,* a large body of drama, much lyric and didactic poetry, and numerous works of a scientific and philosophical character. It is still cultivated as a learned language and formerly held a place in India similar to that occupied by Latin in medieval Europe. At an early date it ceased to be a spoken language.

Alongside of Sanskrit there existed a large number of local dialects in colloquial use, known as Prakrits. A number of these eventually attained literary form; one in particular, Pâli, about the middle of the sixth century B.C. became the language of Buddhism. From these various colloquial dialects have descended the present languages of India, Pakistan, and Bangladesh, spoken by some 600 million people. The most important of these are Hindi, Urdu (the official language of Pakistan), Bengali (the official language of Bangladesh), Punjabi, and Marathi. Urdu is by origin and present structure closely related to Hindi, both languages deriving from Hindustani, the colloquial form of speech that for four centuries was widely used for intercommunication throughout northern India. Urdu differs from Hindi mainly in its considerable mixture of Persian and Arabic and in being written in the Perso-Arabic script instead of Sanskrit characters. Romany, the language of the Gypsies, represents a dialect of northwestern India which from about the fifth century A.D. was carried through Persia and into Armenia and from there has spread through Europe and even into America.

Iranian

Northwest of India and covering the great plateau of Iran is the important group of languages called Iranian. The Indo-European population that settled this region had lived and probably traveled for a considerable time in company with the members of the Indian branch. Such an association accounts for a number of linguistic features that the two groups have in common. Of the people engaged in this joint migration a part seem to have decided to settle down on this great tableland while the rest continued on into India.

Subsequent movements have carried Iranian languages into territories as remote as southern Russia and central China. From early times the region has been subjected to Semitic influence, and many of the early texts are preserved in Semitic scripts that make accurate interpretation difftcult. Fortunately the past few decades have seen the recovery of a number of early documents, some containing hitherto unknown varieties of Iranian speech, which have contributed greatly to the elucidation of this important group of languages.

The earliest remains of the Iranian branch fall into two divisions, an eastern and a western, represented respectively by Avestan and Old Persian. Avestan is the language of the Avesta, the sacred book of the Zoroastrians. It is some-times called Zend, although the designation is not wholly accurate. Strictly speaking, Zend is the language only of certain late commentaries on the sacred text. The Avesta consists of two parts, the Gathas or metrical sermons of Zoroaster, which in their original form may go back as far as 1000 B.C., and the Avesta proper, an extensive collection of hymns, legends, prayers, and legal prescriptions that seem to spring from a period several hundred years later. There is considerable difference in the language of the two parts. The other division of Iranian, Old Persian, is preserved only in certain cuneiform inscriptions which record chiefly the conquests and achievements of Darius (522-486 B.C.) and Xerxes (486-466 B.C.). The most extensive is a trilingual record (in Persian, Assyrian, and Elamite) carved in the side of a mountain at

Behistan, in Media, near the city of Kirmanshah. Besides a representation of Darius with nine shackled prisoners, the rebel chieftains subjugated by him, there are many columns of text in cuneiform characters. A later form of this language, found in the early centuries of our era, is known as Middle Iranian or Pahlavi, the official language of church and state during the dynasty of the Sassanids (A.D. 226-652). This is the ancestor of modern Persian. Persian, also known as Farsi, has been the language of an important culture and an extensive literature since the ninth century. Chief among the literary works in this language is the great Persian epic the *Shahnamah.* Persian contains a large Arabic admixture so that today its vocabulary seems almost as much Arabic as Iranian. In addition to Persian, several other languages differing more or less from it are today in use in various provinces of the old empire—Afghan or Pashto and Baluchi in the eastern territories of Afghanistan and Pakistan, and Kurdish in the west, in Kurdistan. Besides these larger groups there are numerous languages and dialects in the highlands of the Pamir, on the shores of the Caspian Sea, and in the valleys of the Caucasus.

Armenian

Armenian is found in a small area south of the Caucasus Mountains and the eastern end of the Black Sea. The penetration of Armenians into this region is generally put between the eighth and sixth centuries B.C. They evidently came into their present location by way of the Balkans and across the Hellespont. The newcomers conquered a population of which remnants are still perhaps to be found in the Caucasus and whose language may have influenced Armenian in matters of accent and phonology. Armenian shows a shifting of certain consonants that recalls the shifts in Germanic described above and which, like those, may be due to contact with other languages. Moreover, like the south Caucasus languages, Armenian lacks grammatical gender. Armenian is not linked to any other special group of the Indo-European family by common features such as connect Indian with Iranian. It occupies a somewhat isolated position. But in ancient times Thrace and Macedonia were occupied by two peoples—the

Thraco-Phrygians, whom Herodotus mentions as very numerous, and the Macedonians, whose kings for a time adopted Greek and enjoyed a short but brilliant career in Greek history. The Phrygians, like the Armenians, passed into Asia Minor and are familiar to us as the Trojans of Homer. Their language shows certain affinities with Armenian; and, if we knew more about it, we should probably find in it additional evidence for the early association of the two peoples. Unfortunately we have only scanty remains of Phrygian and Macedonian—chiefly place names, glosses, and inscriptions—enough merely to prove their Indo-European character and give a clue to the linguistic affiliation.

Armenian is known to us from about the fifth century of our era through a translation of the Bible in the language. There is a considerable Armenian literature, chiefly historical and theological. The Armenians for several centuries were under Persian domination, and the vocabulary shows such strong Iranian influence that Armenian was at one time classed as an Iranian language. Numerous contacts with Semitic languages, with Greek, and with Turkish have contributed further to give the vocabulary a rich character.

Hellenic

At the dawn of history the Aegean was occupied by a number of populations that differed in race and in language from the Greeks who entered these regions later. In Lemnos, in Cyprus, and Crete especially, and also on the Greek mainland and in Asia Minor, inscriptions have been found written in languages which may in some cases be Indo-European and in others are certainly not. In the Balkans and in Asia Minor were languages such as Phrygian and Armenian, already mentioned, and certainly Indo-European, as well as others (Lydian, Carian, and Lycian) that show some resemblance to the Indo-European type but whose relations are not yet determined. In Asia Minor the Hittites, who spoke an Indo-European language, possessed a kingdom that lasted from about 2000 to 1200 B.C.; and in the second millennium B.C. the eastern Mediterranean was dominated, at least commercially, by a Semitic people, the Phoenicians, who exerted a considerable influence upon the Hellenic world.

Into this mixture of often little-known populations and languages the Greeks penetrated from the north shortly after a date about 2000 B.C. The entrance of the Hellenes into the Aegean was a gradual one and proceeded in a series of movements by groups speaking different dialects of the common language. They spread not only through the mainland of Greece, absorbing the previous populations, but also into the islands of the Aegean and the coast of Asia Minor. The earliest great literary monuments of Greek are the Homeric poems the *Iliad* and the *Odyssey,* believed to date from the eighth century B.C. Of the Greek language we recognize five principal dialectal groups: the Ionic, of which Attic is a subdialect, found (except for Attic) in Asia Minor and the islands of the Aegean Sea; Aeolic in the north and northeast; Arcadian-Cyprian in the Peloponnesus and Cyprus; Doric, which later replaced Arcadian in the Peloponnesus; and Northwest Greek in the north central and western part of the Greek mainland. Of these, Attic, the dialect of the city of Athens, is by far the most studied. It owes its supremacy partly to the dominant political and commercial position attained by Athens in the fifth century, partly to the great civilization that grew up there. The achievements of the Athenians in architecture and sculpture, in science, philosophy, and literature in the great age of Pericles (495-429 B.C.) and in the century following were extremely important for subsequent civilization. In Athens were assembled the great writers of Greece—the dramatists Æchylus, Euripides, and Sophocles in tragedy, Aristophanes in comedy, the historians Herodotus and Thucydides, the orator Demosthenes, the philosophers Plato and Aristotle. Largely because of the political and cultural prestige of Athens, the Attic dialect became the basis of a *koiné* or common Greek that from the fourth century superseded the other dialects; the conquests of Alexander (336-323 B.C.) established this language in Asia Minor and Syria, in Mesopotamia and Egypt, as the general language of the eastern Mediterranean for purposes of international communication. It is chiefly familiar to modern times as the language of the New Testament and, through its employment in Constantinople and the Eastern Empire, as the medium of an extensive Byzantine literature. The various dialects into which the language of modern Greece is divided represent the local differentiation of this *koiné* through the course of centuries. At the present time two varieties of Greek (commonly called Romaic, from its being the language of the eastern Roman Empire) are observable in Greece. One, the popular or demotic, is the natural language of the people; the other, the "pure," represents a conscious effort to restore the vocabulary and even some of the inflections of ancient Greek. Both are used in various schools and universities, but the current official position favors the demotic.

Albanian

Northwest of Greece on the eastern coast of the Adriatic is the small branch named Albanian. It is possibly the modern remnant of Illyrian, a language spoken in ancient times in the northwestern Balkans, but we have too little knowledge of this early tongue to be sure. Moreover, our knowledge of Albanian, except for a few words, extends back only as far as the fifteenth century of our era, and, when we first meet with it, the vocabulary is so mixed with Latin, Greek, Turkish, and Slavonic elements—owing to conquests and other causes—that it is somewhat difficult to isolate the original Albanian. For this reason its position among the languages of the Indo-European family was slow to be recognized. It was formerly classed with the Hellenic group, but since the beginning of the present century it has been recognized as an independent member of the family.

Italic

The Italic branch has its center in Italy, and to most people Italy in ancient times suggests Rome and the language of Rome, Latin. But the predominant position occupied by Latin in the historical period should not make us forget that Latin was only one of a number of languages once found in this area. The geographical situation and agreeable climate of the peninsula seem frequently and at an early date to have invited settlement, and the later population represents a remarkably diverse culture. We do not know much about the early neolithic inhabitants; they had been largely replaced or absorbed before the middle of the first millennium B.C. But we have knowledge of a number of languages spoken in different districts by the sixth century before our era. In the west, especially from the Tiber north, a powerful and aggressive people spoke Etruscan, a non-Indo-European language. In northwestern Italy was situated the little known Ligurian. Venetic in the northeast and Messapian in the extreme southeast were apparently offshoots of Illyrian, already mentioned. And in southern Italy and Sicily, Greek was the language of numerous Greek colonies. All these languages except Etruscan were apparently Indo-European. More important were the languages of the Italic branch itself. Chief of these in the light of subsequent history was Latin, the language of Latium and its principal city, Rome. Closely related to Latin were Umbrian, spoken in a limited area northeast of Latium, and Oscan, the language of the Samnites and of most of the southern peninsula except the extreme projections. All of these languages were in time driven out by Latin as the political influence of Rome became dominant throughout Italy. Nor was the extension of Latin limited to the Italian peninsula. As Rome colonized Spain and Gaul, the district west of the Black Sea, northern Africa, the islands of the Mediterranean, and even Britain, Latin spread into all these regions until its limits became practically co-terminous with those of the Roman Empire. And in the greater part of this area it has remained the language, though in altered form, to the present day.

The various languages that represent the survival of Latin in the different parts of the Roman Empire are known as the Romance or Romanic languages. Some of them have since spread into other territory, particularly in the New World. The most extensive of the Romance languages are French, Spanish, Portuguese, and Italian. French is primarily the language of northern France, although it is the language of literature and education throughout the country. In the Middle Ages it was divided into a number of dialects, especially Norman, Picard, Burgundian, and that of the Ile-de-France. But with the establishment of the Capetians as kings of France and the rise of Paris as the national capital, the dialect of Paris or the Ile-de-France gradually won recognition as the official and literary language. Since the thirteenth century the Paris dialect has been standard French. In the southern half of France the language differed markedly from that of the north. From the word for *yes* the language of the north was called the *langue d'oïl,* that of the south the *langue d'oc.* Nowadays the latter is more commonly known as Provençal. In the twelfth and thirteenth centuries it was the language of an innovative literature, the lyrics of the troubadours, but it has since yielded to the political and social prestige of French. A patriotic effort at the close of the nineteenth century, corresponding to similar movements on behalf of Irish, Norwegian, and other submerged languages, failed to revive the language as a medium of literature, and Provençal is today merely the regional speech of southern France. In the Iberian peninsula Spanish and Portuguese, because of their proximity and the similar conditions under which they have developed, have remained fairly close to each other. In spite of certain differences of vocabulary and inflection and considerable differences in the sounds of the spoken language, a Spaniard can easily read Portuguese. The use of Spanish and Portuguese in Central and South America and in Mexico has already been referred to. Italian has had the longest continuous history in its original location of any of the Romance languages, because it is nothing more than the Latin language as this language has continued to be spoken in the streets of Rome from the founding of the city. It is particularly important as the language of Dante, Petrarch, and Boccaccio, and the vernacular language in which the cultural achievements of the Renaissance first found expression. Romanian is the easternmost of the Romance languages, representing the continued influence of Roman legions in ancient Dacia. In addition to these six languages, about a dozen Romance languages are spoken by smaller populations. Other languages on the Iberian peninsula are Catalan, a language of the northeast but also found in Corsica, and one with an extensive literature, and Galician in the northwest, similar to both Spanish and Portuguese, having features of each, just as Catalan shares features of Provençal and Spanish. The Rhaeto-Romanic group in southeastern Switzerland and adjacent parts of the Tyrol includes Romansch and dialects in which Germanic elements are especially prominent. Walloon is a dialect of French spoken in southern Belgium.

The Romance languages, while representing a continuous evolution from Latin, are not derived from the Classical Latin of Cicero and Virgil. Classical Latin was a literary language with an elaborate and somewhat artificial grammar. The spoken language of the masses, Vulgar Latin (from Latin *vulgus,* the common people), differed from it not only in being simpler in inflection and syntax but also to a certain extent divergent in vocabulary. In Classical Latin the word for horse was *equus,* but the colloquial word was *caballus.* It is from the colloquial word that French *cheval,* Provençal *caval,* Spanish *caballo,* Italian *cavallo,* etc., are derived. In like manner where one wrote *pugna* (fight), *urbs* (city), *os* (mouth), the popular, spoken word was *battualia* (Fr. *bataille), villa* (Fr. *ville), bucca* (Fr. *bouche).* So *verberare=battuere* (Fr. *battre), osculari=basiare* (Fr. *baiser), ignis=focus* (Fr. *feu), ludus=jocus* (Fr. *jeu).* It was naturally the Vulgar Latin of the marketplace and camp that was carried into the different Roman provinces. That this Vulgar Latin developed differently in the different parts of Europe in which it was introduced is explained by a number of factors. In the first place, as Gustav Gröber observed, Vulgar Latin, like all language, was constantly changing, and because the Roman provinces were established at different times and the language carried into them would be more or less the language then spoken in the streets of Rome, there would be initial differences in the Vulgar Latin of the different colonies.[5] These differences would be increased by separation and the influence of the languages spoken by the native populations as they adopted the new language. The Belgae and the Celts in Gaul, described by Caesar, differed from the Iberians in Spain. Each of these peoples undoubtedly modified Latin in accordance with the grammars of their own languages, as normally happens when languages come into contact.[6] It is not difficult to understand the divergence of the Romance languages, and it is not the least interesting feature of the Romance group that we can observe here in historical time the formation of a number of distinct languages from a single parent speech. Such a process of progressive differentiation has brought about, over a greater area and a longer period of time, the differences among the languages of the whole Indo-European family.

Balto-Slavic

The Balto-Slavic branch covers a vast area in the eastern part of Europe. It falls into two groups, the Baltic and the Slavic, which, in spite of differences, have sufficient features in common to justify their being classed together.

There are three Baltic languages: Prussian, Latvian, and Lithuanian. Prussian is now extinct, having been displaced by German since the seventeenth century. Latvian is the language of about two million people in Latvia. Lithuanian is spoken by about three million people in the Baltic state of Lithuania. It is important among the Indo-European languages because of its conservatism. It is sometimes said that a Lithuanian peasant can understand certain simple phrases in Sanskrit. Although the statement implies too much, Lithuanian preserves some very old features that have disappeared from practically all the other languages of the family.

The similarities among the various languages of the Slavic group indicate that as late as the seventh or eighth century of our era they were practically identical or at least were united by frequent intercourse. At the present time they fall into three divisions: East Slavic, West Slavic, and South Slavic. The first two still cover contiguous areas, but the South Slavs, in the Balkan peninsula, are now separated from the rest by a belt of non-Slavic people, the Hungarians and the Romanians.

The earliest form in which we possess a Slavic language is a part of the Bible and certain liturgical texts translated by the missionaries Cyril and Methodius in the ninth century. The language of these texts is South Slavic, but it probably approximates with considerable closeness the common Slavic from which all the Slavic languages have come. It is known as Old Church Slavonic or Old Bulgarian and continued to be used throughout the Middle Ages and indeed well into modern times as the ecclesiastical language of the Orthodox Church.

East Slavic includes three varieties. Chief of these is Russian, the language of about 175 million people. It is found throughout the north, east, and central parts of Russia, was formerly the court language, and is still the official and literary language of the country. Belorussian (White Russian) is the language of about 9 million people in Belarus and adjacent parts of Poland. Ukrainian is spoken by about 50 million people in Ukraine. Nationalist ambitions have led the Ukrainians to stress the difference between their language and Russian, a difference that, from the point of view of mutual intelligibility, causes some difficulty with the spoken language. Russian, Belorussian, and Ukrainian constitute the largest group of Slavic languages.

West Slavic includes four languages. Of these Polish is the largest, spoken by about 36 million people within Poland, by about 5 million in the United States, and by smaller numbers in the former Soviet Union and other countries. Next in size are the mutually intelligible languages of the Czech Republic and Slovakia: Czech, spoken by about 10 million people, and Slovak, spoken by 5 million. The fourth language, Sorbian, is spoken by only 100,000 people in Germany, in a district a little northeast of Dresden.

South Slavic includes Bulgarian, Serbo-Croatian, Slovene, and modern Macedonian, not to be confused with ancient Macedonian, an Indo-European language of uncertain affinity. Bulgarian was spoken in the eastern part of the Balkan peninsula when the region was overrun by a non-Slavic people. But the conqueror was absorbed by the conquered and adopted their language. Modern Bulgarian has borrowed extensively from Turkish for the language of everyday use, while the literary language is much closer to

Russian. The history of Yugoslavia and the fortunes of its languages illustrate tragically the quip that "a language is a dialect with an army and a navy." Serbo-Croatian represents the union of Serbian, formerly the language of Serbia, and Croatian, spoken before World War I by the Croats of Bosnia and Croatia. The two languages are practically identical but use different alphabets. With the breakup of Yugoslavia we can expect references to Serbo-Croatian to be replaced by references separately to Serbian and Croatian. Slovene is spoken by about 1.5 million people in Slovenia, at the head of the Adriatic.

The Slavic languages constitute a more homogeneous group than the languages of some of the other branches. They have diverged less from the common type than those, for example, of the Germanic branch and in a number of respects preserve a rather archaic aspect. Moreover the people speaking the Baltic languages must have lived for many centuries in fairly close contact with the Slavs after the two had separated from the parent Indo-European community.

Germanic

The common form that the languages of the Germanic branch had before they became differentiated is known as Germanic or Proto-Germanic. It antedates the earliest written records of the family and is reconstructed by philologists in the same way as is the parent Indo-European. The languages descended from it fall into three groups: East Germanic, North Germanic, and West Germanic.

The principal language of East Germanic is Gothic. By the third century the Goths had spread from the Vistula to the shore of the Black Sea and in the following century they were Christianized by a missionary named Ulfilas (311-383), whose father seems to have been a Goth and his mother a Greek (Cappadocian). Our knowledge of Gothic is almost wholly due to a translation of the Gospels and other parts of the New Testament made by Ulfilas. Except for some runic inscriptions in Scandinavia it is the earliest record of a Germanic language we possess. For a time the Goths played a prominent part in European history, including in their extensive conquests both Italy, by the Ostrogoths, and Spain, by the Visigoths. In these districts, however, their language soon gave place to Latin, and even elsewhere it seems not to have maintained a very tenacious existence. Gothic survived longest in the Crimea, where vestiges of it were noted down in the sixteenth century. To the East Germanic branch belonged also Burgundian and Vandalic, but our knowledge of these languages is confined to a small number of proper names.

North Germanic is found in Scandinavia, Denmark, Iceland, and the Faroe Islands. Runic inscriptions from the third century preserve our earliest traces of the language. In its earlier form the common Scandinavian language is conveniently spoken of as Old Norse. From about the eleventh century on, dialectal differences become noticeable. The Scandinavian languages fall into two groups: an eastern group including Swedish and Danish, and a western group including Norwegian and Icelandic. Norwegian ceased to be a literary language in the fourteenth century, and Danish (with Norwegian elements) is one written language of Norway.[7] Of the early Scandinavian languages Old Icelandic is by far the most literary. Iceland was colonized by settlers from Norway about A.D. 874 and early preserved a body of heroic literature unsurpassed among the Germanic peoples. Among the more important monuments are the Elder or Poetic Edda, a collection of poems that probably date from the tenth or eleventh century, the Younger or Prose Edda compiled by Snorri Sturluson (1178-1241), and about forty sagas, or prose epics, in which the lives and exploits of various traditional figures are related.

West Germanic is of chief interest to us as the group to which English belongs. It is divided into two branches, High and Low German, by the operation of a Second (or High German) Sound-Shift analogous to that described above as Grimm's Law. This change, by which West Germanic *p, t, k, d,* etc. were changed into other sounds, occurred about A.D. 600 in the southern or mountainous part of the Germanic area but did not take place in the lowlands to the north. Accordingly in early times we distinguish as Low German tongues Old Saxon, Old Low Franconian, Old Frisian, and Old English. The last two are closely related and constitute a special or Anglo-Frisian subgroup.[8] Old Saxon has become the essential constituent of modern Low German or Plattdeutsch; Old Low Franconian, with some mixture of Frisian and Saxon elements, is the basis of modern Dutch in the Netherlands and Flemish in northern Belgium; and Frisian survives in the Netherland province of Friesland, in a small part of Schleswig, in the islands along the coast, and other places. High German comprises a number of dialects (Middle, Rhenish, and East Franconian, Bavarian, Alemannic, etc.). It is divided chronologically into Old High German (before 1100), Middle High German (1100-1500), and Modern High German (since 1500). High German, especially as spoken in the midlands and used in the imperial chancery, was popularized by Luther's translation of the Bible (1522-1532) and since the sixteenth century has gradually established itself as the literary language of Germany.

Celtic

The Celtic languages formed at one time one of the most extensive groups in the Indo-European family. At the beginning of the Christian era the Celts were found in Gaul and Spain, in Great Britain, in western Germany, and northern Italy—indeed, they covered the greater part of Western Europe. A few centuries earlier their triumphal progress had extended even into Greece and Asia Minor. The steady retreat of Celtic before advancing Italic and Germanic tongues is one of the surprising phenomena of history. Today Celtic languages are found only in the far corners of France and the British Isles; in the areas in which they were once dominant they have left but little trace of their presence.

The language of the Celts in Gaul who were conquered by Caesar is known as Gallic. Since it was early replaced by Latin we know next to nothing about it. A few inscriptions, some proper names (cf. *Orgetorix)*, one fragmentary text, and a small number of words preserved in modern French are all that survive. With respect to the Celtic languages in Britain we are better off, although the many contradictory theories of Celticists[9] make it impossible to say with any confidence how the Celts came to England. The older view, which is now questioned, holds that the first to come were Goidelic or Gaelic Celts. Some of these may have been driven to Ireland by the later invaders and from there may have spread into Scotland and the Isle of Man. Their language is represented in modern times by Irish, Scottish Gaelic, and Manx. The later Brythonic Celts, after occupying for some centuries what is now England, were in turn driven westward by Germanic invaders in the fifth century. Some of the fugitives crossed over into Brittany. The modern representatives of the Brythonic division are Welsh, Cornish, and Breton.The remnants of this one-time extensive group of languages are everywhere losing ground at the present day. Spoken by minorities in France and the British Isles, these languages are faced with the competition of two languages of wider communication, and some seem destined not to survive this competition. Cornish became extinct in the eighteenth century, and Manx, once spoken by all the native inhabitants of the Isle of Man, has died out since World War II. In Scotland Gaelic is found only in the Highlands. It is spoken by 75,000 people, of whom fewer than 5,000 do not know English as well. Welsh is still spoken by about one-quarter of the people, but the spread of English among them is indicated by the fact that the number of those who speak only Welsh had dropped from 30 percent in 1891 to 2 percent in 1950 and is still slowly decreasing. Irish is spoken by about 500,000 people, most of whom are bilingual. Whether nationalist sentiment will succeed in arresting the declining trend that has been observable here as in the other Celtic territory remains to be seen. If language planning efforts fail, it seems inevitable that eventually another branch of the Indo-European family of languages will disappear.

Twentieth-century Discoveries

Besides the nine branches described above, discoveries in the twentieth century added two new groups to the family: Hittite and Tocharian. Until recently the Hittites have been known to us chiefly from references in the Old Testament. Abraham bought the burial place for Sarah from a Hittite (Gen. 23), and Bathsheba, whom David coveted, was the wife of Uriah the Hittite (2 Sam. 11). Their language was preserved only in a few uninterpreted documents. In 1907, however, an archaeological expedition uncovered the site of the Hittite capital in Asia Minor, at Boghazköi, about ninety miles east of Ankara, containing the royal archives of nearly 10,000 clay tablets. The texts were written in Babylonian cuneiform characters, and some were in the Babylonian language (Akkadian), the diplomatic language of the day. Most of the tablets, however, were in an unknown language. Although a number of different languages seem to have been spoken in the Hittite area, nine-tenths of the tablets are in the principal language of the kingdom. It is apparently not the original language of the district, but it has been given the name Hittite. The sudden opening up of so extensive a collection of texts has permitted considerable progress to be made in the study of this language. The most remarkable effect upon Indo-European studies has been the confirmation of a hypothesis made by Ferdinand de Saussure in 1879. On the basis of internal evidence Saussure had proposed for Indo-European certain sound patterns that did not occur in any of the languages then known. Twenty years after the discovery of the Hittite tablets it could be demonstrated that Saussure's phonological units, which had become known as "laryngeals," occurred in Hittite much as he had proposed for Indo-European. The number and phonetic features of laryngeals in Indo-European are still a matter of debate, but there is general agreement that at least one laryngeal must be posited for the parent language.[10] In the reconstruction of Indo-European syntax, Hittite has provided invaluable evidence. A strong argument can now be made that Hittite and the oldest hymns of the *Rig-veda* represent the Object-Verb structure of Indo-European, which by the time of Classical Greek and Latin had been largely modified to a Verb-Object pattern.[11] A large proportion of the Hittite vocabulary comes from a non-Indo-European source. The blending with foreign elements appears to be as great as in Albanian. By some scholars Hittite is treated as coordinate with Indo-European, and the period of joint existence is designated Indo-Hittite. It is sufficient, however, to think of Hittite as having separated from the Indo-European community some centuries (perhaps 500 years or more) before any of the other groups began to detach themselves.

Tocharian is the name given to the language in which some fragmentary texts were discovered in the early part of the present century in western China (Xinjiang Uygur). Some of them contain the name of a king who according to Chinese evidence reigned in the early part of the seventh century of our era. To the philologist the discovery is of some importance because the language belongs with the Hellenic, Italic, Germanic, and Celtic groups as a *centum* language rather than with the eastern or *satem* groups, with which we should expect it to be most closely related.[12]

The Home of the Indo-Europeans

It is obvious that if the languages just described represent the progressive differentiation of an original speech, this speech, which we may for convenience call the Indo-European language, must have been spoken by a population somewhere at some time. What can be learned of these people and their early location?

Concerning their physical character, practically nothing can be discerned. Continuity in language and culture does not imply biological descent. It is not an uncommon phenomenon in history for a people to give up their own language and adopt another. Sometimes they adopt the language of their conquerors, or of those whom they have conquered, or that of a people with whom they have simply become merged in a common territory. The Indo-European languages are spoken today in many cultures that until recently have had completely unrelated heritages. And to judge by the large variety of people who have spoken these languages from early times, it is quite possible that the people of the original Indo-European community already represented a wide ethnic diversity. Neither can we form any very definite idea of the date at which this people lived as a single, more or less coherent community. The period of their common life must have extended over a considerable stretch of time. It is customary to place the end of their common existence somewhere between 3500 and 2500 B.C.

With respect to the location of this community at a time shortly before their dispersal, we have at least a basis for inference. To begin with, we may assume that the original home was in that part of the world in which the languages of the family are chiefly to be found today, and we may omit from consideration Africa, Australia, and the American continents because we know that the extension of Indo-European languages in these areas has occurred in historical times. History and its related sciences, anthropology and archaeology, enable us also to eliminate certain other regions, such as the British Isles and the peninsulas of Southern Europe. Early literary tradition occasionally preserves traces of a people at a former stage in their history. The earliest books of the Hindus, for example, the Vedas, show an acquaintance with the Indus but not with the Ganges, indicating that the Indo-Europeans entered India from the northwest. In general, we may be fairly sure that the only regions in which it is reasonable to seek the original home of the Indo-European family are the mainland of Europe and the western part of Asia.Prior to the middle of the nineteenth century it was customary to assume an Asiatic home for the family. Such an opinion was the natural result of biblical tradition that placed the Garden of Eden in the neighborhood of Mesopotamia. This notion seemed to find confirmation in the discovery that Sanskrit, situated in Asia, not only was an Indo-European language but was also in many ways closest in form to the parent speech. Finally, Europe had seen the invasion of the Hun and the Turk and other Asiatic peoples, and it seemed natural to think of the movements of population as generally westward. But it was eventually recognized that such considerations formed a very slender basis for valid conclusions. It was observed that by far the larger part of the languages of this family have been in Europe from the earliest times to which our knowledge extends. Was it not more natural to suppose that the few representatives of the family in Asia should have made their way eastward than that nearly all the languages of Europe should have been the result of Asiatic incursions? In the course of the nineteenth century the comparative study of the Indo-European languages brought to light a number of facts that seemed to support such a supposition.

The evidence of language itself furnishes the most satisfactory criterion yet discovered on which to base a solution of the problem. It is obvious that those elements of the vocabulary which all or a considerable number of the branches of the family have in common must have formed a part of the original word-stock. In fact, a word common to two or three branches of the family, if the branches have not been in such proximity to each other as to suggest mutual influence, is likely to have been in the original language. Now the Indo-European languages generally have a common word for *winter* and for *snow.* It is likely that the original home of the family was in a climate that at certain seasons at least was fairly cold. On the other hand it is not certain that there was a common word for the sea. Instead, some branches of the family, when in the course of their wanderings they came into contact with the sea, had to develop their own words for the new conception. The original community was apparently an inland one, although not necessarily situated at a great distance from the coast. Still more instructive is the evidence of the fauna and flora known to the Indo-European community. As Harold H.Bender, whose *Home of the Indo-Europeans* is an admirable survey of the problem, puts it, "There are no anciently common Indo-European words for elephant, rhinoceros, camel, lion, tiger, monkey, crocodile, parrot, rice, banyan, bamboo, palm, but there are common words, more or less widely spread over Indo-European territory, for snow and freezing cold, for oak, beech, pine, birch, willow, bear, wolf, otter, beaver, polecat, marten, weasel, deer, rabbit, mouse, horse, ox, sheep, goat, pig, dog, eagle, hawk, owl, jay, wild goose, wild duck, partridge or pheasant, snake, tortoise, crab, ant, bee, etc." The force of this list is not in the individual items but in the cumulative effect of the two groups. Two words in it, however, have been the object of special consideration, *beech* and *bee.* A word corresponding to English *beech* is found in a number of Indo-

European languages and was undoubtedly part of the parent vocabulary. The common beech *(Fagus silvatica* Linnaeus) is of relatively limited range: It is practically confined to central Europe and is not native east of Poland and Ukraine.[13] The testimony of this word as to the original home of the Indo-European family would be persuasive if we could be sure that in the parent speech the word always designated what we know as the beech tree. But although this is its meaning in Latin and the Germanic languages, the word means "oak" in Greek, "elder" and "elm" in other languages.[14] In like manner the familiarity of the Indo-European community with the bee is evident from a common word for honey (Latin *mel,* Greek r[1] . * English *mildew,* etc.) and a common word for an intoxicating drink made from honey, called *mead* in Old English. The honeybee is indigenous over almost all Europe but is not found in those parts of Asia that have ever been considered as possible locations of the Indo-European community. From evidence such as this a European home for the Indo-European family has come to be considered more probable.

One other linguistic consideration that figured prominently in past discussions is worth citing because of its intrinsic interest. The branches of the Indo-European family fall into two well-defined groups according to the modification that certain consonants of the parent speech underwent in each. They are known as the *centum* and *satem* groups from the words for hundred in Latin and Avestan, respectively. The *centum* group includes the Hellenic, Italic, Germanic, and Celtic branches. To the *satem* group belong Indian, Iranian, Armenian, Balto-Slavic, and Albanian. A line running roughly from Scandinavia to Greece separates the two and suggests a line of cleavage from which dispersion eastward and westward might have taken place. Although this division has been cited as supporting a homeland in central Europe—in the general area of the present Baltic states—linguists have been unable to find additional characteristics that would have been associated with such a fundamental split. With increasing knowledge about the classification of dialects and the spread of linguistic change, it has become more plausible to view the *centum-satum* division as the result of a sound change in the eastern section of the Indo-European speech community that spread through Indo-Iranian, Armenian, Slavic, and into Baltic.[1]5 It is still useful to speak of *centum* and *satem* languages, but the classification itself does not permit deductions about early migrations.[16]

From the nature of the case, the original home of the Indo-European languages is still a matter of much uncertainty, and many divergent views are held by scholars. During the past thirty years impressive new discoveries have come from archaeological excavations in Russia and Ukraine. Graves in the steppe area between the River Don and the Urals have yielded evidence of an Indo-European "Kurgan" culture that existed north of the Caspian Sea from the fifth through the third millennia B.C. It is especially interesting to note the characteristic flora and fauna of the area during that period, as described by Marija Gimbutas: "The Kurgan people lived in the steppe and forest-steppe zone, but in the fifth and fourth millennia the climate was warmer and damper than at present and what is now the steppe zone was more forested. Mixed forests, including oak, birch, fir, beech, elder, elm, ash, aspen, apple, cherry and willow, extended along rivers and rivulets in which such forest animals as aurochs, elk, boar, wild horse, wolf, fox, beaver, squirrel, badger, hare, and roe deer were present."[17] Gimbutas, who first proposed the name of the culture, believes that the Kurgan people were the original Indo-Europeans, an opinion shared by many archaeologists and linguists. Some scholars accept the descriptions by American and Soviet archaeologists of the early periods of Kurgan culture but propose different directions of migration.[18] Although the Indo-European homeland may prove impossible to locate precisely, one can expect new evidence and new interpretations of old evidence from both linguistics and archaeology.[19] At present it is sufficient to observe that most of the proposed locations can be accommodated in the district east of the Germanic area stretching from central Europe to the steppes of southern Russia.

The civilization that had been attained by the people of this community at the time of their dispersal was approximately that known as neolithic. Copper was, however, already in use to a limited extent. The Indo-Europeans were no longer purely nomadic but had settled homes with houses and some agriculture. Here the evidence drawn from the vocabulary must be used with caution. We must be careful not to attribute to words their modern significance. The existence of a word for plow does not necessarily indicate anything more than the most primitive kind of implement. The Indo-Europeans raised grain and wool and had learned to spin and weave. They kept cattle and had for food not only the products of their own labor but such fruit and game as have always served the needs of primitive communities. They recognized the existence of a soul, believed in gods, and had developed certain ethical ideas. Without assuming complete uniformity of achievement throughout the area covered by this linguistic group, we may believe that the cultural development attained by the Indo-European was already considerable.

REFERENCES

1. In a famous paper of 1786, Sir William Jones, who served as a Supreme Court justice in India, proposed that the affinity of Sanskrit to Greek and Latin could be explained by positing a common, earlier source. See Garland Cannon, *The Life and Mind of Oriental Jones: Sir William Jones, the Father of Modern Linguistics* (Cambridge, UK, 1990), pp. 241-70.

2. The aspirates *(bh, dh, gh)* became voiced fricatives (í, ð, ã) then voiced stops *(b, d, g)*.

3. Cf. the change of s to *z* (which became r medially in West Germanic) in the form of *cçosan—cças—curon—-coren* noted in § 46.

4. For a recent theory of a "superfamily" called Nostratic, which would include a number of Eurasian language families, see Mark Kaiser and V.Shevoroshkin, "Nostratic," *Annual Review of Anthropology,* 17 (1988), 309-29. Vladislav M.Illich-Svitych and Aron Dolgopolsky have proposed that the Indo-European, the Afro-Asiatic, and the Dravidian language families, among others, are related in this superfamily. See also Colin Renfrew, "The Origins of Indo-European Languages," *Scientific American,* 261 (October 1989), 106-14.

5. The Roman colonies were established in Corsica and Sardinia in 231 B.C.Spain became a province in 197 B.C., Provence in 121 B.C., Dacia in A.D. 107.

6. The principle can be illustrated by a modern instance. The Portuguese spoken in Brazil has no sound like the English *th.* Brazilians who learn English consequently have difficulty in acquiring this sound and tend to substitute some other sound of their own language for it. They say *dis* for *this* and *I sink so for I think so.* If we could imagine English introduced into Brazil as Latin was introduced into Gaul or Spain, we could only suppose that the 165 million people of Brazil would universally make such a substitution, and the *th* would disappear in Brazilian English.

7. The union of Norway and Denmark for 400 years made Danish the language of culture. The latter half of the nineteenth century witnessed the beginning of a movement to make the Norwegian dialects into a national language *(Landsmål),* but this regeneration of the national speech has not succeeded in displacing Dano-Norwegian *(Bokmål* 'book language,' formerly *Riksmål* 'national language') as the dominant language. An amalgam of rural speech in normalized form *(Nynorsk* 'New Norwegian') is trying to compete in literature, the theater, etc. and is further complicating the linguistic problem. The whole conflict is treated historically in Einar Haugen, *Language Conflict and Language Planning: The Case of Modern Norwegian* (Cambridge, MA, 1966).

8. The West Germanic languages may be classified in different ways according to the features selected as the basis of division. Thus it is very common to divide them into an Anglo-Frisian group and a German group that includes Old Saxon. The division given in the text is none the less basic and is here retained for the sake of simplicity.

9. For a summary of these theories, see T.Rice Holmes, *Ancient Britain and the Invasions of Julius Caesar* (2nd ed., Oxford, 1936), pp. 444-58. See also Myles Dillon and Nora K.Chadwick, *The Celtic Realms* (2nd ed., London, 1972), chaps. 1, 2, and 9.

10. See Winfred P.Lehmann, *Proto-Indo-European Phonology* (Austin, TX, 1952), pp. 22-35, 85-114, *et passim,* and the essays in *Evidence for Laryngeals,* ed. Werner Winter (The Hague, 1965).

11. See Winfred P.Lehmann, *Proto-Indo-European Syntax* (Austin, TX, 1974), pp. 34-35, 238-51, *et passim.* See also Calvert Watkins, "Preliminaries to the Reconstruction of Indo-European Sentence Structure," in *Proceedings of the Ninth International Congress of Linguists,* ed. Horace G.Lunt (The Hague, 1964).

12. It has been suggested that the Tocharians, perhaps originally from the Balkans, formed part of the extensive migration from Europe into eastern Asia in the eighth and ninth centuries B.C., a migration that resulted in the overthrow of the Chou dynasty in China in 771 B.C. On the basis of archaeological and other evidence it is believed that Illyrians, Thracians, Phrygians, and Germanic peoples (especially Scandinavians) were among those that took part in the movement. See Robert Heine-Geldern, "Das Tocharerproblem und die Pontische Wanderung," *Saeculum, 2* (1951), 225-55.

13. This is the area of the "beech line," which earlier arguments drew while ignoring that the eastern beech *(Fagus orientalis)* differs very little from the common beech and constitutes about one-quarter of the tree population of the Caucasus east to the Caspian Sea. See Paul Friedrich, *Proto-Indo-European Trees* (Chicago, 1970), pp. 112-13.

14. The validity of the evidence drawn from the beech tree receives strong support from Wilhelm Wissmann, *Der Name der Buche* (Berlin, 1952; *Deutsche Akad. der Wissenschaften zu Berlin, Vorträge und Schriften,* Heft 50). Problems in the etymologies of the various forms are treated by George S.Lane, "The Beech Argument: A Re-evaluation of the Linguistic Evidence," *Zeitschrift für vergleichende Sprachforschung,* 81 (1967), 197-212.

15. See Winfred P.Lehmann, *Historical Linguistics* (3rd ed., New York, 1992), pp. 27-28.

16. Accordingly Tocharian, as a *centum* language in *satem* territory, is no longer regarded as the anomalous problem that it was in earlier studies. See George S.Lane, "Tocharian: Indo-European and Non-Indo-European Relationships," in *Indo-European and Indo-Europeans,* p. 79.

17. "Proto-Indo-European Culture: The Kurgan Culture during the Fifth, Fourth, and Third Millennia B.C.," in *Indo-European and Indo-Europeans,* pp. 159-60.

18. It has been argued that the traditional linguistic evidence in favor of the north European plain is sufficient to assume that the Kurgans migrated east at an early date. See Ward H.Goodenough, "The Evolution of Pastoralism and Indo-European Origins," in *Indo-European and Indo-Europeans,* pp. 253-65.

19. A significant example is Colin Renfrew's theory that reverses the direction of influence between the steppes and western Europe and sees the Indo-European culture spreading through the peaceful diffusion of agriculture rather than through conquest. See his *Archaeology and Language: ThePuzzle of Indo-European Origins* (Cambridge, UK, 1988).

3

The Contact of English with Other Languages

The language that was described in the preceding chapter was not merely the product of the dialects brought to England by the Jutes, Saxons, and Angles. These formed its basis, the sole basis of its grammar and the source of by far the largest part of its vocabulary. But other elements entered into it. In the course of the first 700 years of its existence in England it was brought into contact with at least three other languages, the languages of the Celts, the Romans, and the Scandinavians. From each of these contacts it shows certain effects, especially additions to its vocabulary. The nature of these contacts and the changes that were effected by them will form the subject of this chapter.

The Celtic Influence

Nothing would seem more reasonable than to expect that the conquest of the Celtic population of Britain by the Anglo-Saxons and the subsequent mixture of the two peoples should have resulted in a corresponding mixture of their languages; that consequently we should find in the Old English vocabulary numerous instances of words that the Anglo-Saxons heard in the speech of the native population and adopted. For it is apparent that the Celts were by no means exterminated except in certain areas, and that in most of England large numbers of them were gradually assimilated into the new culture. The Anglo-Saxon Chronicle reports that at Andredesceaster or Pevensey a deadly struggle occurred between the native population and the newcomers and that not a single Briton was left alive. The evidence of the place-names in this region lends support to the statement. But this was probably an exceptional case. In the east and southeast, where the Germanic conquest was fully accomplished at a fairly early date, it is probable that there were fewer survivals of a Celtic population than elsewhere. Large numbers of the defeated fled to the west. Here it is apparent that a considerable Celtic-speaking population survived until fairly late times. Some such situation is suggested by a whole cluster of Celtic place-names in the northeastern corner of Dorsetshire.[1] It is altogether likely that many Celts were held as slaves by the conquerors and that many of the Anglo-Saxons chose Celtic mates. In parts of the island, contact between the two peoples must have been constant and in some districts intimate for several generations.

Celtic Place-Names and Other Loanwords

When we come, however, to seek the evidence for this contact in the English language, investigation yields very meager results. Such evidence as there is survives chiefly in place-names.[2] The kingdom of *Kent,* for example, owes its name to the Celtic word *Canti* or *Cantion,* the meaning of which is unknown, while the two ancient Northumbrian kingdoms of *Deira* and *Bernicia* derive their designations from Celtic tribal names. Other districts, especially in the west and southwest, preserve in their present-day names traces of their earlier Celtic designations. *Devonshire* contains in the first element the tribal name *Dumnonii, Cornwall* means the 'Cornubian Welsh', and the former county *Cumberland* (now part of *Cumbria)* is the 'land of the Cymry or Britons'. Moreover, a number of important centers in the Roman period have names in which Celtic elements are embodied. The name *London* itself, although the origin of the word is somewhat uncertain, most likely goes back to a Celtic designation. The first syllable of *Winchester, Salisbury, Exeter, Gloucester, Worcester,*

Lichfield, and a score of other names of cities is traceable to a Celtic source, and the earlier name of Canterbury *(Durovernum)* is originally Celtic. But it is in the names of rivers and hills and places in proximity to these natural features that the greatest number of Celtic names survive. Thus the *Thames* is a Celtic river name, and various Celtic words for river or water are preserved in the names *Avon, Exe, Esk, Usk, Dover,* and *Wye.* Celtic words meaning 'hill' are found in place-names like *Barr* (cf. Welsh *bar* 'top', 'summit'), *Bredon* (cf. Welsh *bre* 'hill), *Bryn Mawr* (cf. Welsh *bryn* 'hill and *mawr* 'great'), *Creech, Pendle* (cf. Welsh *pen* 'top'), and others. Certain other Celtic elements occur more or less frequently such as *cumb* (a deep valley) in names like *Duncombe, Hòlcombe, Winchcombe; torr* (high rock, peak) in *Torr, Torcross, Torhill; pill* (a tidal creek) in *Pylle, Huntspill;* and *brocc* (badger) in *Brockholes, Brockhall,* etc. Besides these purely Celtic elements a few Latin words such as *castra, fontana, fossa, portus,* and *vîcus* were used in naming places during the Roman occupation of the island and were passed on by the Celts to the English. These will be discussed later. It is natural that Celtic place-names should be more common in the west than in the east and southeast, but the evidence of these names shows that the Celts impressed themselves upon the Germanic consciousness at least to the extent of causing the newcomers to adopt many of the local names current in Celtic speech and to make them a permanent part of their vocabulary.

Outside of place-names, however, the influence of Celtic upon the English language is almost negligible. Not more than a score of words in Old English can be traced with reasonable probability to a Celtic source. Within this small number it is possible to distinguish two groups: (1) those that the AngloSaxons learned through everyday contact with the natives, and (2) those that were introduced by the Irish missionaries in the north. The former were transmitted orally and were of popular character; the latter were connected with religious activities and were more or less learned. The popular words include *binn* (basket, crib), *bratt* (cloak), and *brocc* (brock or badger); a group of words for geographical features that had not played much part in the experience of the Anglo-Saxons in their continental home—*crag, luh* (lake), *cumb* (valley), and torr[3] (outcropping or projecting rock, peak), the two latter chiefly as elements in place-names; possibly the words *dun* (dark colored), and *ass* (ultimately from Latin *asinus).* Words of the second group, those that came into English through Celtic Christianity, are likewise few in number. In 563 St. Columba had come with twelve monks from Ireland to preach to his kinsmen in Britain. On the little island of lona off the west coast of Scotland he established a monastery and made it his headquarters for the remaining thirty-four years of his life. From this center many missionaries went out, founded other religious houses, and did much to spread Christian doctrine and learning. As a result of their activity the words *ancor* (hermit), (magician), *cine* (a gathering of parchment leaves), *cross, clugge* (bell), *gabolrind* (compass), *mind* (diadem), and perhaps *StCBf* (history) and *cursian* (to curse), came into at least partial use in Old English.

It does not appear that many of these Celtic words attained a very permanent place in the English language. Some soon died out, and others acquired only local currency. The relation of the two peoples was not such as to bring about any considerable influence on English life or on English speech. The surviving Celts were a submerged people. The Anglo-Saxon found little occasion to adopt Celtic modes of expression, and the Celtic influence remains the least of the early influences that affected the English language.

Three Latin Influences on Old English

If the influence of Celtic upon Old English was slight, it was doubtless so because the relation of the Celt to the Anglo-Saxon was that of a submerged culture and because the Celt was not in a position to make notable contributions to Anglo-Saxon civilization. It was quite otherwise with the second great influence exerted upon English—that of Latin—and the circumstances under which they met. Latin was not the language of a conquered people. It was the language of a highly regarded civilization, one from which the Anglo-Saxons wanted to learn. Contact with that civilization, at first commercial and military, later religious and intellectual, extended over many centuries and was constantly renewed. It began long before the Anglo-Saxons came to England and continued throughout the Old English period. For several hundred years, while the Germanic tribes who later became the English were still occupying their continental homes, they had various relations with the Romans through which they acquired a considerable number of Latin words. Later when they came to England they saw the evidences of the long Roman rule in the island and learned from the Celts additional Latin words that had been acquired by them. And a century and a half later still, when Roman missionaries reintroduced Christianity into the island, this new cultural influence resulted in a quite extensive adoption of Latin elements into the language. There were thus three distinct occasions on which borrowing from Latin occurred before the end of the Old English period, and it will be of interest to consider more in detail the character and extent of these borrowings.

Chronological Criteria

In order to form an accurate idea of the share that each of these three periods had in extending the resources of the English vocabulary it is first necessary to determine as closely as possible the date at which each of the borrowed words entered the language. This is naturally somewhat difftcult to do, and in the case of some words it is impossible. But in a large number of cases it is possible to assign a word to a given period with a high degree of probability and often with certainty. It will be instructive to pause for a moment to inquire how this is done.

The evidence that can be employed is of various kinds and naturally of varying value. Most obvious is the appearance of the word in literature. If a given word occurs with fair frequency in texts such as *Beowulf,* or the poems of Cynewulf, such occurrence indicates that the word has had time to pass into current use and that it came into English not later than the early part of the period of Christian influence. But it does not tell us how much earlier it was known in the language, because the earliest written records in English do not go back beyond the year 700. Moreover the late appearance of a word in literature is no proof of late adoption. The word may not be the kind of word that would naturally occur very often in literary texts, and so much of Old English literature has been lost that it would be very unsafe to argue about the existence of a word on the basis of existing remains. Some words that are not found recorded before the tenth century (e.g., *pîpe* 'pipe', *cîese* 'cheese') can be assigned confidently on other grounds to the period of continental borrowing.

The character of the word sometimes gives some clue to its date. Some words are obviously learned and point to a time when the church had become well established in the island. On the other hand, the early occurrence of a word in several of the Germanic dialects points to the general circulation of the word in the Germanic territory and its probable adoption by the ancestors of the English on the continent. Testimony of this kind must of course be used with discrimination. A number of words found in Old English and in Old High German, for example, can hardly have been borrowed by either language before the Anglo-Saxons migrated to England but are due to later independent adoption under conditions more or less parallel, brought about by the introduction of Christianity into the two areas. But it can hardly be doubted that a word like *copper,* which is rare in Old English, was nevertheless borrowed on the continent when we find it in no less than six Germanic languages.

Much the most conclusive evidence of the date at which a word was borrowed, however, is to be found in the phonetic form of the word. The changes that take place in the sounds of a language can often be dated with some definiteness, and the presence or absence of these changes in a borrowed word constitutes an important test of age. A full account of these changes would carry us far beyond the scope of this book, but one or two examples may serve to illustrate the principle. Thus there occurred in Old English, as in most of the Germanic languages, a change known as *i-umlaut4* This change affected certain accented vowels and diphthongs when they were followed in the next syllable by an ' or *j*. Under such circumstances *œ* and *ã* became *e*, and *O* became *â a* became and W became *f'* The diphthongs became later ' Thus **baKkiz>benc* (bench), **mûsiz>* " ' plural of *mûs* (mouse), etc. The change occurred in English in the course of the seventh century, and when we find it taking place in a word borrowed from Latin it indicates that the Latin word had been taken into English by that time. Thus Latin *monçta* (which became **munit* in Prehistoric *OE)>mynet* (a coin, Mod. E. *mint)* and is an early borrowing. Another change (even earlier) that helps us to date a borrowed word is that known as *palatal diphthongization.* By this sound-change an æ *ore* in early Old English was changed to a diphthong when preceded by certain palatal consonants. OE *cîese* (L. *câseus,* cheese), mentioned above, shows both *i-umlaut* and palatal diphthongization words evidence for date is furnished by the sound-changes of Vulgar Latin. Thus, for example, an intervocalic *p* (and *p* in the combination *pr)* in the late Latin of northern Gaul (seventh century) was modified to a sound approximating a *v,* and the fact that L. *cuprum, coprum* (copper) appears in OE as *copor* with the *p* unchanged indicates a period of borrowing prior to this change (cf. F. *cuivre).* Again Latin *i* changed to *e* before A.D. 400 so that words like OE *biscop* (L. *episcopus), disc* (L. *discus), sigel,* 'brooch' (L. *sigillum),* etc., which do not show this change, were borrowed by the English on the continent. But enough has been said to indicate the method and to show that the distribution of the Latin words in Old English among the various periods at which borrowing took place rests not upon guesses, however shrewd, but upon definite facts and upon fairly reliable phonetic inferences.

Continental Borrowing (Latin Influence of the Zero Period)

The first Latin words to find their way into the English language owe their adoption to the early contact between the Romans and the Germanic tribes on the continent. Several hundred Latin words found in the various Germanic dialects at an early date—some in one dialect only, others in several—testify to the extensive intercourse between the two peoples. The Germanic population within the empire by the fourth century is estimated at several million. They are found in all ranks and classes of society, from slaves in the fields to commanders of important divisions of the Roman army. Although they were scattered all over the empire, they were naturally most numerous along the northern frontier. This stretched along the Rhine and the Danube and bordered on Germanic territory. Close to the border was Treves, in the third and fourth centuries the most flourishing city in Gaul, already boasting Christian churches, a focus of eight military roads, where all the luxury and splendor of Roman civilization were united almost under the gaze of the Germanic tribes on the Moselle and the Rhine. Traders, Germanic as well as Roman, came and went, while Germanic youth returning from within the empire must have carried back glowing accounts of Roman cities and Roman life. Such intercourse between the two peoples was certain to carry words from one language to the other.

The frequency of the intercourse may naturally be expected to diminish somewhat as one recedes from the borders of the empire. Roman military operations, for example, seldom extended as far as the district occupied by the Angles or the Jutes. But after the conquest of Gaul by Caesar, Roman merchants quickly found their way into all parts of the Germanic territory, even into Scandinavia, so that the inhabitants of these more remote sections were by no means cut off from Roman influence. Moreover, intercommunication between the different Germanic tribes was frequent and made possible the transference of Latin words from one tribe to another. In any case some sixty words from the Latin can be credited with a considerable degree of probability to the ancestors of the English in their continental homes.

The adopted words naturally indicate the new conceptions that the Germanic peoples acquired from this contact with a higher civilization. Next to agriculture the chief occupation of the Germanic tribes in the empire was war, and this experience is reflected in words like *camp* (battle), *segn* (banner), *pîl* (pointed stick, javelin), *weall* (wall), *pytt* (pit), *Stræt* (road, street), *mîl* (mile), and *miltestre* (courtesan). More numerous are the words connected with trade. They traded amber, furs, slaves, and probably certain raw materials for the products of Roman handicrafts, articles of utility, luxury, and adornment. The words *cçap* (bargain; cf. Eng., *cheap, chapman)* and *mangian* (to trade) with its derivatives *mangere* (monger), *mangung* (trade, commerce), and *mangunghûs* (shop) are fundamental, while *pund* (pound), *mydd* (bushel), *sçam* (burden, loan), and *mynet* (coin) are terms likely to be employed. From the last word Old English formed the words *mynetian* (to mint or coin) and *mynetere* (money-changer). One of the most important branches of Roman commerce with the Germanic peoples was the wine trade: hence such words in English as *wîn* (wine), *must* (new wine), *eced* (vinegar), and *flasce*[5] (flask, bottle). To this period are probably to be attributed the words *cylle* (L. *culleus,* leather bottle), *cyrfette* (L. *curcurbita,* gourd), and *sester* (jar, pitcher). A number of the new words relate to domestic life and designate household articles, clothing, and the like: *cytel* (kettle; L. *catillus, catînus) mçse* (table), *scamol* (L. *scamellum,* bench, stool; cf. modern *shambles), teped* (carpet, curtain; L. *tapç tum), pyle* (L. *pulvinus,* pillow), *pilece* (L. *pellicia,* robe of skin), and *sigel* (brooch, necklace; L. *sigillum).* Certain other words of a similar kind probably belong here, although the evidence for their adoption thus early is not in every case conclusive: *cycene* (kitchen; L. *coquîna), cuppe* (L. *cuppa,* cup), *disc* (dish; L. *discus), cucler* (spoon; L. *cocleârium), mortere* (L. *mortârium,* a mortar, a vessel of hard material), *lînen* (cognate with or from L. *lînum,* flax), *lîne* (rope, line; L. *lînea),* and *gimm* (L. *gemma,* gem). The speakers of the Germanic dialects adopted Roman words for certain foods, such as *cîese* (L. *câseus* cheese), *spelt* (wheat), *pipor* (pepper), *senep* (mustard; L. *sinâpi), cisten* (chestnut tree; L. *castanea), cires (bçam)* (cherry tree; L. *cerasus),* while to this period are probably to be assigned *butere* (butter; L. butyrum) ,[6]*ynne (lçac)* (L. *ûnio,* onion), *plûme* (plum), *pise* (L. *pisum,* pea), and *minte* (L. *mentha,* mint). Roman contributions to the building arts are evidenced by such words as *cealc* (chalk), *copor* (copper), *pic* (pitch), and *tigele* (tile), while miscellaneous words such as *mûl* (mule), *draca* (dragon), *pâwa* (peacock), the adjectives *sicor* (L. *sçcûrus,* safe) and *calu* (L. *calvus,* bald), *segne* (seine), *pîpe* (pipe, musical instrument), *biscop* (bishop), *câsere* (emperor), and *Sæternesdæg* (Saturday) may be mentioned. OE *cirice* (church) derives from a word borrowed into West Germanic during this period, though probably from Greek *êõñéêóv covrather* than from Latin.[7]

In general, if we are surprised at the number of words acquired from the Romans at so early a date by the Germanic tribes that came to England, we can see nevertheless that the words were such as they would be likely to borrow and such as reflect in a very reasonable way the relations that existed between the two peoples.

Latin through Celtic Transmission (Latin Influence of the First Period).

The circumstances responsible for the slight influence that Celtic exerted on Old English limited in like manner the Latin influence that sprang from the period of Roman occupation. From what has been said above (see page 45) about the Roman rule in Britain, the extent to which the country was Romanized, and the employment of Latin by certain elements in the population, one would expect a considerable number of Latin words from this period to have remained in use and to appear in the English language today. But this is not the case. It would be hardly too much to say that not five words outside of a few elements found in place-names can be really proved to owe their presence in English to the Roman occupation of Britain.[8] It is probable that the use of Latin as a spoken language did not long survive the end of Roman rule in the island and that such vestiges as remained for a time were lost in the disorders that accompanied the Germanic invasions. There was thus no opportunity for direct contact between Latin and Old English in England, and such Latin words as could have found their way into English would have had to come in through Celtic transmission. The Celts, indeed, had adopted a considerable number of Latin words—more than 600 have been identified—but the relations between the Celts and the English were such, as we have already seen, that these words were not passed on. Among the few Latin words that the Anglo-Saxons seem likely to have acquired upon settling in England, one of the most likely, in spite of its absence from the Celtic languages, is *ceaster.* This word, which represents the Latin *castra* (camp), is a common designation in Old English for a town or enclosed community. It forms a familiar element in English place-names such as *Chester, Colchester, Dorchester, Manchester, Winchester, Lancaster, Doncaster, Gloucester, Worcester,* and many others. Some of these refer to sites of Roman camps, but it must not be thought that a Roman settlement underlies all the towns whose names contain this common element. The English attached it freely to the designation of any enclosed place intended for habitation, and many of the places so designated were known by quite different names in Roman times. A few other words are thought for one reason or another to belong to this period: *port* (harbor, gate, town) from L. *portus* and *porta; munt* (mountain) from L. *mōns, montem; torr* (tower, rock) possibly from L. *turris,* possibly from Celtic; *me* (village) from L. *vîcus.* All of these words are found also as elements in place-names. It is possible that some of the Latin words that the Germanic speakers had acquired on the continent, such as *street* (L. *strâta via), wall, wine,* and others, were reinforced by the presence of the same words in Celtic. At best, however, the Latin influence of the First Period remains much the slightest of all the influences that Old English owed to contact with Roman civilization.

Latin Influence of the Second Period: The Christianizing of Britain

The greatest influence of Latin upon Old English was occasioned by the conversion of Britain to Roman Christianity beginning in 597. The religion was far from new in the island, because Irish monks had been preaching the gospel in the north since the founding of the monastery of lona by Columba in 563. However, 597 marks the beginning of a systematic attempt on the part of Rome to convert the inhabitants and make England a Christian country. According to the well-known story reported by Bede as a tradition current in his day, the mission of St. Augustine was inspired by an experience of the man who later became Pope Gregory the Great. Walking one morning in the marketplace at Rome, he came upon some fair-haired boys about to be sold as slaves and was told that they were from the island of Britain and were pagans. "'Alas! what pity,' said he, 'that the author of darkness is possessed of men of such fair countenances, and that being remarkable for such a graceful exterior, their minds should be void of inward grace?' He therefore again asked, what was the name of that nation and was answered, that they were called Angles. 'Right,' said he, 'for they have an angelic face, and it is fitting that such should be co-heirs with the angels in heaven. What is the name,' proceeded he, 'of the province from which they are brought?' It was replied that the natives of that province were called Deiri. 'Truly are they *de ira'* said he, 'plucked from wrath, and called to the mercy of Christ. How is the king of that province called?' They told him his name was Ælla; and he, alluding to the name, said 'Alleluia, the praise of God the Creator, must be sung in those parts.'" The same tradition records that Gregory wished himself to undertake the mission to Britain but could not be spared. Some years later, however, when he had become pope, he had not forgotten his former intention and looked about for someone whom he could send at the head of a missionary band. Augustine, the person of his choice, was a man well known to him. The two had lived together in the same monastery, and Gregory knew him to be modest and devout and thought him well suited to the task assigned him. With a little company of about forty monks Augustine set out for what seemed then like the end of the earth.

It is not easy to appreciate the difficulty of the task that lay before this small band. Their problem was not so much to substitute one ritual for another as to change the philosophy of a nation. The religion that the Anglo-Saxons shared with the other Germanic tribes seems to have had but a slight hold on the people at the close of the sixth century; but their habits of mind, their ideals, and the action to which these gave rise were often in sharp contrast to the teachings of the New Testament. Germanic philosophy exalted physical courage, independence even to haughtiness, loyalty to one's family or leader that left no wrong unavenged. Christianity preached meekness, humility, and patience under suffering and said that if a man struck you on one cheek you should turn the other. Clearly it was no small task that Augustine and his forty monks faced in trying to alter the age-old mental habits of such a people. They might even have expected difficulty in obtaining a respectful hearing. But they seem to have been men of exemplary lives, appealing personality, and devotion to purpose, and they owed their ultimate success as much to what they were as to what they said. Fortunately, upon their arrival in England one circumstance was in their favor. There was in the kingdom of Kent, in which they landed, a small number of Christians. But the number, though small, included no less a person than the queen. Æthelberht, the king, had sought his wife among the powerful nation of the Franks, and the princess Bertha had been given to him only on condition that she be allowed to continue undisturbed in her Christian faith. Æthelberht set up a small chapel near his palace in Kentwara-byrig (Canterbury), and there the priest who accompanied Bertha to England conducted regular services for her and the numerous dependents whom she brought with her. The circumstances under which Æthelberht received Augustine and his companions are related in the extract from Bede given in § 47 above. Æthelberht was himself baptized within three months, and his example was followed by numbers of his subjects. By the time Augustine died seven years later, the kingdom of Kent had become wholly Christian.

The conversion of the rest of England was a gradual process. In 635 Aidan, a monk from the Scottish monastery of Iona, independently undertook the reconversion of Northumbria at the invitation of King Oswald. Northumbria had been Christianized earlier by Paulinus but had reverted to paganism after the defeat of King Edwin by the Welsh and the Mercians in 632. Aidan was a man of great sympathy and tact. With a small band of followers he journeyed from town to town, and wherever he preached he drew crowds to hear him. Within twenty years he had made all Northumbria Christian. There were periods of reversion to paganism, and some clashes between the Celtic and the Roman leaders over doctrine and authority, but England was slowly won over to the faith. It is significant that the Christian missionaries were allowed considerable freedom in their labors. There is not a single instance recorded in which any of them suffered martyrdom in the cause they espoused. Within a hundred years of the landing of Augustine in Kent all England was Christian.

Effects of Christianity on English Civilization

The introduction of Christianity meant the building of churches and the establishment of monasteries. Latin, the language of the services and of ecclesiastical learning, was once more heard in England. Schools were established in most of the monasteries and larger churches. Some of these became famous through their great teachers, and from them trained men went out to set up other schools at other centers. The beginning of this movement was in 669, when a Greek bishop, Theodore of Tarsus, was made archbishop of Canterbury. He was accompanied by Hadrian, an African by birth, a man described by Bede as "of the greatest skill in both the Greek and Latin tongues." They devoted considerable time and energy to teaching. "And because," says Bede, "they were abundantly learned in sacred and profane literature, they gathered a crowd of disciples...and together with the books of Holy Writ, they also taught the arts of poetry, astronomy, and computation of the church calendar; a testimony of which is that there are still living at this day some of their scholars, who are as well versed in the Greek and Latin tongues as in their own, in which they were born." A decade or two later Aldhelm carried on a similar work at Malmesbury. He was a remarkable classical scholar. He had an exceptional knowledge of Latin literature, and he wrote Latin verse with ease. In the north the school at York became in time almost as famous as that of Canterbury. The two monasteries of Wearmouth and Jarrow were founded by Benedict Biscop, who had been with Theodore and Hadrian at Canterbury, and who on five trips to Rome brought back a rich and valuable collection of books. His most famous pupil was the Venerable Bede, a monk at Jarrow. Bede assimilated all the learning of his time. He wrote on grammar and prosody, science and chronology, and composed numerous commentaries on the books of the Old and New Testament. His most famous work is the *Ecclesiastical History of the English People* (731), from which we have already had occasion to quote more than once and from which we derive a large part of our knowledge of the early history of England. Bede's spiritual grandchild was Alcuin, of York, whose fame as a scholar was so great that in 782 Charlemagne called him to be the head of his Palace School. In the eighth century England held the intellectual leadership of Europe, and it owed this leadership to the church. In like manner vernacular literature and the arts received a new impetus. Workers in stone and glass were brought from the continent for the improvement of church building. Rich embroidery, the illumination of manuscripts, and church music occupied others. Moreover the monasteries cultivated their land by improved methods of agriculture and made numerous contributions to domestic economy. In short, the church as the carrier of Roman civilization influenced the course of English life in many directions, and, as is to be expected, numerous traces of this influence are to be seen in the vocabulary of Old English.

The Earlier Influence of Christianity on the Vocabulary

From the introduction of Christianity in 597 to the close of the Old English period is a stretch of more than 500 years. During all this time Latin words must have been making their way gradually into the English language. It is likely that the first wave of religious feeling that resulted from the missionary zeal of the seventh century, and that is reflected in intense activity in church building and the establishing of monasteries during this century, was responsible also for the rapid importation of Latin words into the vocabulary. The many new conceptions that followed in the train of the new religion would naturally demand expression and would at times find the resources of the language inadequate. But it would be a mistake to think that the enrichment of the vocabulary that now took place occurred overnight. Some words came in almost immediately, others only at the end of this period.

In fact, it is fairly easy to divide the Latin borrowings of the Second Period into two groups, more or less equal in size but quite different in character. The one group represents words whose phonetic form shows that they were borrowed early and whose early adoption is attested also by the fact that they had found their way into literature by the time of Alfred. The other contains words of a more learned character first recorded in the tenth and eleventh centuries and owing their introduction clearly to the religious revival that accompanied the Benedictine Reform. It will be well to consider them separately.

It is obvious that the most typical as well as the most numerous class of words introduced by the new religion would have to do with that religion and the details of its external organization. Words are generally taken over by one language from another in answer to a definite need. They are adopted because they express ideas that are new or because they are so intimately associated with an object or a concept that acceptance of the thing involves acceptance also of the word. A few words relating to Christianity such as *church* and *bishop* were, as we have seen, borrowed earlier. The Anglo-Saxons had doubtless plundered churches and come in contact with bishops before they came to England. But the great majority of words in Old English having to do with the church and its services, its physical fabric and its ministers, when not of native origin were borrowed at this time. Because most of these words have survived in only slightly altered form in Modern English, the examples may be given in their modern form. The list includes *abbot, alms, altar, angel, anthem, Arian, ark, candle, canon, chalice, cleric, cowl, deacon, disciple, epistle, hymn, litany, manna, martyr, mass, minster, noon, nun, offer, organ, pall, palm, pope, priest, provost, psalm, psalter, relic, rule, shrift, shrine, shrive, stole, subdeacon, synod, temple,* and *tunic*. Some of these were reintroduced later. But the church also exercised a profound influence on the domestic life of the people. This is seen in the adoption of many words, such as the names of articles of clothing and household use—*cap, sock, silk, purple, chest, mat, sack;*[9] words denoting foods, such as *beet, caul* (cabbage), *lentil* (OE *lent), millet* (OE *mil), pear, radish, doe, oyster* (OE *ostre), lobster, mussel,* to which we may add the noun *cook;*[10] names of trees, plants, and herbs (often cultivated for their medicinal properties), such as *box, pine,*[11] *aloes, balsam, fennel, hyssop, lily, mallow, marshmallow, myrrh, rue, savory* (OE *sæþrige),* and the general word *plant.* A certain number of words having to do with education and learning reflect another aspect of the church's influence. Such are *school, master, Latin* (possibly an earlier borrowing), *grammatic(al), verse, meter, gloss, notary* (a scribe). Finally we may mention a number of words too miscellaneous to admit of profitable classification, like *anchor, coulter, fan* (for winnowing), *fever, place* (cf. *marketplace), spelter* (asphalt), *sponge, elephant, phoenix, mancus* (a coin), and some more or less learned or literary words, such as *calend, circle, legion, giant, consul,* and *talent.* The words cited in these examples are mostly nouns, but Old English borrowed also a number of verbs and adjectives such as *âspendan* (to spend; L. *expendere), bemûtian* (to exchange; L. *mûtâre). dihtan* (to compose; L. *dictâre) pînian* (to torture; L. *poena), pinsian* (to weigh; L. *pçnsâre), pyngan* (to prick; L. *pungere), sealtian* (to dance; L. *saltâre), temprian* (to temper; L. *temperâre), trifolian* (to grind; L. *trîbulâre), tyrnan* (to turn; L. *tornâre),* and *crisp* (L. *crispus,* 'curly'). But enough has been said to indicate the extent and variety of the borrowings from Latin in the early days of Christianity in England and to show how quickly the language reflected the broadened horizon that the English people owed to the church.

The Benedictine Reform

The flourishing state of the church that resulted in these significant additions to the English language unfortunately did not continue uninterrupted. One cause of the decline is to be attributed to the Danes, who at the end of the eighth century began their ravages upon the country. Lindisfarne was burnt in 793, and Jarrow, Bede's monastery, was plundered the following year. In the ninth century throughout Northumbria and Mercia churches and monasteries lay everywhere in ruins. By the tenth century the decline had affected the moral fiber of the church. It would seem as though once success had been attained and a reasonable degree of security, the clergy relaxed their efforts. Wealthy men had given land freely to religious foundations in the hope of laying up spiritual reserves for themselves against the life in the next world. Among the clergy poverty gave way to ease, and ease by a natural transition passed into luxury. Probably a less worthy type was drawn by these new conditions into the religious profession. We hear much complaint about immoderate feasting and drinking and vanity in dress. In the religious houses discipline became lax, services were neglected, monasteries were occupied by groups of secular priests, many of them married; immorality was flagrant. The work of education was neglected, and learning decayed. By the time of Alfred things had reached such a pass that he looked upon the past as a golden age which had gone, "when the Kings who ruled obeyed God and His evangelists," and when "the religious orders were earnest about doctrine, and learning, and all the services they owed to God"; and he lamented that the decay of learning was so great at the beginning of his reign "that there were very few on this side of the Humber who could understand their rituals in English, or translate a letter from Latin into English, and I believe not many beyond the Humber. So few were there that I cannot remember a single one south of the Thames when I came to the kingship." A century later Ælfric, abbot of Eynsham, echoed the same sentiment when he said, "Until Dunstan and Athelwold revived learning in the monastic life no English priest could either write a letter in Latin, or understand one." It is hardly likely, therefore, that many Latin words were added to the English language during these years when religion and learning were both at such a low ebb.

But abuses when bad enough have a way of bringing about their own reformation. What is needed generally is an individual with the zeal to lead the way and the ability to set an example that inspires imitation. King Alfred had made a start. Besides restoring churches and founding monasteries, he strove for twenty years to spread education in his kingdom and foster learning. His efforts bore little fruit. But in the latter half of the tenth century three great religious leaders, imbued with the spirit of reform, arose in the church: Dunstan, archbishop of Canterbury (d. 988), Athelwold, bishop of Winchester (d. 984), and Oswald, bishop of Worcester and archbishop of York (d. 992). With the sympathetic support of King Edgar these men effected a genuine revival of monasticism in England. The true conception of the monastic life was inseparable from the observance of the Benedictine Rule. Almost everywhere in England this had ceased to be adhered to. As the first step in the reform the secular clergy were turned out of the monasteries and their places filled by monks pledged to the threefold vow of chastity, obedience, and poverty. In their work of restoration the reformers received powerful support from the example of continental monasteries, notably those at Fleury and Ghent. These had recently undergone a similar reformation under the inspiring leadership of Cluny, where in 910 a community had been established on even stricter lines than those originally laid down by St. Benedict. Dunstan had spent some time at the Abbey of Blandinium at Ghent; Oswald had studied the system at Fleury; and Athelwold, although wanting to go himself, had sent a representative to Fleury for the same purpose. On the pattern of these continental houses a number of important monasteries were recreated in England, and Athelwold prepared a version of the Benedictine Rule, known as the *Concordia Regularis,* to bring about a general uniformity in their organization and observances. The effort toward reform extended to other divisions of the church, indeed to a general reformation of morals, and brought about something like a religious revival in the island. One of the objects of special concern in this work of rehabilitation was the improvement of education—the establishment of schools and the encouragement of learning among the monks and the clergy. The results were distinctly gratifying. By the close of the century the monasteries were once more centers of literary activity. Works in English for the popularizing of knowledge were prepared by men who thus continued the example of King Alfred, and manuscripts both in Latin and the vernacular were copied and preserved. It is significant that the four great codices in which the bulk of Old

English poetry is preserved date from this period. We doubtless owe their existence to the reform movement.

Influence of the Benedictine Reform on English

The influence of Latin upon the English language rose and fell with the fortunes of the church and the state of learning so intimately connected with it. As a result of the renewed literary activity just described, a new series of Latin importations took place. These differed somewhat from the earlier Christian borrowings in being words of a less popular kind and expressing more often ideas of a scientific and learned character. They are especially frequent in the works of Ælfric and reflect not only the theological and pedagogical nature of his writings but also his classical tastes and attainments. His literary activity and his vocabulary are equally representative of the movement. As in the earlier Christian borrowings a considerable number of words have to do with religious matters: *alb, Antichrist, antiphoner, apostle, canticle, cantor, cell, chrism, cloister, collect, creed, dalmatic, demon, dirge, font, idol, nocturn, prime, prophet, sabbath, synagogue, troper.* But we miss the group of words relating to everyday life characteristic of the earlier period. Literary and learned words predominate. Of the former kind are *accent, brief* (the verb), *decline* (as a term of grammar), *history, paper, pumice, quatern* (a quire or gathering of leaves in a book), *term(inus), title.* A great number of plant names are recorded in this period. Many of them are familiar only to readers of old herbals. Some of the better known include *celandine, centaury, coriander, cucumber, ginger, hellebore, lovage, periwinkle, petersili* (parsley), *verbena.*[12] A few names of trees might be added, such as *cedar, cypress, fig, laurel,* and *magdâla* (almond).[13] Medical terms, like *cancer, circulâdl* (shingles), *paralysis, scrofula, plaster,* and words relating to the animal kingdom, like *aspide* (viper), *camel, lamprey, scorpion, tiger,* belong apparently to the same category of learned and literary borrowings. It would be possible to extend these lists considerably by including words that were taken over in their foreign form and not assimilated. Such words as *epactas, corporale, confessores, columba* (dove), *columne, cathedra, catacumbas, apostata, apocalipsin, acolitus, absolutionem, invitatorium, unguentum, cristalla, cometa, bissexte, bibliothece, basilica, adamans,* and *prologus* show at once by their form their foreign character. Although many of them were later reintroduced into the language, they do not constitute an integral part of the vocabulary at this time. In general, the later borrowings of the Christian period come through books. An occasional word assigned to this later period may have been in use earlier, but there is nothing in the form to indicate it, and in the absence of any instance of its use in the literature before Alfred it is safer to put such borrowings in the latter part of the Old English period.

The Application of Native Words to New Concepts

The words that Old English borrowed in this period are only a partial indication of the extent to which the introduction of Christianity affected the lives and thoughts of the English people. The English did not always adopt a foreign word to express a new concept. Often an old word was applied to a new thing and by a slight adaptation made to express a new meaning. The Anglo-Saxons, for example, did not borrow the Latin word *deus,* because their own word *God* was a satisfactory equivalent. Likewise *heaven* and *hell* express conceptions not unknown to Anglo-Saxon paganism and are consequently English words. *Patriarch* was rendered literally by *hçahfœder* (high father), *prophet* by *wîtega* (wise one), *martyr* often by the native word *þrô were* (one who suffers pain), and saint by *hâlga* (holy one). Specific members of the church organization such as *pope, bishop,* and *priest,* or *monk* and *abbot* represented individuals for which the English had no equivalent and therefore borrowed the Latin terms; however they did not borrow a general word for clergy but used a native expression, *ðœt gâstlice folc* (the spiritual folk). The word *Easter* is a Germanic word taken over from a pagan festival, likewise in the spring, in honor of Eostre, the goddess of dawn. Instead of borrowing the Latin word *praedicâre* (to preach) the English expressed the idea with words of their own, such as *iOBTOH*(to teach) or bodian (to bring a message); to pray (L. *precâre)* was rendered by *biddan* (to ask) and other words of similar meaning, *prayer* by a word from the same root, *gebed.* For *baptize* (L. *baptizâre)* the English adapted a native word *fullian* (to consecrate) while its derivative *fulluht* renders the noun *baptism.* The latter word enters into numerous compounds, such as *fulluhtbœþ* (font), *fulwere* (baptist), *fulluht-fœder* (baptizer), *fulluht-hâd* (baptismal vow), *fulluht-nama* (Christian name), *fulluht-stôw* (baptistry), *fulluht-tîd* (baptism time), and others. Even so individual a feature of the Christian faith as the sacrament of the Lord's Supper was expressed by the Germanic word *hûsl* (modern *housel),* while *lâc,* the general word for sac-rifice to the gods, was also sometimes applied to the Sacrifice of the Mass. The term *Scriptures* found its exact equivalent in the English word *gewritu,* and *çvangelium* was rendered by *godspell,* originally meaning good tidings. *Trinity* (L .*trinitas)* was translated *þrines* (three-ness), the idea of God the Creator was expressed by *scieppend* (one who shapes or forms), *fruma* (creator, founder), or *metod* (measurer). Native words like *fœder* (father), *dryhten* (prince), *wealdend* (ruler), *þçoden* (prince), *weard* (ward, protector), *hlâford* (lord) are frequent synonyms. Most of them are also applied to *Christ,* originally a Greek word and the most usual name for the Second Person of the Trinity, but *nil'lvnd* (Savior) is also commonly employed. The Third Person (Spiritus Sanctus) was translated *Hâlig Gäst* (Holy Ghost). Latin *diabolus* was borrowed as *deoM* (devil) but we find *fçond* (fiend) as a common synonym. Examples might be multiplied. Cross is *rôd* (rood), *trçow* (tree), *gealga* (gallows), etc.; resurrection is from *ârîsan* (to arise); *peccatum* is *synn* (sin), while other words like *mân, firen, leahtor, wôh,* and *scyld,* meaning 'vice', 'crime', 'fault', and the like, are commonly substituted. The Judgment Day is *Doomsday.* Many of these words are translations of their Latin equivalents and their vitality is attested by the fact that in a great many cases they have continued in use down to the present day. It is important to recognize that the significance of a foreign influence is not to be measured simply by the foreign words introduced but is revealed also by the extent to which it stimulates the language to independent creative effort and causes it to make full use of its native resources.

The Extent of the Influence

To be sure, the extent of a foreign influence is most readily seen in the number of words borrowed. As a result of the Christianizing of Britain some 450 Latin words appear in English writings before the close of the Old English period. This number does not include derivatives or proper names, which in the case of biblical names are very numerous. But about 100 of these were purely learned or retained so much of their foreign character as hardly to be considered part of the English vocabulary. Of the 350 words that have a right to be so considered, some did not make their way into general use until later—were, in fact, reintroduced later. On the other hand, a large number of them were fully accepted and thoroughly incorporated into the language. The real test of a foreign influence is the degree to which the words that it brought in were assimilated. This is not merely a question of the power to survive; it is a question of how completely the words were digested and became indistinguishable from the native word-stock, so that they could enter into compounds and be made into other parts of speech, just like native words. When, for example, the Latin noun *planta* comes into English as the noun *plant* and later is made into a verb by the addition of the infinitive ending -*ian (plantian)* and other inflectional elements, we may feel sure that the word has been assimilated. This happened in a number of cases as in *gemartyrian* (to martyr), *sealmian* (to play on the harp), *culpian* (to humiliate oneself), *fersian* (to versify), *glçsan* (to gloss), and *crispian* (to curl). Assimilation is likewise indicated by the use of native formative suffixes such as *-dôm, -hâd, -ung* to make a concrete noun into an abstract *(martyrdôm, martyrhâd, martyrung).* The Latin influence of the Second Period was not only extensive but thorough and marks the real beginning of the English habit of freely incorporating foreign elements into its vocabulary.

The Scandinavian Influence: The Viking Age

Near the end of the Old English period English underwent a third foreign influence, the result of contact with another important language, the Scandinavian. In the course of history it is not unusual to witness the spectacle of a nation or people, through causes too remote or complex for analysis, suddenly emerging from obscurity, playing for a time a conspicuous, often brilliant, part, and then, through causes equally difficult to define, subsiding once more into a relatively minor sphere of activity. Such a phenomenon is presented by the Germanic inhabitants of the Scandinavian peninsula and Denmark, one-time neighbors of the Anglo-Saxons and closely related to them in language and blood. For some centuries the Scandinavians had remained quietly in their northern home. But in the eighth century a change, possibly economic, possibly political, occurred in this area and provoked among them a spirit of unrest and adventurous enterprise. They began a series of attacks upon all the lands adjacent to the North Sea and the Baltic. Their activities began in plunder and ended in conquest. The Swedes established a kingdom in Russia; Norwegians colonized parts of the British Isles, the Faroes, and Iceland, and from there pushed on to Greenland and the coasts of Labrador and Newfoundland; the Danes founded the dukedom of Normandy and finally conquered England. The pinnacle of their achievement was reached in the beginning of the eleventh century when Cnut, king of Denmark, obtained the throne of England, conquered Norway, and from his English capital ruled the greater part of the Scandinavian world. The daring sea rovers to whom these unusual achievements were due are commonly known as Vikings,[14] and the period of their activity, extending from the middle of the eighth century to the beginning of the eleventh, is popularly known as the Viking Age. It was to their attacks upon, settlements in, and ultimate conquest of England that the Scandinavian influence upon Old English was due.

The Scandinavian Invasions of England

In the Scandinavian attacks upon England three well-marked stages can be distinguished. The first is the period of early raids, beginning according to the Anglo-Saxon Chronicle in 787 and continuing with some intermissions until about 850. The raids of this period were simply plundering attacks upon towns and monasteries near the coast. Sacred vessels of gold and silver, jeweled shrines, costly robes, and valuables of all kinds were carried off, and English people were captured to be made slaves. Noteworthy instances are the sacking of Lindisfarne and Jarrow in 793 and 794. But with the plundering of these two famous monasteries the attacks apparently ceased for forty years, until renewed in 834 along the southern coast and in East Anglia. These early raids were apparently the work of small isolated bands.

The second stage is the work of large armies and is marked by widespread plundering in all parts of the country and by extensive settlements. This new development was inaugurated by the arrival in 850 of a Danish fleet of 350 ships. Their pirate crews wintered in the isle of Thanet and the following spring captured Canterbury and London and ravaged the surrounding country. Although defeated by a West Saxon army, they soon renewed their attacks. In 866 a large Danish army plundered East Anglia and in 867 captured York. In 869 the East Anglian king, Edmund, met a cruel death in resisting the invaders. The incident made a deep impression on all England, and the memory of his martyrdom was vividly preserved in English tradition for nearly two centuries. The eastern part of England was now largely in the hands of the Danes, and they began turning their attention to Wessex. The assault upon Wessex began shortly before the accession of King Alfred (871-899). Even the greatness of this greatest of English kings threatened to prove insufficient to withstand the repeated attacks of the Northmen. After seven years of resistance, in which temporary victories were invariably succeeded by fresh defeats, Alfred was forced to take refuge with a small band of personal followers in the marshes of Somerset. But in this darkest hour for the fortunes of the English, Alfred's courage and persistence triumphed. With a fresh levy of men from Somerset, Wiltshire, and Hampshire, he suddenly attacked the Danish army under Guthrum at Ethandun (now Edington, in Wiltshire). The result was an overwhelming victory for the English and a capitulation by the Danes (878).

The Treaty of Wedmore (near Glastonbury), which was signed by Alfred and Guthrum the same year, marks the culmination of the second stage in the Danish invasions. Wessex was saved. The

Danes withdrew from Alfred's territory. But they were not compelled to leave England. The treaty merely defined the line, running roughly from Chester to London, to the east of which the foreigners were henceforth to remain. This territory was to be subject to Danish law and is hence known as the Danelaw. In addition the Danes agreed to accept Christianity, and Guthrum was baptized. This last provision was important. It might secure the better observance of the treaty, and, what was more important, it would help to pave the way for the ultimate fusion of the two groups.

The third stage of the Scandinavian incursions covers the period of political adjustment and assimilation from 878 to 1042. The Treaty of Wedmore did not put an end to Alfred's troubles. Guthrum was inclined to break faith, and there were fresh invasions from outside. But the situation slowly began to clear. Under Alfred's son Edward the Elder (900-925) and grandson Athelstan (925-939) the English began a series of counterattacks that put the Danes on the defensive. One of the brilliant victories of the English in this period was Athelstan's triumph in 937 in the battle of Brunanburh, over a combined force of Danes and Scots, a victory celebrated in one of the finest of Old English poems. By the middle of the century a large part of eastern England, though still strongly Danish in blood and custom, was once more under English rule.

Toward the end of the century, however, when England seemed at last on the point of solving its Danish problem, a new and formidable succession of invasions began. In 991 a substantial Viking fleet, which may have been under the command of Olaf Tryggvason, attacked and pillaged various towns along the southeast coast of England. It then sailed up the Blackwater to the vicinity of Maldon, where it was met by Byrhtnoth, the valiant earl of the East Saxons, in a battle celebrated in another famous Old English war poem, *The Battle of Maldon.* Here the English, heroic in defeat, lost their leader, and soon the invaders were being bribed by large sums to refrain from plunder. The invasions now began to assume an official character. In 994 Olaf, who shortly became king of Norway, was joined by Svein, king of Denmark, in a new attack on London. The sums necessary to buy off the enemy became greater and greater, rising in 1012 to the amazing figure of £48,000. In each case the truce thus bought was temporary, and Danish forces were soon again marching over England, murdering and pillaging. Finally Svein determined to make himself king of the country. In 1014, supported by his son Cnut, he crowned a series of victories in different parts of England by driving Æthelred, the English king, into exile and seizing the throne. Upon his sudden death the same year his son succeeded him. Three years of fighting established Cnut's claim to the throne, and for the next twenty-five years England was ruled by Danish kings.

The Settlement of the Danes in England

The events here rapidly summarized had as an important consequence the settlement of large numbers of Scandinavians in England. However temporary may have been the stay of many of the attacking parties, especially those that in the beginning came simply to plunder, many individuals remained behind when their ships returned home. Often they became permanent settlers in the island. Some indication of their number may be had from the fact that more than 1,400 places in England bear Scandinavian names. Most of these are naturally in the north and east of England, the district of the Danelaw, for it was here that the majority of the invaders settled. Most of the new inhabitants were Danes, although there were considerable Norwegian settlements in the northwest, especially in what is now Cumbria, and in a few of the northern counties. The presence of a large Scandinavian element in the population is indicated not merely by placenames but by peculiarities of manorial organization, local government, legal procedure, and the like. Thus we have to do not merely with large bands of marauders, marching and countermarching across England, carrying hardship and devastation into all parts of the country for upward of two centuries, but also with an extensive peaceable settlement by farmers who intermarried with the English, adopted many of their customs, and entered into the everyday life of the community. In the districts where such settlements took place, conditions were favorable for an extensive Scandinavian influence on the English language.

The Amalgamation of the Two Peoples

The amalgamation of the two peoples was greatly facilitated by the close kinship that existed between them The problem of the English was not the assimilation of an alien people representing an alien culture and speaking a wholly foreign tongue. The policy of the English kings in the period when they were reestablishing their control over the Danelaw was to accept as an established fact the mixed population of the district and to devise a *modus vivendi* for its component elements. In this effort they were aided by the natural adaptability of the Scandinavian. Generations of contact with foreign communities, into which their many enterprises had brought them, had made the Scandinavians a cosmopolitan people. The impression derived from a study of early English institutions is that in spite of certain native customs that the Danes continued to observe, they assimilated to most of the ways of English life. That many of them early accepted Christianity is attested by the large number of Scandinavian names found not only among monks and abbots, priests and bishops, but also among those who gave land to monasteries and endowed churches. It would be a great mistake to think of the relation between Anglo-Saxon and Dane, especially in the tenth century, as uniformly hostile. One must distinguish, as we have said, between the predatory bands that continued to traverse the country and the large numbers that were settled peacefully on the land. Alongside the ruins of English towns—Symeon of Durham reports that the city of Carlisle remained uninhabited for 200 years after its destruction by the Danes—there existed important communities established by the newcomers. They seem to have grouped themselves at first in concentrated centers, parceling out large tracts of land from which the owners had fled, and preferring this form of settlement to too scattered a distribution in a strange land. Among such centers the Five Boroughs—Lincoln, Stamford, Leicester, Derby, and Nottingham—became important *foci* of

Scandinavian influence. It was but a question of time until these large centers and the multitude of smaller communities where the Northmen gradually settled were absorbed into the general mass of the English population.

The Relation of the Two Languages

The relation between the two languages in the district settled by the Danes is a matter of inference rather than exact knowledge. Doubtless the situation was similar to that observable in numerous parts of the world today where people speaking different languages are found living side by side in the same region. Although in some places the Scandinavians gave up their language early[15] there were certainly communities in which Danish or Norse remained for some time the usual language. Up until the time of the Norman Conquest the Scandinavian language in England was constantly being renewed by the steady stream of trade and conquest. In some parts of Scotland, Norse was still spoken as late as the seventeenth century. In other districts in which the prevailing speech was English there were doubtless many of the newcomers who continued to speak their own language at least as late as 1100 and a considerable number who were to a greater or lesser degree bilingual. The last-named circumstance is rendered more likely by the frequent intermarriage between the two peoples and by the similarity between the two tongues. The Anglian dialect resembled the language of the Northmen in a number of particulars in which West Saxon showed divergence. The two may even have been mutually intelligible to a limited extent. Contemporary statements on the subject are conflicting, and it is difficult to arrive at a conviction. But wherever the truth lies in this debatable question, there can be no doubt that the basis existed for an extensive interaction of the two languages upon each other, and this conclusion is amply borne out by the large number of Scandinavian elements subsequently found in English.

The Tests of Borrowed Words

The similarity between Old English and the language of the Scandinavian invaders makes it at times very difficult to decide whether a given word in Modern English is a native or a borrowed word. Many of the more common words of the two languages were identical, and if we had no Old English literature from the period before the Danish invasions, we should be unable to say that many words were not of Scandinavian origin. In certain cases, however, we have very reliable criteria by which we can recognize a borrowed word. These tests are not such as the lay person can generally apply, although occasionally they are sufficiently simple. The most reliable depend upon differences in the development of certain sounds in the North Germanic and West Germanic areas. One of the simplest to recognize is the development of the sound *sk*. In Old English this was early palatalized to *sh* (written *sc)*, except possibly in the combination *scr,* whereas in the Scandinavian countries it retained its hard *sk* sound. Consequently, while native words like *ship, shall, fish* have *sh* in Modern English, words borrowed from the Scandinavians are generally still pronounced with *sk: sky, skin, skill, scrape, scrub, bask, whisk.* The OE *scyrte* has become *shirt,* while the corresponding ON form *skyrta* gives us *skirt.* In the same way the retention of the hard pronunciation of *k* and *g* in such words as *kid, dike*[16] (cf. *ditch), get, give, gild,* and *egg is* an indication of Scandinavian origin. Occasionally, though not very often, the vowel of a word gives clear proof of borrowing. For example, the Germanic diphthong *ai* becomes *â* in Old English (and has become ô in Modern English) but became *ei* or *ç* in Old Scandinavian. Thus *aye, nay* (beside *no* from the native word), *hale* (cf. the English form *(w)hole), reindeer,* and *swain* are borrowed words, and many more examples can be found in Middle English and in the modern dialects. Thus there existed in Middle English the forms *geit, gait,* which are from Scandinavian, beside *gât, gôt* from the OE word. The native word has survived in Modern English *goat.* In the same way the Scandinavian word for *loathsome* existed in Middle English as *leiþ, laiþ* beside *lâþ, lôþ.* Such tests as these, based on sound-developments in the two languages, are the most reliable means of distinguishing Scandinavian from native words. But occasionally meaning gives a fairly reliable test. Thus our word *bloom* (flower) could come equally well from OE *blôma* or Scandinavian *blôm.* But the OE word meant an 'ingot of iron', whereas the Scandinavian word meant 'flower, bioom'. It happens that the Old English word has survived as a term in metallurgy, but it is the Old Norse word that has come down in ordinary use. Again, if the initial *g* in *gift* did not betray the Scandinavian origin of this word, we should be justified in suspecting it from the fact that the cognate OE word *gift* meant the 'price of a wife', and hence in the plural 'marriage', whereas the ON word had the more general sense of 'gift, present'. The word *plow* in Old English meant a measure of land, in Scandinavian the agricultural implement, which in Old English was called a *sulh.* When neither the form of a word nor its meaning proves its Scandinavian origin we can never be sure that we are dealing with a borrowed word. The fact that an original has not been preserved in Old English is no proof that such an original did not exist. Nevertheless when a word appears in Middle English that cannot be traced to an Old English source but for which an entirely satisfactory original exists in Old Norse, and when that word occurs chiefly in texts written in districts where Danish influence was strong, or when it has survived in dialectal use in these districts today, the probability that we have here a borrowed word is fairly strong. In every case final judgment must rest upon a careful consideration of all the factors involved.

Scandinavian Place-Names

Among the most notable evidences of the extensive Scandinavian settlement in England is the large number of places that bear Scandinavian names. When we find more than 600 places like *Grimsby, Whitby, Derby, Rugby,* and *Thoresby,* with names ending in *-by,* nearly all of them in the district occupied by the Danes, we have a striking evidence of the number of Danes who settled in England. For these names all contain the Danish word *by,* meaning 'farm' or 'town', a word that is also seen in our word *by-law* (town law). Some 300 names like *Althorp, Bishopsthorpe, Gawthorpe,* and *Linthorpe* contain the Scandinavian word *thorp* (village). An almost equal number contain the word *thwaite* (an isolated piece of land)—*Applethwaite, Braithwaite, Cowperthwaite, Langthwaite, Satterthwaite.* About a hundred places bear names ending in *toft* (a piece of ground, a messuage)—*Brimtoft, Eastoft, Langtoft, Lowestoft, Nortoft.* Numerous other Scandinavian elements enter into English place-names, which need not be particularized here. It is apparent that these elements were commonplace in the speech of the people of the Danelaw. It has been remarked above that more than 1,400 Scandinavian place-names have been counted in England, and the number will undoubtedly be increased when a more careful survey of the material has been made. These names are not uniformly distributed over the Danelaw. The largest number are found in Yorkshire and Lincolnshire. In some districts in these counties as many as 75 percent of the place-names are of Scandinavian origin. Cumbria contributes a large number, reflecting the extensive Norse settlements in the northwest, while Norfolk, with a fairly large representation, shows that the Danes were numerous in at least this part of East Anglia. It may be remarked that a similarly high percentage of Scandinavian personal names has been found in the medieval records of these districts. Names ending in *-son,* like *Stevenson* or *Johnson,* conform to a characteristic Scandinavian custom, the equivalent of Old English patronymic being *-ing,* as in *Browning.*

The Earliest Borrowing

The extent of this influence on English place-nomenclature would lead us to expect a large infiltration of other words into the vocabulary. But we should not expect this infiltration to show itself at once. The early relations of the invaders with the English were too hostile to lead to much natural intercourse, and we must allow time for such words as the Anglo-Saxons learned from their enemies to find their way into literature. The number of Scandinavian words that appear in Old English is consequently small, amounting to only about two score. The largest single group of these is such as would be associated with a sea-roving and predatory people. Words like *barda* (beaked ship), *cnearr* (small warship), *scegþ* (vessel), *liþ* (fleet), *scegþmann* (pirate), *dreng* (warrior), *hâ* (oarlock) and (rower in a warship), *bâtswegen* (boatman, source of Modern English *boatswain), hofding* (chief, ringleader), *orrest* (battle), *rân* (robbery, rapine), and *fylcian* (to collect or marshal a force) show in what respects the invaders chiefly impressed the English. A little later we find a number of words relating to the law or characteristic of the social and administrative system of the Danelaw. The word *la w* itself is of Scandinavian origin, as is the word *outlaw.* The word *mâl* (action at law), *hold* (freeholder), *wapentake* (an administrative district), *hûsting* (assembly), and *riding* (originally *thriding,* one of the former divisions of Yorkshire) owe their use to the Danes. In addition to these, a number of genuine Old English words seem to be translations of Scandinavian terms: *bôtlças* (what cannot be compensated), *hâmsôcn* (attacking an enemy in his house), *lahcçap* (payment for reentry into lost legal rights), *landcçap* (tax paid when land was bought) are examples of such translations.[17] English legal terminology underwent a complete reshaping after the Norman Conquest, and most of these words have been replaced now by terms from the French. But their temporary existence in the language is an evidence of the extent to which Scandinavian customs entered into the life of the districts in which the Danes were numerous.

Scandinavian Loanwords and Their Character

It was after the Danes had begun to settle down peaceably in the island and enter into the ordinary relations of life with the English that Scandinavian words began to enter in numbers into the language. If we examine the bulk of these words with a view to dividing them into classes and thus discovering in what domains of thought or experience the Danes contributed especially to English culture and therefore to the English language, we shall not arrive at any significant result. The Danish invasions were not like the introduction of Christianity, bringing the English into contact with a different civilization and introducing them to many things, physical as well as spiritual, that they had not known before. The civilization of the invaders was very much like that of the English themselves. Consequently the Scandinavian elements that entered the English language are such as would make their way into it through the give-and-take of everyday life. Their character can best be conveyed by a few examples, arranged simply in alphabetical order. Among nouns that came in are *axle-tree, band, bank, birth, boon, booth, brink, bull, calf* (of leg), *crook, dirt, down* (feathers), *dregs, egg, fellow, freckle, gait, gap, girth, guess, hap, keel, kid, leg, link, loan, mire, race, reef* (of sail), *reindeer, rift, root, scab, scales, score, scrap, seat, sister, skill, skin, skirt, sky, slaughter, snare, stack, steak, swain, thrift, tidings, trust, want, window.* The list has been made somewhat long in order to better illustrate the varied and yet simple character of the borrowings. Among adjectives we find *awkward, flat, ill, loose, low, meek, muggy, odd, rotten, rugged, scant, seemly, sly, tattered, tight,* and *weak.* There are also a surprising number of common verbs among the borrowings, like *to bait, bask, batten, call, cast, clip, cow, crave, crawl, die, droop, egg (on), flit, gape, gasp, get, give, glitter, kindle, lift, lug, nag, raise, rake, ransack, rid, rive, scare, scout* (an idea), *scowl, screech, snub, sprint, take, thrive, thrust.* Lists such as these suggest better than any explanation the familiar, everyday character of the words that the Scandinavian invasions and subsequent settlement brought into English.

The Relation of Borrowed and Native Words

It will be seen from the words in the above lists that in many cases the new words could have supplied no real need in the English vocabulary. They made their way into English simply as the result of the mixture of the two peoples. The Scandinavian and the English words were being used side by side, and the survival of one or the other must often have been a matter of chance. Under such circumstances a number of things might happen. (1) Where words in the two languages coincided more or less in form and meaning, the modern word stands at the same time for both its English and its Scandinavian ancestors.

Examples of such words are *burn, cole, drag, fast, gang, murk(y) scrape, thick.* (2) Where there were differences of form, the English word often survived. Beside such English words as *bench, goat, heathen, yarn, few, grey, loath, leap, flay,* corresponding Scandinavian forms are found quite often in Middle English literature and in some cases still exist in dialectal use. We find *screde, skelle, skere* with the hard pronunciation of the initial consonant group beside the standard English *shred, shell, sheer; wae* beside *woe,* the surviving form except in *welaway; trigg* the Old Norse equivalent of OE *trçowe* (true). Again where the same idea was expressed by different words in the two languages it was often, as we should expect, the English word that lived on. We must remember that the area in which the two languages existed for a time side by side was confined to the northern and eastern half of England. Examples are the Scandinavian words *attlen* beside

English *think* (in the sense of *purpose, intend), bolnen* beside *swell, tinen* (ON *)* beside *lose, site* (ON *J)* beside *sorrow, roke* (fog) beside *mist, reike* beside *path.* (3) In other cases the Scandinavian word replaced the native word, often after the two had long remained in use concurrently. Our word *awe* from Scandinavian, and its cognate *eye (aye)* from Old English are both found in the *Ormulum* (c. 1200). In the earlier part of the Middle English period the English word is more common, but by 1300 the Scandinavian form begins to appear with increasing frequency and finally replaces the Old English word. The two forms must have been current in the everyday speech of the northeast for several centuries, until finally the pronunciation *awe* prevailed. The Old English form is not found after the fourteenth century. The same thing happened with the two words for egg, *ey* (English) and *egg* (Scandinavian). Caxton complains at the close of the fifteenth century (see the passage quoted in § 151) that it was hard even then to know which to use. In the words *sister* (ON *syster,* OE *sweostor), boon* (ON *bôn,* OE *bçn) loan* (ON *lân,* OE), *weak* (ON *veikr,* OE *wâc)* the Scandinavian form lived. Often a good Old English word was lost, since it expressed the same idea as the foreign word. Thus the verb *take* replaced the OE *niman;'8 cast* superseded the OE *weorpan,* while it has itself been largely displaced now by *throw; cut*took the place of OE *snîðan* and *ceorfan,* which survives as *carve.* Old English had several words for *anger* (ON *angr)*, including *torn, grama,* and *irre,* but the Old Norse word prevailed. In the same way the Scandinavian word *bark* replaced OE *rind, wing* replaced OE *feþra, sky* took the place of *ûprodor* and *wolcen* (the latter now being preserved only in the poetical word *welkin)*, and *window* (=wind-eye) drove out the equally appropriate English word (eye-thirl, i.e., eye-hole; cf. *nostril=nose* thirl, nose hole). (4) Occasionally both the English and the Scandinavian words were retained with a difference of meaning or use, as in the following pairs (the English word is given first): *no—nay, whole—hale, rear—raise, from—fro, craft—skill, hide—skin, sick—ill.* (5) In certain cases a native word that was apparently not in common use was reinforced, if not reintroduced, from the Scandinavian. In this way we must account for such words as *till, dale, rim, blend, run,* and the Scottish *bairn.* (6) Finally, the English word might be modified, taking on some of the character of the corresponding Scandinavian word. *Give* and get with their hard *g* are examples, as are *scatter* beside *shatter,* and *Thursday* instead of the OE *Thunresdæg.* Some confusion must have existed in the Danish area between the Scandinavian and the English form of many words, a confusion that is clearly betrayed in the survival of such hybrid forms as *shriek* and *screech.* All this merely goes to show that in the Scandinavian influence on the English language we have to do with the intimate mingling of two tongues. The results are just what we should expect when two rather similar languages are spoken for upwards of two centuries in the same area.

Form Words

If further evidence were needed of the intimate relation that existed between the two languages, it would be found in the fact that the Scandinavian words that made their way into English were not confined to nouns and adjectives and verbs but extended to pronouns, prepositions, adverbs, and even a part of the verb *to be.* Such parts of speech are not often transferred from one language to another. The pronouns *they, their,* and *them* are Scandinavian. Old English used *hîe, hiera, him* (see § 45). Possibly the Scandinavian words were felt to be less subject to confusion with forms of the singular. Moreover, though these are the most important, they are not the only Scandinavian pronouns to be found in English. A late Old English inscription contains the Old Norse form *hanum* for *him. Both* and *same,* though not primarily pronouns, have pronominal uses and are of Scandinavian origin. The preposition *till* was at one time widely used in the sense of *to,* besides having its present meaning; and *fro,* likewise in common use formerly as the equivalent of *from,* survives in the phrase *to and fro.* Both words are from the Scandinavian. From the same source comes the modern form of the conjunction *though,* the Old Norse equivalent of OE *þçah.* The Scandinavian use of *at* as a sign of the infinitive is to be seen in the English *ado (at-do)* and was more widely used in this construction in Middle English. The adverbs *aloft, athwart, aye* (ever), and *seemly,* and the earlier *heþen* (hence) and *hweþen* (whence), are all derived from the Scandinavian. Finally the present plural *are* of the verb *to be* is a most significant adoption. While *we aron* was the Old English form in the north, the West Saxon plural was *syndon* (cf. German *sind),* and the form *are* in Modern English undoubtedly owes its extension to the influence of the Danes. When we remember that in the expression *they are* both the pronoun and the verb are Scandinavian we realize once more how intimately the language of the invaders has entered into English.

Scandinavian Influence outside the Standard Speech

We should miss the full significance of the Scandinavian influence if we failed to recognize the extent to which it is found outside the standard speech. Our older literature and the modern dialects are full of words that are not now in ordinary use. The ballads offer many examples. When the *Geste of Robin Hood* begins "*Lythe* and listin, gentilmen" it has for its first word an Old Norse synonym for *listen.* When a little later on the Sheriff of Nottingham says to Little John, "Say me no we, *wightyonge* man, What is nowe thy name?" he uses the ON *vigt* (strong, courageous). In the ballad of *Captain Car* the line "*Busk* and *bowne,* my merry men all" contains two words from the same source meaning *prepare.* The word *gar,* meaning *to cause* or *make one do something,* is of frequent occurrence. Thus, in *Chevy Chace* we are told of Douglas' men that "Many a doughetë the(y) *garde* to dy"—that is, they made many a doughty man die. In *Robin Hood and Guy of Gisborne* the Virgin Mary is addressed: "Ah, deere Lady! sayd Robin Hoode, Thou art both mother and *may,*" in which *may* is a Scandinavian form for *maid.* Bessie Bell and Mary Gray, in the ballad of that name, "*bigget* a bower on yon burn-brae," employing in the process another word of Norse origin, *biggen* (to build), a word also used by Burns in *To a Mouse:* "Thy wee bit housie, too, in ruin!.. And naething now to big a new ane." In Burns and Scott we find the comparative *worse* in the form *waur:* "A' the warld kens that they maun either marry or do waur" *(Old Mortality)*, also an old word (ON *verre)* more commonly found in the form used by Chaucer in the *Book of the Duchess:* "Allas! how myghte I fare werre?" Examples could be multiplied, but it is sufficiently evident that there is much Scandinavian material in the dialects besides what has found its way into the standard speech.

Effect on Grammar and Syntax

That the Scandinavian influence not only affected the vocabulary but also extended to matters of grammar and syntax as well is less capable of exact demonstration but is hardly to be doubted. Inflections are seldom transferred from one language to another. A certain number of inflectional elements peculiar to the Northumbrian dialect have been attributed to Scandinavian influence,[19] among others the *-s* of the third person singular, present indicative, of verbs and the participial ending *-and (bindand),* corresponding to *-end* and *-ind* in the Midlands and South, and now replaced by *-ing.* The words *scant, want, athwart* preserve in the final *t the* neuter adjective ending of Old Norse. But this is of no great significance. It is much more important to recognize that in many words the English and Scandinavian languages differed chiefly in their inflectional elements. The body of the word was so nearly the same in the two languages that only the endings would put obstacles in the way of mutual understanding. In the mixed population that existed in the Danelaw these endings must have led to much confusion, tending gradually to become obscured and finally lost. It seems but natural that the tendency toward the loss of inflections, which was characteristic of the English language in the north even in Old English times, was strengthened and accelerated by the conditions that prevailed in the Danelaw, and that some credit must be given the Danes for a development that, spreading to other parts and being carried much farther, resulted after the Norman Conquest in so happily simplifying English grammar. Likewise, the way words are put together in phrases and clauses—what we call syntax—is something in which languages less often influence one another than in matters of vocabulary. The probability of such influence naturally varies with the degree of intimacy that exists between the speakers of two languages. In those parts of Pennsylvania—the "Pennsylvania Dutch" districts—where German and English have mingled in a jargon peculiar to itself, German turns of expression are frequently found in the English spoken there. It is quite likely that the English spoken in the districts where there were large numbers of Danes acquired certain Danish habits of expression. A modern Dane like Jespersen[20] notes that the omission of the relative pronoun in relative clauses (rare in Old English) and the retention or omission of the conjunction *that are* in conformity with Danish usage; that the rules for the use of *shall* and *will* in Middle English are much the same as in Scandinavian; and that some apparently illogical uses of these auxiliaries in Shakespeare (e.g., "besides it *should* appear" in the *Merchant of Venice,* III, ii, 289) do not seem strange to a Dane, who would employ the same verb. Logeman[21] notes the tendency, common to both languages, to put a strong stress at times on the preposition and notes the occurrence of locutions such as "he has some one to work for" that are not shared by the other Germanic languages. It is possible, of course, that similarities such as these are merely coincidences, that the Scandinavian languages and English happened to develop in these respects along similar lines. But there is nothing improbable in the assumption that certain Scandinavian turns of phrase and certain particular usages should have found their way into the idiom of people in no small part Danish in descent and living in intimate contact with the speakers of a Scandinavian tongue.

Period and Extent of the Influence

It is hardly possible to estimate the extent of the Scandinavian influence by the number of borrowed words that exist in Standard English. That number, if we restrict the list to those for which the evidence is fully convincing, is about 900. These, as the examples given above show, are almost always words designating common everyday things and fundamental concepts. To this group we should probably be justified in adding an equal number in which a Scandinavian origin is probable or in which the influence of Scandinavian forms has entered. Furthermore there are, according to Wright, the editor of the *English Dialect Dictionary,* thousands of Scandinavian words that are still a part of the everyday speech of people in the north and east of England and in a sense are just as much a part of the living language as those that are used in other parts of the country and have made their way into literature. He notes that "if we exclude all *sc-* words of various origins which are common to the standard language and the dialects, it is a remarkable fact that the *English Dialect Dictionary* contains 1,154 simple words beginning with *sc-(sk-).* Locally, at least, the Scandinavian influence was tremendous. The period during which this large Danish element was making its way into the English vocabulary was doubtless the tenth and eleventh centuries. This was the period during which the merging of the two peoples was taking place. The occurrence of many of the borrowed words in written records is generally somewhat later. A considerable number first make their appearance in the *Ormulum* at the beginning of the thirteenth century. But we must attribute this fact to the scarcity of literary texts of an earlier date, particularly from the region of the Danelaw. Because of its extent and the intimate way in which the borrowed elements were incorporated, the Scandinavian influence is one of the most interesting of the foreign influences that have contributed to the English language.

REFERENCES

1. R.E.Zachrisson, *Romans, Kelts, and Saxons in Ancient Britain* (Uppsala, Sweden, 1927), p. 55.
2. An admirable survey of the Celtic element in English place-names is given by E.Ekwall in the *Introduction to the Survey of English Place-Names,* ed. A.Mawer and F.M.Stenton for the English Place-Name Society, 1, part 1 (Cambridge, UK, 1924), pp. 15-35.
3. Cf. E.Ekwall, "Zu zwei keltischen Lehnwörtern in Altenglischen," *Englische Studien,* 54 (1920), 102-10.
4. *Umlaut is* a German word meaning 'alteration of sound'. In English this is sometimes called *mutation.*
5. The OE *flasce* should have become *flash* in Modern English, so that the word was probably reintroduced later and may have been influenced (as the *OED* suggests) by the Italian *fiasco.*
6. *Butter is* a difficult word to explain. The unweakened *t* suggests early borrowing. Butter was practically unknown to the Romans; Pliny has to explain its meaning and use. But a well-known allusion in Sidonius Apollinaris testifies to its use among the Burgundians on their hair. The bishop complains of the rancid odor of Burgundian chiefs with buttered hair.
7. The *OED* has an interesting essay on the uncertainties of the etymology of *church.* Other words that probably belong to the period of continental borrowing are *ynce* (ounce, inch), *palenise* (palace), *solor* (upper room), *tæfel* (chessboard), *miscian* (to mix), and *olfend* (camel), but there is some uncertainty about their origin or history.
8. J.Loth in *Les Mots latins dans les langues brittoniques* (Paris, 1892, p. 29) assigns fifteen words to this period. Some of these, however, are more probably to be considered continental borrowings.
9. Other words of this sort, which have not survived in Modern English, are *cemes* (shirt), *swiftlere* (slipper), *sûtere* (shoemaker), *byden* (tub, bushel), *bytt* (leather bottle), *cçac* (jug), *læfel* (cup), *orc* (pitcher), and *Strtsl* (blanket, rug).
10. Cf. also OE *cîepe* (onion, L. *cçpa),* [illegible] (turnip, L. *nâpus),* *sigle* (rye, V.L. *sigale).*
11. Also *sæppe* (spruce-fir), *môrbçam* (mulberry tree).
12. A number of interesting words of this class have not survived in modern usage, such as *aprotane* (wormwood), *armelu* (wild rue), *caric* (dry fig),

elehtre (lupin), *mârûfie* (horehound), *nepte* (catnip), *pollegie* (pennyroyal), *hymele* (hop-plant).

13. Most of these words were apparently bookish at this time and had to be reintroduced later from French.

14. The term *viking is* usually thought to be derived from Old Norse *vîk,* a bay, as indicating "one who ca me out from, or frequented, inlets of the sea." It may, however, come from OE *wîc,* a camp, "the formation of temporary encampments being a prominent feature of viking raids" *(OED).*

15. On this question see E.Ekwall, "How Long Did the Scandinavian Language Survive in England?" *Jespersen Miscellany,* pp. 17-30, and R.I.Page, "How Long Did the Scandinavian Language Survive in England? The Epigraphical Evidence," in *England Before the Conquest: Studies in Primary Sources Presented to Dorothy Whitelock,* ed. P.Clemoes and K.Hughes (Cambridge, UK, 1971), pp. 165-81.

16. The *k* in this could be accounted for on the basis of the oblique cases, but it is more probably due to Scandinavian influence. It is possible that the retention of the hard *k* and *g* is due to Anglian rather than Scandinavian tendencies.

4

The Norman Conquest and the Subjection of English

On the northern coast of France directly across from England is a district extending some seventy-five miles back from the Channel and known as Normandy. It derives its name from the bands of Northmen who settled there in the ninth and tenth centuries, at the same time that similar bands were settling in the north and east of England. The Seine offered a convenient channel for penetration into the country, and the settlements of Danes in this region furnish a close parallel to those around the Humber. A generation after Alfred reached an agreement with the North-men in England, a somewhat similar understanding was reached between Rollo, the leader of the Danes in Normandy, and Charles the Simple, king of France. In 912 the right of the Northmen to occupy this part of France was recognized; Rollo acknowledged the French king as his overlord and became the first duke of the Normans. In the following century and a half a succession of masterful dukes raised the dukedom to a position of great influence, over-shadowing at times the power of the king of France.

The adaptability of the Scandinavian, always a marked characteristic of this people, nowhere showed itself more quickly. Readily adopting the ideas and customs of those among whom they came to live, the Normans had soon absorbed the most important elements of French civilization. Moreover they injected fresh vigor into what they borrowed. They profited from their contact with French military forces and, adding French tactics to their own impetuous courage, soon had one of the best armies, if we may use the term, in Europe. They took important features of Frankish law, including the idea of the jury and, with a genius for organization that shows up as clearly in the Norman kingdom of Sicily as in Normandy and later in England, made it one of the outstanding legal systems of the world. They accepted Christianity and began the construction of those great Norman cathedrals that are still marvels to the modern architect. But most important of all, for us, they soon gave up their own language and learned French. So rapidly did the old Scandinavian tongue disappear in the Norman capital that the second duke was forced to send his son to Bayeux so that he might learn something of the speech of his forefathers. In the eleventh century, at the time of the Norman Conquest, the civilization of Normandy was essentially French, and the Normans were among the most advanced and progressive of the peoples of Europe.

For some years before the Norman Conquest the relations between England and Normandy had been fairly close. In 1002 Æthelred the Unready had married a Norman wife and, when driven into exile by the Danes, took refuge with his brother-in-law, the duke of Normandy. His son Edward, who had thus been brought up in France, was almost more French than English. At all events, when in 1042 the Danish line died out and Edward, known as the Confessor, was restored to the throne from which his father had been driven, he brought with him a number of his Norman friends, enriched them, and gave them important places in the government. A strong French atmosphere pervaded the English court during the twenty-four years of his reign.

When in January 1066, after a reign of twenty-four years, Edward the Confessor died childless, England was again faced with the choice of a successor. And there was not much doubt as to where the choice would fall. At his succession Edward had found England divided into a few large districts, each under the control of a powerful earl. The most influential of these nobles was Godwin, earl of the West Saxon earldom. He was a shrewd, capable man and was soon Edward's principal adviser. Except for one brief interval, he was the virtual ruler of England until the time of his death. His eldest son, Harold, succeeded to his title and influence and during the last twelve years of Edward's reign exercised a firm and capable influence over national affairs. The day after Edward's death Harold was elected king.

His election did not long go unchallenged. William, the duke of Normandy at this time, was a second cousin to the late king. Although this relationship did not give him any right of inheritance to the English throne, he had nevertheless been living in expectation of becoming Edward's successor. Edward seems to have encouraged him in this hope. While William had been on a brief visit in England, Edward had assured him that he should succeed him. Even Harold had been led, though unwillingly, to acknowledge his claim. Having on one occasion fallen into William's hands, it seems he had been forced to swear, as the price of his freedom, not to become a candidate or oppose William's election. But the English had had enough of French favorites, and when the time came Harold did not consider himself bound by his former pledge.

Only by force could William hope to obtain the crown to which he believed himself entitled. Perhaps the difftculty involved in an armed invasion of England would have discouraged a less determined claimant. But William was an exceptionally able man. From infancy he had surmounted difftculties. Handicapped by the taint of illegitimacy, the son of his father by a tanner's daughter of Falaise, he had succeeded to the dukedom of Normandy at the age of six. He was the object of repeated attempts upon his life, and only the devoted care of his regents enabled him to reach maturity. In early manhood he had had to face a number of crucial contests with rebellious barons, powerful neighbors, and even his overlord, the French king. But he had emerged triumphantly from them all, greatly strengthened in position and admirably schooled for the final test of his fortune. William the Great, as the chroniclers called him, was not the man to relinquish a kingdom without a struggle.

Having determined upon his course of action, he lost no time in beginning preparations. He secured the cooperation of his vassals by the promise of liberal rewards, once England was his to dispose of. He came to terms with his rivals and enemies on the continent. He appealed to the pope for the sanction of his enterprise and received the blessing of the Church. As a result of these inducements, the ambitious, the adventurous, and the greedy flocked to his banner from all over France and even other parts of Europe. In September he landed at Pevensey, on the south coast of England, with a formidable force.

His landing was unopposed. Harold was occupied in the north of England meeting an invasion by the king of Norway, another claimant to the throne, who had been joined by a brother of Harold's, Tostig, returning from exile. Hardly had Harold triumphed in battle over the invaders when word reached him of William's landing. The news was scarcely unexpected, but the English were not fully prepared for it. It was difficult to keep a medieval army together over a protracted period. William's departure had been delayed, and with the coming of the harvest season many of those whom Harold had assembled a few months before, in anticipation of an attack, had been sent home. Harold was forced to meet the invader with such forces as he had. He called upon his brothers-in-law in the earldoms of Mercia and Northumbria to join him and repel the foreigner by a united effort. But they hung back. Nevertheless, hurrying south with his army, Harold finally reached a point between the Norman host and London. He drew up his forces on a broad hill at Senlac, not far from Hastings, and awaited William's attack. The battle began at about nine o'clock in the morning. So advantageous was Harold's position and so well did the English defend themselves that in the afternoon they still held their ground. For William the situation was becoming desperate, and he resorted to a desperate stratagem. His only hope lay in getting the English out of their advantageous position on the hill. Because he could not drive them off, he determined to try to lure them off and ordered a feigned retreat. The English fell into the trap. Thinking the Normans were really fleeing, a part of the English army started in pursuit, intending to cut them down in their flight. But the Normans made a stand, and the battle was renewed on more even terms. Then happened one of those accidents more easily possible in medieval than in modern warfare. Harold, always in the thick of the fight, was killed during the battle. According to tradition, he was pierced in the eye by a Norman arrow (although the Bayeux Tapestry supplies contradictory evidence about the arrow). In any event, his death seems to have been instantaneous. Two of his brothers had already fallen. Deprived of their leaders, the English became disorganized. The confusion spread. The Normans were quick to profit by the situation, and the English were soon in full retreat. When night fell they were fleeing in all directions, seeking safety under the cover of darkness, and William was left in possession of the field.

Although William had won the battle of Hastings and eliminated his rival, he had not yet attained the English crown. It was only after he had burnt and pillaged the southeast of England that the citizens of London decided that further resistance would be useless. Accordingly they capitulated, and on Christmas Day 1066, William was crowned king of England.

The Norman Settlement

William's victory at Hastings and his subsequent coronation in London involved more than a mere substitution of one monarch for another. It was not as though he had been chosen originally as the successor of Edward. In that case there would doubtless have been more French favorites at court, as in the time of the Confessor, and Normans in certain important offices. But the English nobility would have remained intact, and the English government would have continued with its tradition unbroken. But William's possession of the throne had been a matter of conquest and was attended by all the consequences of the conquest of one people by another.

One of the most important of these consequences was the

introduction of a new nobility.[1] Many of the English higher class had been killed on the field at Hastings. Those who escaped were treated as traitors, and the places of both alike were filled by William's Norman followers. This process was repeated several times during the next four years while the Conquest was being completed. For William's coronation did not win immediate recognition throughout England. He was in fact acknowledged only in the southeast. Upon his return from a visit to Normandy the following year he was faced with serious rebellions in the southwest, the west, and the north. It was necessary for him to enter upon a series of campaigns and to demonstrate, often with ruthless severity, his mastery of the country. As a result of these campaigns the Old English nobility was practically wiped out. Although many lesser landholders kept small estates, the St. Albans Chronicler was but slightly exaggerating when he said that scarcely a single noble of English extraction remained in the kingdom.[2] In 1072 only one of the twelve earls in England was an Englishman, and he was executed four years later.[3] What was true in the time of the Conqueror was true also in the reigns of his sons, and later. For several generations after the Conquest the important positions and the great estates were almost always held by Normans or men of foreign blood. As an English poet, Robert of Brunne (1338), sums up the situation,

> To Frankis & Normanz, for þar grete laboure,
> To Flemmynges & Pikardes, þat were with him in stoure,
>
> He gaf londes bityme, of whilk þer successoure
> Hold Zit þe seysyne, with fulle grete honoure.[4]

In like manner Norman prelates were gradually introduced into all important positions in the church. The two archbishops were Normans. Wulfstan of Worcester was the only Old English bishop who retained his office until the end of the Conqueror's reign, and even his exceptional personality did not prevent him from being scorned by Lanfranc as a simple and untutored man, ignorant of the French language and unable to assist in the king's councils.[5] The English abbots were replaced more slowly, but as fast as vacancies occurred through death or deprivation they were filled generally by foreigners. In 1075 thirteen of the twenty-one abbots who signed the decrees of the Council of London were English; twelve years later their number had been reduced to three. Foreign monks and priests followed the example of their superiors and sought the greater opportunities for advancement that England now offered. A number of new foundations were established and entirely peopled by monks brought over from Norman houses.

It is less easy to speak with certainty of the Normans in the lower walks of life who came into England with William's army. Many of them doubtless remained in the island, and their number was increased by constant accretions throughout the rest of the eleventh century and the whole of the next. The numerous castles that the Conqueror built were apparently garrisoned by foreign troops.[6] In the chronicles of the period we find instances extending all through the twelfth century of foreign forces being brought to England. Many of these doubtless made but a short stay in the island, but it is safe to say that every Norman baron was surrounded by a swarm of Norman retainers. William of Newburgh speaks of the bishop of Ely, in the reign of Richard I, as surrounding his person with an army of friends and foreign soldiers, as well as arranging marriages between Englishmen of position and his relations, "of whom he brought over from Normandy multitudes for this purpose."[7] Ecclesiastics, it would seem, sometimes entered upon their office accompanied by an armed band of supporters. Turold, who became abbot of Peterborough in 1070, is

> To French and Normans, for their great labor,
> To Flemings and Picards, that were with him in battle,
>
> He gave lands betimes, of which their successors
> Hold yet the seizin, with full great honor.

described as coming at the head of 160 armed Frenchmen to take possession of his monastery;[8] and Thurston, appointed abbot of Glastonbury in 1082, imposed certain innovations in the service upon the monks of the abbey by calling for his Norman archers, who entered the chapter house fully armed and killed three of the monks, besides wounding eighteen.[9] Likewise merchants and craftsmen from the continent seem to have settled in England in considerable numbers.[10] There was a French town beside the English one at Norwich and at Nottingham,[11] and French Street in Southampton, which retains its name to this day, was in the Middle Ages one of the two principal streets of the town.[12] It is quite impossible to say how many Normans and French people settled in England in the century and a half following the Conquest,[13] but because the governing class in both church and state was almost exclusively made up from among them, their influence was out of all proportion to their number.

The Use of French by the Upper Class

Whatever the actual number of Normans settled in England, it is clear that the members of the new ruling class were sufficiently predominant to continue to use their own language. This was natural enough at first, as they knew no English; but they continued to do so for a long time to come, picking up some knowledge of English gradually but making no effort to do so as a matter of policy. For 200 years after the Norman Conquest, French remained the language of ordinary intercourse among the upper classes in England. At first those who spoke French were those of Norman origin, but soon through intermarriage and association with the ruling class numerous people of English extraction must have found it to their advantage to learn the new language, and before long the distinction between those who spoke French and those who spoke English was not ethnic but largely social. The language of the masses remained English, and it is reasonable to assume that a French soldier settled on a manor with a few hundred English peasants would soon learn the language of the people among whom his lot was cast. The situation was well described, about the year 1300, by the writer of a chronicle which goes by the name of *Robert of Gloucester:*

> Þus com lo engelond in to normandies hond.
> & þe normans ne couþe speke þo bote hor owe speche
> & speke french as hii dude atom, & hor children dude also teche;

So þat heiemen of þis lond þat of hor blod come
Holdeþ alle þulke spreche þat hii of hom nome.
Vor bote a man conne frenss me telþ of him lute.
Ac lowe men holdeþ to engliss & to hor owe speche 3ᵘte-
Ich wene þer ne beþ in al þe world contreyes none
Pat ne holdeþ to hor owe speche bote engelond one.
Ac wel me wot uor to conne boþe wel it is,
Vor þe more þat a mon can, þe more wurþe he is.[14] (7537-47)

An instructive parallel to the bilingual character of England in this period is furnished by the example of Belgium today. Here we find Flemish and French (Walloon) in use side by side. (Flemish is only another name for the Dutch spoken in Belgium, which is practically identical to that of the southern Netherlands.) Although the use of the two languages here is somewhat a matter of geography—Flemish prevailing in the north and French in the part of the country lying toward France—it is also to some extent dependent upon the social and cultural position of the individual. French is often spoken by the upper classes, even in Flemish districts, while in such a city as Brussels it is possible to notice a fairly clear division between the working classes, who speak Flemish, and the higher economic and social groups, who attend French schools, read French newspapers, and go to French theaters. In the interest of accuracy, it may be noted parenthetically that fluency in French is becoming less common in the north, especially among the younger generation.

Circumstances Promoting the Continued Use of French

The most important factor in the continued use of French by the English upper class until the beginning of the thirteenth century was the close connection that existed through all these years between England and the continent. From the time of the Conquest the kings of England were likewise dukes of Normandy. To the end of his life William the Conqueror seems to have felt more closely attached to his dukedom than to the country he governed by right of conquest. Not only was he buried there, but in dividing his possessions at his death he gave Normandy to his eldest son and England to William, his second son. Later the two domains were united again in the hands of Henry I. Upon the accession of Henry II, English possessions in France were still further enlarged. Henry, as count of Anjou, inherited from his father the districts of Anjou and Maine. By his marriage with Eleanor of Aquitaine he came into possession of vast estates in the south, so that when he became king of England he controlled about two-thirds of France, all the western part of the country from the English Channel to the Pyrenees.

Under the circumstances it is not surprising that the attention of the English should often be focused upon affairs in France. Indeed, English kings often spent a great part of their time there. The Conqueror and his sons were in France for about half of their respective reigns. Henry I (1100-1135) was there for a total of more than seventeen out of the thirty-five years of his reign, sometimes for periods of three and four years at a time.[15] Although conditions at home kept Stephen (1135-1154) for the most part in England, Henry II (1154-1189) spent nearly two-thirds of his long reign in France. When we remember that, except for Henry I, no English king until Edward IV (1461-1483) sought a wife in England, it is easy to see how continentally minded English royalty was and how natural a thing would seem the continued use of French at the English court.

What was true of the royal family was equally true of the nobility in general. The English nobility was not so much a nobility of England as an Anglo-French aristocracy. Nearly all the great English landowners had possessions likewise on the continent, frequently contracted continental marriages, and spent much time in France, either in pursuance of their own interests or those of the king. When we remember that on many of the occasions when the king and his nobles crossed the Channel they were engaged in military operations and were accompanied by military forces, that the business of ecclesiastics and merchants constantly took them abroad, we can readily see how this constant going and coming across the narrow seas made the continued use of French by those concerned not only natural but inevitable.

The Attitude toward English

There is no reason to think that the preference that the governing class in England showed for French was anything more than a natural result of circumstances. The idea that the newcomers were actively hostile to the English language is without foundation.[16] It is true that English was now an uncultivated tongue, the language of a socially inferior class, and that a bishop like Wulfstan might be subjected to Norman disdain in part, at least, because of his ignorance of that social shibboleth.[17] Henry of Huntington's statement that it was considered a disgrace to be called an Englishman may be set down to rhetorical exaggeration. It is unreasonable to expect a conquered people to feel no resentment or the Norman never to be haughty or overbearing. But there is also plenty of evidence of mutual respect and peaceful cooperation, to say nothing of intermarriage, between the Normans and the English from the beginning. The chronicler Orderic Vitalis, himself the son of a Norman father and an English mother, in spite of the fact that he spent his life from the age of ten in Normandy, always refers to himself as an Englishman.

According to the same chronicler[18] William the Conqueror made an effort himself at the age of forty-three to learn English, that he might understand and render justice in the disputes between his subjects, but his energies were too completely absorbed by his many other activities to enable him to make much progress. There is nothing improbable in the statement. Certainly the assertion of a fourteenth-century writer[19] that the Conqueror considered how he might destroy the "Saxon" tongue in order that English and French might speak the same language seems little less than silly in view of the king's efforts to promote the belief that he was the authentic successor of the Old English kings and in the light of his use of English alongside of Latin, to the exclusion of French, in his charters. His youngest son, Henry I, may have known some English, though we must give up the pretty story of his interpreting the English words in a charter to the monks of Colchester.[20] If later kings for a time seem to have been ignorant of the language,[21] their lack of acquaintance with it is not to be attributed to any fixed purpose. In the period with which we are at the moment concerned—the period up to 1200—the attitude of the king and the upper classes toward the English language may be characterized as one of simple indifference. They did not cultivate English—which is not the same as saying that they had no acquaintance with it—because their activities in England did not necessitate it and their constant concern with continental affairs made French for them much more useful.

French Literature at the English Court

How completely French was the English court at this time is clearly shown by the literature produced for royal and noble patronage. In an age that had few of our modern means of entertainment, literature played a much more important part in the lives of the leisured class. And it is interesting to find a considerable body of French literature being produced in England from the beginning of the twelfth century, addressed to English patrons and directed toward meeting their special tastes and interests. We do not know much about the literary conditions at the court of the Conqueror himself, although his recognition of learning is to be seen in many of his appointments to high ecclesiastical positions. His daughter Adela was a patron of poets, and his son Henry I, whether or not he deserved the title Beauclerc that contemporaries gave him,[22] was at least married successively to two queens who were generous in their support of poets. His court was the center of much literary activity[23] Matilda, his first wife, was especially partial to foreign poets.[24] For Adelaide of Louvain, his second wife, David related the achievements of her husband, the king, in French verse. The work is lost, but we know of it from the statement of a contemporary poet, Geoffrey Gaimar, who boasted that he knew more tales than David ever knew or than Adelaide had in books. Likewise for Adelaide, Philippe de Thaun wrote his *Bestiary,* a poem describing rather fancifully the nature of various animals and adding to each description a moral still more fanciful. Gaimar wrote his *History of the English,* likewise in French verse, for Lady Custance "li Gentil," who also paid him a mark of silver for a copy of David's poem, which she kept in her chamber. At the same time Samson de Nanteuil devoted 11,00 lines of verse to be *Proverbs of Solomon* for Lady Adelaide de Condé, wife of a Lincolnshire baron. In the reign of Henry II Wace wrote his celebrated *Roman de Brut* and presented it to the queen, Eleanor of Aquitaine. It is a legendary history of Britain, in which the exploits of King Arthur occupy a prominent place, and was certain to interest a royal family anxious to know something about the history of the country over which it had come to rule. Later Wace undertook in his *Roman de Rou* to write a similar account of the dukes of Normandy. Works of devotion and edification, saints' lives, allegories, chronicles, and romances of Horn, Havelok, Tristan, and other heroes poured forth in the course of the twelfth century. It is indicative of the firm roots that French culture had taken on English soil that so important a body of literature in the French language could be written in or for England, much of it under the direct patronage of the court.

Fusion of the Two Peoples

As we look back over any considerable stretch of history we are likely to experience in the perspective a foreshortening that makes a period of 150 years seem relatively small, and we fail to realize that changes that seem sudden are in rality quite a natural in the course of a lifetime or a succession of generations. In the years following the Norman Conquest the sting of defeat and the hardships incident to so great a political and social disturbance were gradually forgotten. People accepted the new order as something accomplished; they accepted it as a fact and adjusted themselves to it. The experience of our own time shows how quickly national antagonisms and the biterness of war can be allayed, and what a decade or two in the twentieth century can accomplish in this respect must be allowed to have been possible also in the eleventh. The fusion of Normans and English was rapid, but not more rapid than national interest and the intercourse of everyday life would normally bring about. The distinction between French and English that appears among the Domesday jurors[25] or a document of 1100 addressed by Henry I "to all his faithful people, both French and English, in Hertfordshire" does not long survive. When a distinction is made it soon comes to be between the English, meaning all people of England, and the French, meaning the inhabitants of Franch. This early fusion of French and English in England is quite clear from a variety of evidences. It is evident in the marriage of Normans to English women, as when Robert d'Oily further enriched himself by marrying Eadgyth, the daughter of a great English landowner, or when the parents of Orderic Vitalis, already mentioned, were united.[26] It is evident from the way in which the English gave their support to their rulers and Norman prelates, as when William II and Henry I drove off foreign invaders with armies made up almost wholly of English troops or when, Anselm and Becket found their staunchest supporters among the English.[27] It is evident in many other ways. Between 1072 and 1079 Wulfstan brought about some sort of spiritual federation between the monks of Worcester and six other English monasteries—Evesham, Chertsey, Bath, Pershore, Winchecombe, and Gloucester—in which we find "the heads of these great monasteries, some Norman, some English,...binding themselves together without respect of birth or birthplace, in the closest spiritual fellowship."[28] Norman nobles identified themselves with their new country by founding monasteries on their estates and chose burial for themselves and their families in their adopted land rather than in Normandy.[29] In the towns the associations incident to trade are spoken of by Orderic Vitalis as another factor in bringing about a union between the two peoples.[30] Everywhere there are signs of convergence. The fusion seems to have gone forward rapidly in the reign of Henry I, and by the end of the twelfth century an English jurist was able to write: "Now that the English and Normans have been dwelling together, marrying and giving in marriage, the two nations have become so mixed that it is scarcely possible to-day, speaking of free men, to tell who is English, who of Norman race."[31] Only the events of the next century, the loss of Normandy, and the growing antagonism toward France were necessary to complete the union, psychological as well as physical, of all the inhabitants of England.

The Diffusion of French and English

The difftcult question of the extent to which English and French were used in England after the Norman Conquest is not easily answered. The evidence on which we can base a conclusion is scattered, must be carefully appraised, and is not always easy to harmonize. From time to time writers of the period tell us that such a one spoke both French and English or that he was ignorant of one or the other language. At times incidents in the chroniclers enable us to draw a pretty safe inference. Books and treatises, such as the *Ancrene Riwle* and the various thirteenth-century works on husbandry, when we know the individuals for whom they were written, or the social class, at least, to which they belong, shed some light on the problem. From the thirteenth century on, something can be gleaned from the proceedings of the courts, where the language in which a man testifies is occasionally noted. The appearance of manuals from about 1250 for the teaching of French is significant. In the fourteenth century poets and writers often preface their works with an explanation of the language employed and incidentally indulge from time to time in valuable observations of a more general linguistic nature. In the fifteenth century the evidence becomes fairly abundant—letters public and private, the acts and records of towns, guilds, and the central government, and a variety of incidental allusion. From all of this accumulated testimony the situation can be easily enough stated in general terms, as, indeed, has already been done (§ 85): French was the language of the court and the upper classes, English the speech of the mass of the people. Can we, however, define the position of the two languages more specifically? The question to be asked is really twofold: (1) When and how generally did the upper class learn English? (2) How far down in the social scale was a knowledge of French at all general?

Knowledge of English among the Upper Class

We have already remarked that the use of French was not confined to persons of foreign extraction, but that all those who were brought into association with the governing class soon acquired a command of it. It was a mark of social distinction. On the other hand, the fact that English was the language of the greater part of the population made it altogether likely that many of the upper class would acquire some familiarity with it. Such appears to have been the case, at least by the twelfth century. The evidence comes mostly from the reign of Henry II.[32] The most striking instance is that reported (c. 1175) by William of Canterbury in his life of Becket. On one occasion Helewisia de Morville, wife of a man of Norman descent and mother of one of Becket's murderers, invoked the aid of her husband in an emergency by crying out, "Huge de Morevile, ware, ware, ware, Lithulf heth his swerd adrage!"[33] Clearly her husband, whatever language he spoke, understood English. Henry II himself seems to have understood English, though he did not speak it. According to a story twice told by Giraldus Cambrensis[34] he was once addressed by a Welshman in English. Understanding the remark, "the king, in French, desired Philip de Mercros, who held the reins of his horse, to ask the rustic if he had dreamt this." When the knight explained the king's question in English, the peasant replied in the same language he had used before, addressing himself to the king, not the interpreter. That the king's knowledge of English did not extend to an ability to speak the language is in harmony with the testimony of Walter Map, who credits him with "having a knowledge of all the languages which are spoken from the Bay of Biscay to the Jordan, but making use only of Latin and French." [5] His wife, however, Eleanor of Aquitaine, always required an interpreter when people spoke English.[36] The three young women of aristocratic family for whom the *Ancrene Riwle,* or *Rule for Anchoresses,* was probably written about 1200 were advised to do their reading in either French or English, and the original language of the *Rule* itself was almost certainly English.

That English survived for a considerable time in some monasteries is evident from the fact that at Peterborough the Anglo-Saxon Chronicle was continued until 1154. Among churchmen the ability to speak English was apparently fairly common. Gilbert Foliot, bishop of London, a man of Norman descent, was, according to Walter Map,[37] very fluent in Latin,

French, and English. Hugh of Nonant, bishop of Coventry, a native of Normandy, must have known English, since he criticizes a fellow bishop for his ignorance of it,[38] while Giraldus Cambrensis, bishop-elect of St. Davids, had such a knowledge of English that he could read and comment upon the language of Alfred and compare the dialects of northern and southern England.[39] At the same date Abbot Samson, head of the great abbey of Bury St. Edmunds, is thus described by Jocelyn de Brakelond: "He was an eloquent man, speaking both French and Latin, but rather careful of the good sense of that which he had to say than of the style of his words. He could read books written in English very well, and was wont to preach to the people in English, but in the dialect of Norfolk where he was born and bred."

From these instances we must not make the mistake of thinking such a knowledge of English universal among people of this station. Others could be cited in which bishops and abbots were unable to preach in anything but Latin or French.[40] St. Hugh, bishop of Lincoln in the time of Henry II, did not understand English but required an interpreter.[41] One of the most notorious cases of a man who did not know English and who was not only an important ecclesiastic but also one of the chief men of the kingdom is that of William Longchamp, bishop of Ely and chancellor of England in the reign of Richard I. The incident is alluded to in a number of chroniclers, of his seeking to escape from England in 1191, disguised as a woman and carrying under his arm some cloth as if for sale. When approached at Dover by a possible purchaser, who asked how much he would let her have an ell for, he was unable to reply because he was utterly unacquainted with the English language.[42] It is true that both of these men were foreigners, one a Burgundian, the other a Norman, and the fact of their not knowing English is set down by contemporaries as something worth noting. Among those of lower rank, whose position brought them into contact with both the upper and the lower class—stewards and bailiffs, for example—or men like the knight of Glamorgan, whom we have seen acting as Henry's interpreter, the ability to speak English as well as French must have been quite general. And among children whose parents spoke different languages a knowledge of English is to be assumed even from the days of the Conqueror if we may consider the case of Orderic Vitalis as representative. His father was Norman and his mother (presumably) English. He was taught Latin by an English priest and at the age of ten was sent to St. Evroult in Normandy. There he says "like Joseph in Egypt, I heard a language which I did not know."

The conclusion that seems to be justified by the somewhat scanty facts we have to go on in this period is that a knowledge of English was not uncommon at the end of the twelfth century among those who habitually used French; that among churchmen and men of education it was even to be expected; and that among those whose activities brought them into contact with both upper and lower classes the ability to speak both languages was quite general.

Knowledge of French among the Middle Class

If by the end of the twelfth century a knowledge of English was not unusual among members of the highest class, it seems equally clear that a knowledge of French was often found somewhat further down in the social scale. Among the knightly class French seems to have been cultivated even when the mother tongue was English. In the reign of Henry II a knight in England got a man from Normandy to teach his son French.[43] That an ability to speak French was expected among this class may be inferred from an incident in one of the chroniclers describing a long-drawn-out suit (1191) between the abbey of Croyland and the prior of Spalding. Four supposed knights were called to testify that they had made a view of the abbot. They were neither knights nor holders of a knight's fee, and the abbot testified that they had never come to make a view of him. The chronicler adds that "the third one of them did not so much as know how to speak French."[44] Next to the knights the inhabitants of towns probably contained the largest number of those among the middle class who knew French. In many towns, especially in important trading centers, men with Norman names were the most prominent burgesses and probably constituted a majority of the merchant class.[45] The likelihood that stewards and bailiffs on manors spoke both languages has already been mentioned. In fact, a knowledge of French may sometimes have extended to the free tenants. At any rate Jocelyn de Brakelond relates that the Abbot Samson conferred a manor upon a man bound to the soil "because he was a good farmer and didn't know how to speak French." William Rothwell has discussed the complex situation in medieval England as a result of the presence of three languages—Latin, French, and English—and has noted the greater likelihood of French in regions nearer London: "Latin and French would be found primarily in those places where the business of government was transacted and would be used by men for whom they constituted a professional qualification, not a vernacular."[46] It has sometimes been urged that because preaching to the people was often done in French, such a fact argues for an understanding of the language. But we are more than once told in connection with such notices that the people, although they did not understand what was said, were profoundly moved.[47] It would be a mistake to consider that a knowledge of French was anything but exceptional among the common people as a whole. The observation of a writer at the end of the thirteenth century, Lewede men cune Ffrensch non, Among an hondryd vnneþis on[48] was probably true at all times in the Middle Ages.[49]

Recent insights from sociolinguistics into the structures of pidgin and creole language have led some linguists to ask whether Middle English was a creole. Much of the ensuing controversy hinges on the definitions that are given to *pidgin* and *creole* (for a related problem see § 250.8). A pidgin is a simplified language used for communication between speakers of different languages, typically (during the past five centuries) for trading purposes between speakers of a European language such as Portuguese, Spanish, French, or English and speakers of an African or Asian language. If the simplified language is then learned as a first language by a new generation of speakers and its structures and vocabulary are expanded to serve the needs of its community of speakers, it is known as a creole. The linguistic situation in England during the twelfth and thirteenth centuries had certain external parallels with that in the present-day Caribbean or the South Pacific, where languages are regularly in contact, and pidgins and creoles develop. However, to call Middle English a creole stretches the word beyond its usefulness. Manfred Görlach reviews the evidence, finds a lack of "any texts that could justify the assumption that there was a stable pidgin or creole English in use in thirteenth-century French households," and concludes: "The English-speaking majority among the population of some ninety percent did not unlearn their English after the advent of French, nor did they intentionally modify its structures on the French pattern—as Renaissance writers modelled their English on Latin. Influence of French on inflections and, by and large, on syntactical structures cannot be proved, but appears unlikely from what we know about bilingualism in Middle English times."[50]

Thus in the period preceding the loss of Normandy in 1204 there were some who spoke only French and many more who spoke only English. There was likewise a considerable number who were genuinely bilingual as well as many who had some understanding of both languages while speaking only one. That the latter class—those who were completely or to some extent bilingual—should have been fairly numerous need cause no surprise. Among people accustomed to learn more through the ear than through the eye, learning a second language presents no great problem. The ability to speak one or more languages besides one's native tongue is largely a matter of opportunity, as can be seen in a number of European countries today. In this connection we may again recall the situation of Belgium, where the majority of the people can get along in either Flemish or French, regardless of which of the two languages they habitually use.

REFERENCES

1. On the fate of the Old English aristocracy see F.M.Stenton, "English Families and the Norman Conquest," *Trans. Royal Hist. Soc.*, 4th ser., 26 (1944), 1-12.

2. Roger of Wendover, ed. H.O.Coxe, II, 23 (Eng. Hist. Soc.).
3. P.V.D.Shelly, *English and French in England, 1066-1100* (Philadelphia, 1921), p. 32.
4. *Chronicle,* ed. Hearne, I, 72:
5. Roger of Wendover, II, 52.
6. OrdericVitalis, Bk. IV, *passim.*
7. William of Newburgh, Bk. IV, chap. 14, 16.
8. Freeman, *Norman Conquest,* IV, 457, 459.
9. Freeman, IV, 390-93. Both incidents are related in the Peterborough Chronicle.
10. A contemporary biographer of Thomas Becket tells us that many natives of Rouen and Caen settled in London, preferring to dwell in this city because it was better fitted for commerce and better supplied with the things in which they were accustomed to trade. *Materials for the History of Thomas Becket,* IV, 81 (Rolls Series).
11. W.Cunningham, *Alien Immigrants to England,* pp. 35-36.
12. P.Studer, *Oak Book of Southampton,* I, xii ff.
13. F.York Powell in Traill's *Social England,* I, 346, says: "One may sum up the change in England by saying that some 20,000 foreigners replaced some 20,000 Englishmen; and that these newcomers got the throne, the earldoms, the bishoprics, the abbacies, and far the greater portion of the big estates, mediate and immediate, and many of the burgess holdings in the chief towns." We do not know what the estimate is based upon, but unless it refers, as it seems to do, to the years immediately following the Conquest, it does not seem to be too high.
14. Thus came, lo! England into Normandy's hand.

    And the Normans didn't know how to speak then but their own speech
    And spoke French as they did at home, and their children did also teach;
    So that high men of this land that of their blood come
    Hold all that same speech that they took from them.
    For but a man know French men count of him little.
    But low men hold to English and to their own speech yet.
    I think there are in all the world no countries
    That don't hold to their own speech but England alone.
    But men well know it is well for to know both,
    For the more that a man knows, the more worth he is.
15. W.Farrer, "An Outline Itinerary of King Henry the First," *Eng. Hist. Rev.,* 34 (1919), 303-82, 505-79.

16 On this subject see the excellent discussion in Shelly, *English and French in England.*

17. Roger of Wendover, ed. H.O.Coxe, II, 52.

18. Ordericus Vitalis, ed. Prevost, II, 215.

19. Robert Holkot, on the authority of John Selden, *Eadmeri Monachi Cantuariensis Historiae Novorum siue sui Saeculi Libri VI* (London, 1623), p. 189.

20. The story was considered authentic by so critical a student as J.Horace Round ("Henry I as an English Scholar," *Academy,* Sept. 13, 1884, p. 168), but the charter was proved by J.Armitage Robinson to be a forgery. Cf. C.W.David, "The Claim of King Henry I to Be Called Learned," *Anniversary Essays in the Medieval History by Students of Charles Homer Haskins* (Boston, 1929), pp. 45-56.

21. We do not know whether William Rufus and Stephen knew English. Henry II understood it, although he apparently did not speak it. Richard I was thoroughly French; his whole stay in England amounted to only a few months. He probably knew no English. Concerning John's knowledge of English we have no evidence. As Freeman remarks *(Norman Conquest,* II, 129), the royal family at this time is frequently the least English in England and is not to be used as a norm for judging the diffusion of the two languages.

22. The question is decided in the negative by David, "The Claim of King Henry I."

23. For a fuller treatment of the subject, see an excellent study by K.J.Holzknecht, *Literary Patronage in the Middle Ages* (Philadelphia, 1923), chap. 12.

24. William of Malmesbury, *Gesta Regum Anglorum,* II, 494 (Rolls Series).

25. Round, *Feudal England,* pp.120-21.

26. Matthew Paris speaks of the Conqueror as promoting mariages between the Norrnans and the English. Cf. *Gesta Abbatum,* I, 44 (Rolls Series).

27. Hardy, *Catalogue of Materials,* II, xxiv.

28. Freeman, *Norman Conquest,* IV, 382-87.

29 Shelly, *English and French in England,* p. 42.

30. Freeman, IV, chap. VII.

31 Dialogus de Scaccario (1177). Stubbs, *Select Charters* (4th ed., 1881), p. 168. The *Dialogus de Scaccario* is edited and translated by Charles Johnson (London, 1950). Hardy, *Catalogue of Materials,* II, xxiv.

32. Some of William the Conqueror's English writs were addressed to Normans. But this hardly implies that they understood English any more than the king himself did. It is doubtful whether the recipients in many cases could have read the writ themselves in any language.

33. *Maerials for the History of Thomas Becket,* I, 128 (Rolls Series).

34. *Itinerary through Wales,* Bk. I, chap. 6; *Conquest of Ireland,* Bk. I, chap. 40.

35. *De Nugis Curialium,* V, vi (trans. Tupper and Ogle).

36. Richard of Devizes, in *Chronicles of the Reigns of Stephen, Henry II, and Richard I,* III, 431 (Rolls Series).

37. *De Nugis,* I, xii. However, his fluency in three languages may have been mentioned because it was unusual.

38. Cf. Freeman, *Norman Conquest,* V, 831.

39. *Descr. of Wales,* Bk. I, chap. 6.

40. For example, Jofrid, abbot of Croyland, if we can trust the fourteenth-century continuation of Pseudo-Ingulph. The abbot of Durham who visited St. Godric (died 1170) needed an interpreter because Godric spoke English. Cf. *Libellus de Vita et Miracula S.Godrici,* p. 352 *(Surtees Soc.,* xx).

41. *Magna Vita,* ed. Dimick, pp. 157, 268 (Rolls Series).

42. One of the fullest accounts is in Roger of Hoveden, III, 141-47 (Rolls Series).

43. *Materials for the History of Thomas Becket,* I, 347; Freeman, V, 891.

44. Continuation of Pseudo-Ingulph, trans. H.T.Riley, p. 286. The continuation in which this incident occurs is not to be confused with the fourteenth-century forgery but is a genuine work of considerable value (Gross).

45. At Southampton at the time of the Domesday survey the number of those who settled in the borough "after King William came into England" was sixty-five French born and thirty-one English born. The figures represent men and many of them doubtless had families. Cf. J.S.Davies, *A History of Southampton* (Southampton, UK, 1883), pp. 26-28.

46. "Language and Government in Medieval England," *Zeitschrift für französischen Sprache und Literatur,* 93 (1983), 259.

47. As, for example, by Giraldus Cambrensis, *Itinerary through Wales,* Bk. I, chap. 11. A similar instance, equally specific though less trustworthy,

is in the continuation of Pseudo-Ingulph attributed to Peter of Blois (trans. Riley, p. 238).

48. *The Romance of Richard the Lion-hearted,* ed. Brunner, lines 23-24: Common men know no French. Among a hundred scarcely one.

49. Vising, in his *Anglo-Norman Language and Literature,* pp. 15-18, and in his other contributions mentioned in the bibliography to this chapter, cites a number of passages from poets who explain why they are writing in French as evidence for "the complete dominance of the Anglo-Norman language during the second half of the twelfth and most of the thirteenth century in nearly all conditions of life, and of its penetration even into the lower strata of society." But the point in every case is that their work is "translaté hors de latin en franceys a l'aprise de lay gent" and is intended for those "ke de clergie ne ount apris," that is, who know no Latin. Even in the one instance in which the poet included in his appeal "Li grant e li mendre," his words need apply only to those less than "the great" who can understand his work in French, "Q' en franceis le poent entendre."

50. Manfred Görlach, "Middle English—a Creole?" in *Linguistics across Historical and Geographical Boundaries,* ed. D.Kastovsky and A.Szwedek (2 vols., Berlin, 1986), I, 337, 338.

5

Language Changing after 1200–1500

How long the linguistic situation just described would have continued if the conditions under which it arose had remained undisturbed is impossible to say. As long as England held its continental territory and the nobility of England were united to the continent by ties of property and kindred, a real reason existed for the continued use of French among the governing class in the island. If the English had permanently retained control over the two-thirds of France that they once held, French might have remained permanently in use in England. But shortly after 1200 conditions changed. England lost an important part of its possessions abroad. The nobility gradually relinquished their continental estates. A feeling of rivalry developed between the two countries, accompanied by an antiforeign movement in England and culminating in the Hundred Years' War. During the century and a half following the Norman Conquest, French had been not only natural but more or less necessary to the English upper class; in the thirteenth and fourteenth centuries its maintenance became increasingly artificial. For a time certain new factors helped it to hold its ground, socially and officially. Meanwhile, however, social and economic changes affecting the English-speaking part of the population were taking place, and in the end numbers told. In the fourteenth century English won its way back into universal use, and in the fifteenth century French all but disappeared. We must now examine in detail the steps by which this situation came about.

The Loss of Normandy

The first link in the chain binding England to the continent was broken in 1204 when King John lost Normandy. John, seeing the beautiful Isabel of Angouleme, fell violently in love with her and, no doubt having certain political advantages in mind, married her in great haste (1200), notwithstanding the fact that she was at the time formally betrothed to Hugh of Lusignan, the head of a powerful and ambitious family. To make matters worse, John, anticipating hostility from the Lusignans, took the initiative and wantonly attacked them. They appealed for redress to their common overlord, the king of France. Philip saw in the situation an opportunity to embarrass his most irritating vassal. He summoned John (1202) to appear before his court at Paris, answer the charges against him, and submit to the judgment of his peers. John maintained that as king of England he was not subject to the jurisdiction of the French court; Philip replied that as duke of Normandy he was. John demanded a safe conduct, which Philip offered to grant only on conditions that John could not accept. Consequently, on the day of the trial the English king did not appear, and the court declared his territory confiscated according to feudal law. Philip proceeded at once to carry out the decision of the court and invaded Normandy. A succession of victories soon put the greater part of the duchy in his control. One after another of John's supporters deserted him. His unpopularity was increased by the news of the death of the young prince Arthur, John's nephew and captive, who was married to Philip's daughter and who, it was firmly believed, had been murdered. In 1204 Rouen surrendered, and Normandy was lost to the English crown.

So far as it affected the English language, as in other respects as well, the loss of Normandy was wholly advantageous. King and nobles were now forced to look upon England as their first concern. Although England still retained large continental possessions, they were in the south of France and had never been so intimately connected by ties of language, blood, and property interests as had Normandy. It gradually became apparent that the island kingdom had its own political and economic ends and that these were not the same as those of France. England was on the way to becoming not merely a geographical term but once more a nation.

Separation of the French and English Nobility

One of the important consequences of the event just described was that it brought to a head the question of whether many of the nobility owed their allegiance to England or to France. After the Norman Conquest a large number held lands in both countries. A kind of interlocking aristocracy existed, so that it might be difficult for some of the English nobility to say whether they belonged more to England or to the continent. Some steps toward a separation of their interests had been taken from time to time. The example of the Conqueror, who left Normandy to his son Robert and England to William Rufus, was occasionally followed by his companions. The Norman and English estates of William Fitz Osbern were divided in this way at his death in 1071, and of Roger de Montgomery in 1094, though the latter were afterwards reunited.[1] On several occasions Henry I confiscated the English estates of unruly Norman barons. But in 1204 the process of separation was greatly accelerated, for by a decree of 1204-1205 the king of France announced that he had confiscated the lands of several great barons, including the earls of Warenne, Arundel, Leicester, and Clare, and of all those knights who had their abode in England.[2] For the most part the families that had estates on both sides of the Channel were compelled to give up one or the other. Sometimes they divided into branches and made separate terms; in other cases great nobles preferred their larger holdings in England and gave up their Norman lands.[3] John's efforts at retaliation came to the same effect. It is true that the separation was by no means complete. In one way or another some nobles succeeded in retaining their positions in both countries. But double allegiance was generally felt to be awkward,[4] and the voluntary division of estates went on. The action of Simon de Montfort in

some extent by the enterprise of the Normans themselves, would have constituted in itself a strong reason for the continued use of French among polite circles in England.

English and French in the Thirteenth Century

The thirteenth century must be viewed as a period of shifting emphasis upon the two languages spoken in England. The upper classes continued for the most part to speak French, as they had done in the previous century, but the reasons for doing so were not the same. Instead of being a mother tongue inherited from Norman ancestors, French became, as the century wore on, a cultivated tongue supported by social custom and by business and administrative convention. Meanwhile English made steady advances. A number of considerations make it clear that by the middle of the century, when the separation of the English nobles from their interests in France had been about completed, English was becoming a matter of general use among the upper classes. It is at this time, as we shall see, that the adoption of French words into the English language assumes large proportions. The transference of words occurs when those who know French and have been accustomed to use it try to express themselves in English. It is at this time also that the literature intended for polite circles begins to be made over from French into English (see § 110). There is evidence that by the close of the century some children of the nobility spoke English as their mother tongue and had to be taught French through the medium of manuals equipped with English glosses.

There is no need to heap up evidence of the continued use of French by the upper class in this century. Even at the close of the century it was used in Parliament[19] in the law courts, in public negotiations generally.[20] Treatises on husbandry that have come down to us from this time are all in French. All of them[21] seem intended for the owners of estates, except possibly *Seneschaucie,* which is on the duties of the seneschal. French was read by the educated, including those who could not read Latin.[22] That the ability was on the decline is suggested by the action of a chronicler at the end of the century who, after citing a petition to Parliament "written in the French language in conformity with the usual custom," translates it into Latin in order that it "may be more easily understood by those of posterity who may not be so well versed in the above language."[23]

That the knowledge of French, even of those who attempted to use it in this period, was sometimes imperfect is quite clear. One author of a French poem says he hardly knows how to write the language because he was never in Paris or at the abbey of St. Denis.[24] The most interesting evidence, however, is to be found in the bills or petitions presented to the justices in eyre at the close of the thirteenth and the beginning of the fourteenth centuries by those seeking redress at the law. Custom required these bills to be in French. They are obviously not written by lawyers or by the complainants themselves, but by professional scribes or possibly the parish priest. As the editor of a volume of such petitions[25] says, "The text of the bills makes it plain that the draftsmen were struggling with the forms of a language that was far from being a living tongue with them," and he offers good reason for believing "that they neither spoke French nor were accustomed to hear it spoken in their own neighborhood." Furthermore, declension and conjugation are often incorrect or peculiar, and the writers make the most obvious mistakes in gender, such as using *la* before a man's name and *le* before a woman's *("le* avant dit Aliz"). Yet, edited by E.Lamond, *Walter of Henley's Husbandry* (London, 1890). One was sup-posedly written by Bishop Grosseteste in 1240-1241 for the countess of Lincoln. Walter of Henley's treatise exists in an English version that is attributed in the manuscripts to Grosseteste. If we could trust the attribution, it would constitute evidence that some of the landowners at this time preferred to read English. But the translation belongs probably to a later date. [2] A French poem on the calendar is addressed to "simpli gent lettre," that is, those who could read, while Grosseteste's *Château d'Amour* was "por ceus ki ne sevent mie ne lettrure ne clergie," that is, those who could neither read at all nor understand Latin, but could understand French when it was read to them.

[23]Continuation of Pseudo-Ingulph, *Ingulph's Chronicle,* trans. H.T.Riley, singularly enough, the handwriting of some of the worst is excellent and seems clearly to point to an educated person.[26]

The spread of English among the upper classes was making steady progress. References to a knowledge of the language on the part of members of this class are now seldom found, especially in the latter part of the century, probably because it had become general. We do not know whether Henry III understood English, though he probably did. His brother, Richard, earl of Cornwall, who was elected emperor of Germany in 1257, certainly did, for Matthew Paris tells us that he was chosen partly "on account of his speaking the English language, which is similar in sound to the German."[27] Henry's son, Edward I, notwithstanding his Provengal mother, spoke English readily, perhaps even habitually.[28] While the references to the language are not numerous, they are suggestive. Here a bishop preaches in it;[29] there a judge quotes it,[30] monks joke in it;[31] friars use it to explain to the people of Worcester a legal victory.[32] A royal proclamation is issued in it.[33]

The clearest indication of the extent to which the English language had risen in the social scale by the middle of the thirteenth century is furnished by a little treatise written by Walter of Bibbesworth to teach children French—how to speak and how to reply, "Which every gentleman ought to know." French is treated as a foreign language, and the child is taken on a very practical course through life, learning the names of the parts of the body, the articles of its clothing, food, household utensils and operations, meals, and the like, together with terms of falconry and the chase and other polite accomplishments. The important words are provided with an interlinear English gloss. The person for whom the little manual was prepared was Dionysia, the daughter of William de Munchensy. The latter was among the leaders of the barons in the battle of Lewes and was related, through his sister's marriage, to the half-brother of King Henry III. Dionysia herself was later married to one of the sons of the earl of Oxford. She thus belonged to the upper circle of the nobility, and it is therefore highly significant that the language she knew, and through which she acquired French, was English. Since the treatise was certainly written in the thirteenth century (not later than 1250) and the number of manuscripts that have come down to us shows that it had much wider circulation than in just the family for which it was originally written, we may feel quite sure that the mother tongue of the children of the nobility in the year 1300 was, in many cases, English.[34]

Finally, it is interesting to note the appearance at this time of an attitude that becomes more noticeable later, the attitude that the proper language for Englishmen to know and use is English. In the *Cursor Mundi,* an encyclopedic poem on biblical subjects, written shortly before or shortly after the year 1300, we may detect a mild but nonetheless clear protest against the use of French and a patriotic espousal of English:

Þis ilk bok es translate
Into Inglis tong to rede
For the love of Inglis lede,[35]
Inglis lede of Ingland,
For the commun at[36] understand.
Frankis rimes here I redd
Comunlik in ilka sted;[37]
Mast[38] es it wroght for Frankis man,
Quat[39] is for him na Frankis can?
In Ingland the nacion,
Es Inglis man þar in commun;
Þe speche þat man wit mast may spede;
Mast þarwit to speke war nede.
Selden was for ani chance
Praised Inglis tong in France;
Give we ilkan[40] þare langage,
Me think we do þam non outrage.
To laud[41] and Inglis man I spell
Þat understandes þat I tell...

(CursorMundi, Prologue, II. 232-50)

The Provisions of Oxford, mentioned above, were in Latin,

French, and English. Latin was naturally the language of record. It is certain that the document was sent in English to the sheriffs of every county to be publicized. Whether it was also sent in French is not known but seems likely. At all events, fourteen years before (1244), the *Annals of Burton* record a letter from the dean of Lincoln asking the bishop of Lichfield to proclaim a directive from the pope excommunicating those who broke the provisions of Magna Carta, the pronouncement to be *in lingua Anglicana et Gallicana.*[42] In 1295 a document was read before the county court at Chelmsford, Essex, and explained *in gallico et anglico,*[43] but this may represent no more than the survival of a custom of making important announcements in both languages. We may sum up the situation by saying that in the latter part of the thirteenth century English was widely known among all classes of people, though not necessarily by everyone.

Attempts to Arrest the Decline of French

At the close of the thirteenth century and especially in the course of the next we see clear indications that the French language was losing its hold on England in the measures adopted to keep it in use. The tendency to speak English was becoming constantly stronger even in those two most conservative institutions, the church and the universities. Already in the last decades of the thirteenth century the great Benedictine monasteries of Canterbury and Westminster adopted regulations forbidding the novices to use English in school or cloister and requiring all conversation to be in French.[44] Similar regulations were found necessary at the universities. A fourteenth-century statute of Oxford required the students to construe and translate in both English and French "lest the French language be entirely disused."[45] Supplementary ordinances drawn up for Exeter College by Bishop Stapleton in 1322 and 1325, and the foundation statutes of Oriel (1326) and Queen's (1340), required that the conversation of the students be in Latin or in French. As early as 1284 at Merton, Archbishop Peckham found that Latin was not spoken, as the rules required. Some time later conditions at this fine old college were clearly in a bad way; the Fellows talked English at table and wore "dishonest shoes."[46] Among the Cambridge colleges Peterhouse had a similar rule. Students were expected to speak Latin except that they might use French "for a just or reasonable cause...but very rarely English.[47] The primary purpose of these regulations was of course to insure an easy command of the Latin language, but it is evident that without them the language that would have been spoken, if not Latin, would have been English. According to Froissart, a further effort to keep the French language from going out of use was made by parliament in 1332, which decreed "that all lords, barons, knights, and honest men of good towns should exercise care and diligence to teach their children the French language in order that they might be more able and better equipped in their wards."[48] Such efforts as these indicate how artificial was the use of French in England by the fourteenth century.

If further evidence were needed it would be found in the appearance of numerous manuals for learning French. As early as 1250 we find a short Latin treatise on the French verb. Walter of Bibbesworth's *Traité* of about the same date has already been mentioned. In succeeding years there are several adaptations of it, fuller in treatment and with more attention to pronunclation. They form an unbroken series from that time down to our own textbooks of the present day, and in them all French is treated frankly as a foreign language.[49] These works have traditionally been understood as books for children, but it is possible that they functioned more as manuals for adults, both for the adults' own use and for instructing children. If so, the need for help in French extended at least a generation further back.[50]

Provincial Character of French in England

One factor against the continued use of French in England was the circumstance that Anglo-French was not "good" French. In the Middle Ages there were four principal dialects of French spoken in France: Norman, Picard (in the northeast), Burgundian (in the east), and the Central French of Paris (the Ile-de-France). At the date of the Norman Conquest and for some time after, each enjoyed a certain local prestige,[51] but with the rapid rise of the Capetian power in the thirteenth century the linguistic supremacy of Paris followed upon its political ascendancy. The French introduced into England was possibly a mixture of various northern dialectal features, but with Norman predominating, and under the influence of English linguistic tendencies, it gradually developed into something quite different from any of the continental dialects. The difference was noticed quite early,[52] and before long the French of England drew a smile from continental speakers. It was the subject of humorous treatment in literature,[53] and English writers became apologetic. One poet says, "A false French of England I know, for I have not been elsewhere to acquire it; but you who have learned it elsewhere, amend it where there is need."[54] The more ambitious sent their children to France to have the "barbarity" taken off their speech.[55] But the situation did not mend. Everybody is familiar with the gentle fun that Chaucer makes of the Prioress:

And Frensh she spak ful faire and fetisly, After the scole of Stratford atte Bowe, For Frensh of Paris was to hir unknowe.

One might well feel some hesitancy about speaking a language of which one had to be slightly ashamed.

The Hundred Years' War

In the course of the centuries following the Norman Conquest the connection of England with the continent, as we have seen, had been broken. It was succeeded by a conflict of interests and a growing feeling of antagonism that culminated in a long period of open hostility with France (1337-1453). The causes of this struggle are too complex to be entered into here, but the active interference of France in England's efforts to control Scotland led Edward III finally to put forth a claim to the French throne and to invade France. The great victories of the English at Crécy (1346) and Poitiers (1356) fanned English patriotism to a white heat, though this auspicious beginning of the struggle was followed by a depressing period of reverses and though the contest was interrupted by long periods of truce. In the reign of Henry V

England again enjoyed a brief period of success, notably in the victory against great odds at Agincourt (1415). But the success did not continue after the young king's death, and the exploits of Joan of Arc (1429) marked the beginning of the end. Although this protracted war again turned people's attention to the continent, and the various expeditions might have tended to keep the French language in use, it seems to have had no such effect, but rather the opposite. Probably the intervals between the periods of actual fighting were too long and the hindrances to trade and other intercourse too discouraging. The feeling that remained uppermost in the minds of most people was one of animosity, coupled with a sense of the inevitability of renewed hostilities. During all this time it was impossible to forget that French was the language of an enemy country, and the Hundred Years' War is probably to be reckoned as one of the causes contributing to the disuse of French.

The Rise of the Middle Class

A feature of some importance in helping English to recover its former prestige is the improvement in the condition of the mass of the people and the rise of a substantial middle class. As we have seen, the importance of a language is largely determined by the importance of the people who speak it. During the latter part of the Middle English period the condition of the laboring classes was rapidly improving. Among the rural population villeinage was dying out. Fixed money payments were gradually substituted for the days' work due the lord of the manor, and the status of the villein more nearly resembled that of the free tenants. The latter class was itself increasing; there was more incentive to individual effort and more opportunity for a person to reap the rewards of enterprise. The process by which these changes were being brought about was greatly accelerated by an event that occurred in the year 1349.

In the summer of 1348 there appeared in the southwest of England the first cases of a disease that in its contagiousness and fatality exceeded anything previously known. It spread rapidly over the rest of the country, reaching its height in 1349 but continuing in the north into the early months of 1350. The illness, once contracted, ran a very rapid course. In two or three days the victims either died or showed signs of recovery. Generally they died. Immunity was slight, and in the absence of any system of quarantine the disease spread unimpeded through a community. The mortality was unbelievably high, though it has often been exaggerated. We can no more believe the statement that scarcely one-tenth of the people were left alive than we can the assertion of the same chronicler that all those born after the pestilence had two "cheek-teeth in their head less than they had afore." Careful modern studies based on the data contained in episcopal registers show that 40 percent of the parish clergy died of the plague, and while this is apparently higher than for the population at large, the death rate during the plague approximated 30 percent. It is quite sufficient to justify the name "The Black Death."

The effects of so great a calamity were naturally serious, and in one direction at least are fully demonstrable. As in most epidemics, the rich suffered less than the poor. The poor could not shut themselves up in their castles or retreat to a secluded manor. The mortality was accordingly greatest among the lower social orders, and the result was a serious shortage of labor. This is evident in the immediate rise in wages, a rise which the Statute of Laborers was insufficient to control or prevent. Nor was this result merely temporary if we may judge from the thirteen reenactments of the statute in the course of the next hundred years. Villeins frequently made their escape, and many cotters left the land in search of the high wages commanded by independent workers. Those who were left behind felt more acutely the burden of their condition, and a general spirit of discontent arose, which culminated in the Peasants' Revolt of 1381. By and large, the effect of the Black Death was to increase the economic importance of the laboring class and with it the importance of the English language which they spoke.[56]

We may also note at this time the rise of another important group—the craftsmen and the merchant class. By 1250 there had grown up in England about two hundred towns with populations of from 1,000 to 5,000; some, like London or York, were larger.

These towns became free, self-governing communities, electing their own officers, assessing taxes in their own way, collecting them and paying them to the king in a lump sum, trying their own cases, and regulating their commercial affairs as they saw fit. The townsfolk were engaged for the most part in trade or in the manufacturing crafts and banded together into commercial fraternities or guilds for their mutual protection and advantage. In such an environment there arose in each town an independent, sometimes a wealthy and powerful class, standing halfway between the rural peasant and the hereditary aristocracy.

Such changes in the social and economic life benefited particularly the English-speaking part of the population, and enable us better to understand the final triumph of English in the century in which these changes largely occur.

General Adoption of English in the Fourteenth Century

At the beginning of the fourteenth century English was once more known by everyone. The most conclusive evidence of this is the direct testimony of contemporaries. So much of the polite literature of England until a generation or two before had been in French that writers seemed to feel called upon to justify their use of English. Accordingly they frequently begin with a prologue explaining their intention in the work that follows and incidentally make interesting observations on the linguistic situation. From a number of such statements we may select three quotations. The first is from a collection of metrical homilies written in the north of England about the year 1300:

> Forthi wil I of my povert
> Schau sum thing that Ik haf in hert,
> On Ingelis tong that alle may
> Understand quat I wil say;
> For laued men havis mar mister
> Godes word for to her
> Than klerkes that thair mirour lokes,
> And sees hou thai sal lif on bokes.

And bathe klerk and laued man
Englis understand kan,
That was born in Ingeland,
And lang haves ben thar in wonand,
Bot al men can noht, I-wis,
Understand Latin and Frankis.
Forthi me think almous it isse
To wirke sum god thing on Inglisse,
That mai ken lered and laued bathe.[57]

Therefore will I of my poverty
Show something that I have in heart
In English tongue that all may
Understand what I will say;
For laymen have more need
God's word for to hear
Than clerks that look in their *Mirror*
And see in books how they shall live.
And both clerk and layman
Can understand English,
Who were born in England
And long have been dwelling therein,
But all men certainly cannot
Understand Latin and French.
Therefore methinks it is alms (an act of charity)
To work some good thing in English
That both learned and lay may know.

The allusion to clerks that have their *Mirror* is probably a reference to the *Miroir,* or *Les Evangiles des Domees,* an Anglo-French poem by Robert of Gretham.

Here we are told that both learned and unlearned understand English. A still more circumstantial statement, serving to confirm the above testimony, is found in William of Nassyngton's *Speculum Vitae or Mirror of Life* (c. 1325):

In English tonge I schal ȝow telle

ȝif ȝe wyth me so longe wil dwelle.
No Latyn wil I speke no waste,
But English, þat men vse mast,
Þat can eche man vnderstande,
Þat is born in Ingelande;
For þat langage is most chewyd,
Os wel among lered os lewyd.
Latyn, as I trowe, can nane
But þo, þat haueth it in scole tane,
And somme can Frensche and no
Latyn, vsed han[63] cowrt and dwellen þerein,
And somme can of Latyn a party,
Þat can of Frensche but febly;
And somme vnderstonde wel Englysch,
Þat can noþer Latyn nor Frankys.
Boþe lered and lewed, olde and
Alle vnderstonden english tonge.

Here the writer acknowledges that some people who have lived at court know French, but he is quite specific in his statement that old and young, learned and unlearned, all understand the English tongue. Our third quotation, although the briefest, is perhaps the most interesting of all. It is from the opening lines of a romance called *Arthur and Merlin,* written not later than the year 1325 and probably in the opening years of the century:

Riȝt is, þat Inglische Inglische vnderstond,
Þat was born in Inglond;
Freynsche vse þis gentilman,

Ac euerich Inglische can.

Mani noble ich haue yseiȝe

Þat no Freynsche couþe seye.

The special feature of this passage is not the author's statement that everybody knows English, which we have come to expect, but his additional assertion that at a time when gentlemen still "used" French he had seen many a noble who could not speak that language.

Although, as these quotations show, English was now understood by everyone, it does not follow that French was unknown or had entirely gone out of use. It still had some currency at the court although English had largely taken its place; we may be sure that the court that Chaucer knew spoke English even if its members commonly wrote and often read French. A dozen books owned by Richard II in 1385, most of them romances, seem from their titles to have been all French, though he spoke English fluently and Gower wrote the *Confessio Amantis* for him in English. Robert of Brunne, who wrote his *Chronicle* in 1338, implies that French is chiefly the language of two groups, the educated classes and the French. That in England French was the accomplishment mainly of the educated in the fourteenth century is implied by the words of Avarice in *Piers Plowman* (B-text, V, 239): "I lerned nevere rede on boke, And I can no Frenche in feith but of the ferthest ende of Norfolke." Among the learned we must include the legal profession and the church. French was the language of lawyers and of the law courts down to 1362. We may likewise believe that ecclesiastics could still commonly speak French. We are told that Hugh of Eversdone, the cellarer, who was elected abbot of St. Albans in 1308, knew English and French very well, though he was not so competent in Latin; and an amusing story of the bishop of Durham who was consecrated in 1318 attests his knowledge of French while revealing an even greater ignorance of the language of the service. We have already seen that French was kept up as the language of conversation in the monasteries of St. Augustine at Canterbury and St. Peter at Westminster. It was so also at St. Mary's Abbey, York, as appears from the *Ordinal* drawn up in 1390, and was probably the case generally. Chaucer's prioress spoke French, though she told her tale to the Canterbury pilgrims in English, and the instructions from the abbot of St. Albans to the nuns of Sopwell in 1338 are in French. But clerks of the younger generation in Langland's time seem to have been losing their command of the language. Outside the professions, French seems to have been generally known to government officials and the more substantial burgesses in the towns. It was the language of parliament and local administration. The business of town councils and the guilds seems to have been ordinarily transacted in French, though there are scattered instances of the intrusion of English. French was very common at this time in letters and dispatches and local records, and was probably often written by people who did not habitually speak it. An anonymous chronicle of about 1381 is written in French, but, as the editor remarks, it is the French of a man who is obviously thinking in English; and the poet Gower, who wrote easily in Latin, French, and English, protests that he knows little French. In spite of Trevisa's statement about the efforts of "uplondish" men to learn French in order to liken themselves to gentlemen, French can have had but little currency among the middle classes outside of the towns. It is interesting to note that the chief disadvantage that Trevisa sees in the fact that children no longer learn French is that "it will be harm for them if they shall pass the sea and travel in strange lands," though his scholarly instincts led him to add "and in many other places."

It is clear that the people who could speak French in the fourteenth century were bilingual. Edward III knew English, and Richard II addressed the people in it at the time of Wat Tyler's rebellion. Outside the royal family it would seem that even among the governing class English was the language best understood. When Edward III called a parliament in 1337 to advise him about prosecuting his claim to the throne of France, it was addressed by a lawyer who, according to Froissart, was very competent in

Latin, French, and English. And he spoke in English, although, as we have seen, French was still the usual language of Parliament, "to the end that he might be better understood by all, for one always knows better what one wishes to say and propose in the language to which he is introduced in his infancy than in any other." Ten years before, a similar incident occurred when the privileges which Edward II confirmed to the city of London were read before the mayor, aldermen, and citizens assembled in the Guildhall and were explained to them in English by Andrew Horn, the city chamberlain. In 1362 the chancellor opened Parliament for the first time with a speech in English. English likewise appears at this time in the acts of towns and guilds. In 1388 Parliament required all guilds to submit a report on their foundation, statutes, property, and the like. The returns are mostly in Latin, but forty-nine of them are in English, outnumbering those in French. The Customal of Winchester, which exists in an Anglo-Norman text of about 1275, was translated into English at the end of the fourteenth century. Finally, in the last year of the century, in the proceedings at the deposition of Richard II, the articles of accusation were read to the assembled Parliament in Latin and English, as was the document by which Richard renounced the throne. The order deposing him was read to him in English, and Henry IV's speeches claiming the throne and later accepting it were delivered in English. Thus the proceedings would seem to have been conspicuous for the absence of French. There can be no doubt in the light of instances such as these that in the fourteenth century English is again the principal tongue of all England.

English in the Law Courts

In 1362 an important step was taken toward restoring English to its dominant place as the language of the country. For a long time, probably from a date soon after the Conquest, French had been the language of all legal proceedings. But in the fourteenth century such a practice was clearly without justification, and in 1356 the mayor and aldermen of London ordered that proceedings in the sheriffs' court of London and Middlesex be in English. Six years later, in the Parliament held in October 1362, the *Statute of Pleading* was enacted, to go into effect toward the end of the following January:

> Because it is often shewed to the king by the prelates, dukes, earls, barons, and all the commonalty, of the great mischiefs which have happened to divers of the realm, because the laws, customs, and statutes of this realm be not commonly known in the same realm; for that they be pleaded, shewed, and judged in the French tongue, which is much unknown in the said realm; so that the people which do implead, or be impleaded, in the king's court, and in the courts of others, have no knowledge nor understanding of that which is said for them or against them by their serjeants and other pleaders; and that reasonably the said laws and customs shall be most quickly learned and known, and better understood in the tongue used in the said realm, and by so much every man of the said realm may the better govern himself without offending of the law, and the better keep, save, and defend his heritage and possessions; and in divers regions and countries, where the king, the nobles, and others of the said realm have been, good governance and full right is done to every person, because that their laws and customs be learned and used in the tongue of the country: the king, desiring the good governance and tranquillity of his people, and to put out and eschew the harms and mischiefs which do or may happen in this behalf by the occasions aforesaid, hath ordained and established by the assent aforesaid, that all pleas which shall be pleaded in his courts whatsoever, before any of his justices whatsoever, or in his other places, or before any of his other ministers whatsoever, or in the courts and places of any other lords whatsoever within the realm, shall be pleaded, shewed, defended, answered, debated, and judged in the English tongue, and that they be entered and enrolled in Latin.

All this might have been said in one sentence: Hereafter all lawsuits shall be conducted in English. But it is interesting to note that the reason frankly stated for the action is that "French is much unknown in the said realm." Custom dies hard, and there is some reason to think that the statute was not fully observed at once. It constitutes, however, the official recognition of English.

English in the Schools

From a time shortly after the Conquest, French had replaced English as the language of the schools. In the twelfth century there are patriotic complaints that Bede and others formerly taught the people in English, but their lore is lost; other people now teach our folk. A statement of Ranulph Higden in the fourteenth century shows that in his day the use of French in the schools was quite general. At the end of the first book of his *Polychronicon* (c. 1327), a universal history widely circulated, he attributes the corruption of the English language which he observes in part to this cause:

This apayrynge of þe burþe tunge is bycause of tweie þinges; oon is for children in scole aȝenst þe vsage and manere of alle oþere naciouns beeþ compelled for to leue hire owne langage, and for to construe hir lessouns and here þynges in Frensche, and so þey haueþ seþ þe Normans come first in to Engelond. Also gentil men children beeþ i-tauȝt to speke Frensche from þe tyme þet þey beeþ i-rokked in here cradel, and kunneþ speke and playe wiþ a childes broche; and vplondisshe men wil likne hym self to gentil men, and fondeþ wiþ greet besynesse for to speke Frensce, for to be [more] i-tolde of.

However, after the Black Death, two Oxford schoolmasters were responsible for a great innovation in English education. When the translator of Higden's book, John Trevisa, came to the above passage he added a short but extremely interesting observation of his own:

> Þis manere was moche i-vsed to fore þe firste moreyn and is siþþe sumdel i-chaunged; for Iohn Cornwaile, a maister of grammer, chaunged þe lore in gramer scole and construccioun of Frensche in to Englische; and Richard Pencriche lerned þat manere techynge of hym and oþere men of Pencrich; so þat

> now, þe ȝere of oure Lorde a þowsand þre hundred and foure score and fyue, and of þe secounde kyng Richard after þe conquest nyne, in alle þe gramere scoles of Engelond, children leueþ Frensche and construeþ and lerneþ an Englische, and haueþ þerby auauntage in oon side and disauauntage in anoþer side; here auauntage is, þat þey lerneþ her gramer in lasse tyme þan children were i-woned to doo; disauauntage is þat now children of gramer scole conneþ na more Frensche þan can hir lift heele, and þat is harme for hem and þey schulle passe þe see and trauaille in straunge landes and in many oþer places. Also gentil men haueþ now moche left for to teche here children Frensche.

By a fortunate circumstance we know that there was a John Cornwall licensed to teach Latin grammar in Oxford at this time; his name appears in the accounts of Merton in 1347, as does that of Pencrich a few years later. The innovation was probably due to a scarcity of competent teachers. At any rate, after 1349 English began to be used in the schools and by 1385 the practice had become general.

Increasing Ignorance of French in the Fifteenth Century

The statement already quoted from a writer of the beginning of the fourteenth century to the effect that he had seen many nobles who could not speak French indicates a condition that became more pronounced as time went on. By the fifteenth century the ability to speak French fluently seems to have been looked upon as an accomplishment. Even the ability to write it was becoming less general among people of position. In 1400 George Dunbar, earl of March, in writing to the king in English, says: "And, noble Prince, marvel ye not that I write my letters in English, for that is more clear to my understanding than Latin or French." Another very interesting case is offered by a letter from Richard Kingston, dean of Windsor, addressed to the king in 1403. Out of deference to custom, the dean begins bravely enough in French, but toward the close, when he becomes particularly earnest, he passes instinctively from French to English in the middle of a sentence.

An incident that occurred in 1404 seems at first sight to offer an extreme case. The king of France had refused to recognize Henry IV when he seized the English throne, and his kinsman, the count of Flanders, supported him in his refusal. Outrages were soon committed by the French on English subjects, to which the English retaliated, and finally an attempt was made to settle the matter by negotiation. The English representatives included Sir Thomas Swynford and one Nicholas de Ryssheton, who signs himself "Professor of Both Laws," that is, civil and ecclesiastical. Now there would be nothing remarkable about these negotiations were it not for the fact that several times the English ambassadors complain about the use of French by their French correspondents and ask them to write only in Latin. On two occasions they speak of the French language as being as unknown to them as Hebrew. This statement, if taken at its face value, as has generally been done, is astonishing, to say the least. But it is quite unbelievable. De Ryssheton, as a lawyer, must have known French well. We need not pause over the reasons for the statement." The statement was not true; but the English delegates would not have alleged such a reason for carrying on negotiation in Latin if it had not had a certain plausibility. Ignorance of French must have been quite common among the governing class in England from the beginning of the fifteenth century. Before the middle of the century it was necessary to have a "Secretary in the French language" among the government officials. At the end of the century Caxton could write: "For the mooste quantyte of the people vnderstonde not latyn ne frensshe here in this noble royame of englond."

French as a Language of Culture and Fashion

When French went out of use as a spoken language in England not only was its sphere more restricted but the reasons for its cultivation changed. In the first decade of the fifteenth century, John Barton wrote a *Donet François,* a treatise intended for adults who wished to learn French. It is interesting to note the three reasons he gives for Englishmen's learning the language. He says nothing about their needing it to communicate among themselves but says, first, it will enable them to communicate with their neighbors of the realm of France. In the second place, the laws are largely in French. And finally, he says, gentlemen and women willingly write to each other in French. The first of these reasons would be equally valid today. The other two are a heritage of the past, which in time disappeared. Later Caxton in his *Dialogues in French and English* has the merchant chiefly in mind: "Who this booke shall wylle [wish to] lerne may well enterprise or take on honde marchandises fro one land to anothir." But French had been for so long the mark of the privileged class that such cultivation of it as persisted in this century and in after times was prompted largely by the feeling that it was the language of culture and fashion. This feeling was strengthened in the eighteenth century and it is present in the minds of many people today.

The Use of English in Writing

The last step that the English language had to make in its gradual ascent was its employment in writing. For here it had to meet the competition of Latin as well as French. The use of Latin for written communication and record was due partly to a habit formed at a time when most people who could write at all could write Latin, partly to its international character, and partly to the feeling that it was a language that had become fixed while the modern languages seemed to be variable, unregulated, and in a constant state of change. Modern languages began to encroach upon this field of Latin at a time when French was still the language of the educated and the socially prominent. French accordingly is the first language in England to dispute the monopoly of Latin in written matter, and only in the fifteenth century does English succeed in displacing both. In private and semi-official correspondence French is at its height at about 1350; the earliest English letters appear in the latter part of the century, but there are few before 1400. English letters first occur among the Paston letters and in the Stonor correspondence between 1420 and 1430. After 1450 English letters are everywhere the rule. It is rather similar with wills. The earliest known English will subsequent to the Conquest dates from 1383, and English wills are rare before 1400. But in 1397 the earl of Kent made his will in English, and in 1438 the countess of Stafford in doing likewise said, "I...ordeyne and make my testament in English tonge, for my most profit, redyng, and understandyng in yis wise." The wills of Henry IV, Henry V, and Henry VI are all in English.

The fifteenth century also saw the adoption of English for the records of towns and guilds and in a number of branches of the central government. About 1430 a number of towns are seen translating their ordinances and their books of customs into English, and English becomes general in their transactions after 1450. It is so likewise with the guilds. English was used along with French in the ordinances of the London pepperers as early as 1345. At York the ordinances of the crafts begin to be in English from about 1400 on. An interesting resolution of the London brewers, dating about 1422, shows them adopting English by a formal action:

> Whereas our mother tongue, to wit, the English tongue, hath in modern days begun to be honorably enlarged and adorned; for that our most excellent lord king Henry the Fifth hath, in his letters missive, and divers affairs touching his own person, more willingly chosen to declare the secrets of his will [in it]; and for the better understanding of his people, hath, with a diligent mind, procured the common idiom (setting aside others) to be commended by the exercise of writing; and there are many of our craft of brewers who have the knowledge of writing and reading in the said English idiom, but in others, to wit, the Latin and French, before these times used, they do not in any wise understand; for which causes, with many others, it being considered how that the greater part of the Lords and trusty Commons have begun to make their matters to be noted down in our mother tongue, so we also in our craft, following in some manner their steps, have decreed in future to commit to memory the needful things which concern us.

The records of Parliament tell a similar story. The petitions of the Commons, on which statutes were based if they met with approval, are usually in French down to 1423 and seem to have been enrolled in French even when originally presented in English. After 1423 they are often in English. The statutes themselves are generally in Latin down to about 1300, in French until the reign of Henry VII. In 1485 they begin to appear in English alongside of French, and in 1489 French entirely disappears.

The reign of Henry V (1413-1422) seems to have marked the turning point in the use of English in writing. The example of the king in using English in his letters and certain efforts of his to promote the use of English in writing, which we would gladly know more about, are specifically referred to as a precedent in the resolution of the London brewers quoted above. Apparently his brilliant victories over the French at Agincourt and elsewhere gave the English a pride in things English. The end of his reign and the beginning of the next mark the period at which English begins to be generally adopted in writing. If we want a round number, the year 1425 represents very well the approximate date.

Middle English Literature

The literature written in England during the Middle English period reflects fairly accurately the changing fortunes of English. During the time that French was the language best understood by the upper classes, the books they read or listened to were in French. All of continental French literature was available for their enjoyment, and we have seen above how this source was supplemented by an important body of French poetry written in England (§ 88). The rewards of patronage were seldom to be expected by those who wrote in English; with them we must look for other incentives to writing. Such incentives were most often found among members of the religious body, interested in promoting right living and in the care of souls. Accordingly, the literature in English that has come down to us from this period (1150-1250) is almost exclusively religious or admonitory. The *Ancrene Riwle,* the *Ormulum* (c. 1200), a series of paraphrases and interpretations of Gospel passages, and a group of saints' lives and short homiletic pieces showing the survival of an Old English literary tradition in the southwest are the principal works of this class. The two outstanding exceptions are Layamon's *Brut* (c. 1200), based largely on Wace, and the astonishing debate between *The Owl and the Nightingale* (c. 1195), a long poem in which two birds exchange recriminations in the liveliest fashion. There was certainly a body of popular literature that circulated orally among the people, just as at a later date the English and Scottish popular ballads did, but such literature has left slight traces in this early period. The hundred years from 1150 to 1250 have been justly called the Period of Religious Record. It is not that religious works were not written in French too for the upper classes; it is rather the absence in English of works appealing to courtly tastes that marks the English language at this time as the language of the middle and lower classes.

The separation of the English nobility from France by about 1250 and the spread of English among the upper class is manifest in the next hundred years of English literature. Types of polite literature that had hitherto appeared in French now appear in English. Of these types the most popular was the romance. Only one English romance exists from an earlier date than 1250, but from this time translations and adaptations from the French begin to be made, and in the course of the fourteenth century their number becomes quite large. The religious literature characteristic of the previous period continues; but we now have other types as well. The period from 1250 to 1350 is a Period of Religious and Secular Literature in English and indicates clearly the wider diffusion of the English language.

The general adoption of English by all classes, which had taken place by the latter half of the fourteenth century, gave rise to a body of literature that represents the high point in English literary achievement in the Middle Ages. The period from 1350 to 1400 has been called the Period of Great Individual Writers. The chief name is that of Geoffrey Chaucer (1340-1400), the greatest English poet before Shakespeare. Not to mention his delightful minor poems, he is the author of a long narrative poem telling the story of the unhappy love of *Troilus and Criseyde* and, most famous of his works, the *Canterbury Tales*, which, besides giving us in the general prologue a matchless portrait gallery of contemporary types, constitutes in the variety of the tales a veritable anthology of medieval literature. To this period belong William Langland, the reputed author of along social allegory, *Piers Plowman* (1362-1387); John Wycliffe (d. 1384), putative translator of the Bible and author of a large and influential body of controversial prose; and the unknown poet who wrote not only the finest of the Middle English romances, *Sir Gawain and the Green Knight,* but three allegorical and religious poems of great beauty, including *Pearl.* Any one of these men would have made the later fourteenth century an outstanding period in Middle English literature. Together they constitute a striking proof of the secure position the English language had attained.

The fifteenth century is sometimes known as the Imitative Period because so much of the poetry then written was written in emulation of Chaucer. It is also spoken of as a Transition Period, because it covers a large part of the interval between the age of Chaucer and the age of Shakespeare. The period has been unjustly neglected. Writers like Lydgate, Hoccleve, Skelton, and Hawes are not negligible, though admittedly overshadowed by some of their great predecessors, and at the end of the century we have the prose of Malory and Caxton. In the north the Scottish Chaucerians, particularly Henryson, Dunbar, Gawin Douglas, and Lindsay, produced significant work. These authors carry on the tradition of English as a literary medium into the Renaissance. Thus, Middle English literature follows and throws interesting light on the fortunes of the English language.

REFERENCES

1. For other instances see F.M.Powicke, *The Loss of Normandy* (Manchester, 1913), p. 482.
2. Powicke, pp. 403, 415.
3. Stubbs, *Constitutional History of England.* I, 557; J.R.Strayer, *The Administration of Normandy under Saint Louis* (Cambridge, MA, 1932), p. 7.
4. Confiscations continued, as in 1217 and 1224. Cf. Kate Norgate, *The Minority of Henry III* (London, 1912), pp. 77, 220-21.

5. Charles Bémont, *Simon de Montfort* (Oxford, 1930), p. 4.
6. Matthew Paris, *Chronica Majora,* trans. J.A.Giles, I, 481-82. Although Matthew Paris puts this action of Louis IX and Henry III under the year 1244, it is possible that it belongs to the previous year. As early as July 1243, Henry ordered inquiry to be made to determine what magnates of England had stood with the king of France in the last war *(Cal. Close Rolls, 1242-47,* p. 69), and on January 24, 1244, he granted to his son Edward "a moiety of all the lands which the king has ordered to be taken into his hands and which belonged to men of the fealty of the king of France, and those holding of him" *(Cal. Pat. Rolls, 1232-47,* p. 418).
7. Roger of Wendover, trans. J.A.Giles, II, 565-66.
8. *Ibid.,* II,567-68.
9. *Chronica Major a,* trans. Giles, I, 122.
10. O.H.Richardson, *The National Movement in the Reign of Henry III* (New York, 1897), p.75.
11. Matthew Paris, II, 433.
12. *Ibid.,* II, 247. For the extent to which these foreigners were enriched, see Harold S.Snellgrove,*The Lusignans in England, 1247-1258* (Albuquerque, 1950; *Univ. of New MexicoPub. in History,* No. 2).
13. Nothing can equal the impression that would be gained of this period by reading a hundred pages of Matthew Paris. Perhaps a few quotations will help to complete the picture: "My dear earl, I will no longer conceal from you the secret desire of my heart, which is, to raise and enrich you, and to advance your interests, by marrying your eldest legitimate son to the daughter of Guy, count of Angouleme, my uterine brother" (III, 15). "At the instigation of the queen, Baldwin de Rivers married a foreign lady, a Savoyard, and a relation of the queen's. The county of Devon belonged to this Baldwin, and thus the noble possessions and heritages of the English daily devolved to foreigners" (III, 219). "At the beginning of the month of May [1247],.two ladies of Provence were, by the forethought and arrangement of Peter of Savoy, married to two noble youths, namely, Edmund earl of Lincoln, and Richard de Bourg, whom the king had for some years brought up in his palace. At this marriage the sounds of great discontent and anger were wafted through the kingdom, because, as they said, these females, although unknown, were united to the nobles against their wills" (II, 230). "In the same year, on the 13th of August, by the wish and proposal of the king, Johanna, the daughter of Warin de Muntchesnil, was married to

William de Valence, the king's uterine brother; for, the eldest son and heir of the said Warin being dead, a very rich inheritance awaited this daughter Johanna, who was the only daughter left" (II, 230).

14. III, 151.

15. Roger of Wendover, II, 583-84.

16. Quoted by Richardson, *National Movement* (New York, 1897), pp. 32-33.

17. Avoit une coustume ens el tiois pays
Que tout li grant seignor, li conte et li marchis
Avoient entour aus gent françoise tousdis
Pour aprendre françoise lor filles et lor fis;
Li rois et la roïne et Berte o le cler vis

Sorent près d'aussi bien la françois de Paris
Com se il fussent né au bourc à Saint Denis.

18. Cf. Nyrop, *Grammaire historique de la langue française,* I, 30; Brunot, *Histoire de la langue française,* I, 358-a99. Writers still speak of the wide popularity of French at a much later date. Christine de Pisan at the beginning of the fifteenth century calls it "la plus commune par l'universel monde" *(Le Livre des Trois Vertus,* quoted in R. Thomassy, *Essai sur les écrits politiques de Christine de Pisan* (Paris, 1838), pp. lxxxi-lxxxii) and cf. the anonymous author of *La Manière de langage (1396), ed. P.* Meyer, Rev. Critique, 10 (1870), 373-408.

19. In the reign of Edward I the archbishop of Canterbury presented to the king and the leaders of the army a Latin letter from the pope and explained its contents in French (Matthew of West-minster, trans. C.D.Young, II, 546). The petitions to Parliament at this time are mostly in French, and sometimes the statutes themselves, though these were commonly drawn up in Latin *(Statutes of the Realm,* I, xl, and R.L.Atkinson, "Interim Report on Ancient Petitions," typed transcript bound in the copy of *Lists and Indexes,* no. 1, in the Literary Search Room of the Public Record Office).

20. As when Edward I was called in (1291) to settle the dispute concerning the Scottish succession (Rymer, *Foedera,* II, 553).

21. Four are edited by E.Lamond, *Walter of Henley's Husbandry* (London, 1890). One was supposedly written by Bishop Grosseteste in 1240–1241 for the countess of Lincoln. Walter of Henley's treatise exists in an English version that is attributed in the manuscripts to Grosseteste. If we could trust the attribution, it would constitute evidence that some of the landowners at this time preferred to read English. But the translation belongs probably to a later date.

22. A French poem on the calendar is addressed to "simpli gent lettre," that is, those who could read, while Grosseteste's *Château d'Amour* was "por ceus ki ne sevent mie ne lettrure ne clergie," that is, those who could neither read at all nor understand Latin, but could understand French when it was read to them.

23. Continuation of Pseudo-Ingulph, *Ingulph's Chronicle,* trans. H.T.Riley, p. 330.

24. Je ne sai guers romanz faire... Car jeo ne fu unques a Parye Ne al abbaye de saint Denys. *(Antikrist,* latter part of the thirteenth century, cited by Vising, *Franska Språket i England,* III, 9.)

25. W.C.Bolland, *Select Bills in Eyre, A.D. 1292-1333* (London, 1914), pp. xix-xx, xxx-xxxi (Selden Soc).

26. William Rothwell summarizes the situation well: "The true role of French in thirteenth-century England was not at all that of a vernacular, except possibly in the case of the king's immediate entourage." Also, "French as a vernacular was declining steadily before the twelfth century gave way to the thirteenth, but as a language of culture and administration it prospered all through the thirteenth century and even beyond," in "The Role of French in Thirteenth-Century England," *Bulletin of the John Rylands Library,* 58 (1975-76), 455, 462.

27. *Chronica Majora,* trans. Riley, III, 209.

28. Cf. an incident in Walter of Hemingburgh, I, 337 (Eng. Hist. Soc.); Freeman, V, 533.

29. Grosseteste (cf. Stevenson, *Robert Grosseteste,* p. 32).

30. W.C.Bolland, *The Year Books* (Cambridge, 1921), p. 76.

31. Giraldus Cambrensis, *Opera,* IV, 209 (Rolls Series).

32. Annals of Worcester, *Annales Monastici,* IV, 504 (Rolls Series).

33. The agreement reached by the barons and the king in 1258 and known as the Provisions of Oxford was made public by a proclamation that bound everyone in England to the acceptance of it. The proclamation, issued by the king October 18, 1258, was in French and English and was directed "To alle hise holde ilaerde and ileawede" (to all his faithful subjects, learned and lay) in every county. It is the first proclamation to be issued in English since the Norman Conquest, and, although the only one for a good while, is very likely the result of Simon de Montfort's desire to reach the people of the middle class, the lesser barons, and the inhabitants of the towns.For the text of the proclamation, as entered on the Patent Roll, see A.J.Ellis, "On the Only

English Proclamation of Henry III," *Trans. Philol. Soc.* (1868), pp. 1-135. The actual copy sent to the sheriff of Oxford was later found and published by W.W.Skeat, "The Oxford MS. of the Only English Proclamation of Henry III," *ibid.* (1880-1881), Appendix VI. A facsimile of this copy is given in Octavus Ogle, *Royal Letters Addressed to Oxford* (Oxford, 1892).

34. The treatise has been edited by William Rothwell, *Walter de Bibbesworth: Le Tretiz* (London, 1990). On the date see Baugh, "The Date of Walter of Bibbesworth's Traité," *Festschrift für Walther Fischer* (Heidelberg, 1959), pp. 21-33.
35. people
36. to
37. each place
38. most
39. what
40. each one
41. ignorant, lay
42. *Annales Monastici,* I, 322 (Rolls Series).
43. W.A.Morris, *The Early English County Court* (Berkeley, 1926), p. 173.
44. *Customary of the Benedictine Monasteries of Saint Augustine, Canterbury, and Saint Peter, Westminster,* ed. E.H.Thompson, Henry Bradshaw Soc., XXIII, 210; XXVIII, 164.
45. *Munimenta Academica,* II, 438 (Rolls Series).
46. C.E.Mallet, *A History of the University of Oxford* (3 vols., London, 1924-1927), I, 118.
47. *Documents Relating to the University and Colleges of Cambridge* (1852), II, 31.
48. *Œuvres de Froissart,* ed. Kervyn de Lettenhove, II, 419.
49. A full account of these books is given in K.Lambley, *The Teaching and Cultivation of the French Language in England* (Manchester, 1920), and G.T.Clapton and W.Stewart, *Les Études françaisesdans l 'enseignement en Grande-Bretagne* (Paris, 1929).
50. See William Rothwell, "The Teaching of French in Medieval England," *Mod. Lang. Rev.,* 63 (1968), 37-46.
51. Roger Bacon notes the four dialects and says: "A fitting and intelligible expression in the dialect of the Picards is out of place among the

Burgundians, nay, among their nearer Gallic neighbors." *The Opus Majus of Roger Bacon,* trans. R.B. Burke (Philadelphia, 1928), I, 75.

52. Walter Map says that "if one is faulty in his use of this tongue, we say that he speaketh French of Marlborough." *De Nugis Curialium,* V, vi (trans. Tupper and Ogle).

53. H.Albert, *Mittelalterlicher Englisch-französischer Jargon* (Halle, Germany, 1922).

54. A life of Edward the Confessor in Anglo-French verse of the latter part of the thirteenth century; cf. A.T.Baker in *Mod. Lang. Rev.,* 3 (1907-1908), 374-75. William of Wadington makes a similar excuse: "No one ought to blame me for the French or the verse, for I was born in England and nourished and brought up there." So too does Gower (Vising, *Franska Språket i England,* III, 9).

55. Gervase of Tilbury, *Otia Imperialia* (1212), chap. 20, ed. G.G.Leibnitz, *Scriptores Rerum Brunsvicensium* (Hanover, Germany, 1707), I, 945.

56. As a result of the plague English must also have made its way more rapidly in the monasteries, as we know it did in the schools, and probably elsewhere. Forty-seven monks and the abbot died at St. Albans in 1349. Their places were filled by men who often knew no other language than English. We may judge of the situation from the words of the chronicler Knighton: "But, within a short time, a very great multitude of men whose wives had died of the pestilence flocked to Holy Orders, of whom many were illiterate and almost sheer lay folk, except in so far as they could read, though not understand."

57. North English Homily Cycle, ed. John Small, *English Metrical Homilies from Manuscripts of the Fourteenth Century* (Edinburgh, 1862), pp. 3-4:

6

Middle English a Period of Great Change

The Middle English period (1150-1500) was marked by momentous changes in the English language, changes more extensive and fundamental than those that have taken place at any time before or since. Some of them were the result of the Norman Conquest and the conditions which followed in the wake of that event. Others were a continuation of tendencies that had begun to manifest themselves in Old English. These would have gone on even without the Conquest, but they took place more rapidly because the Norman invasion removed from English those conservative influences that are always felt when a language is extensively used in books and is spoken by an influential educated class. The changes of this period affected English in both its grammar and its vocabulary. They were so extensive in each department that it is difficult to say which group is the more significant. Those in the grammar reduced English from a highly inflected language to an extremely analytic one.[1] Those in the vocabulary involved the loss of a large part of the Old English word-stock and the addition of thousands of words from French and Latin. At the beginning of the period English is a language that must be learned like a foreign tongue; at the end it is Modern English.

Decay of Inflectional Endings

The changes in English grammar may be described as a general reduction of inflections. Endings of the noun and adjective marking distinctions of number and case and often of gender were so altered in pronunciation as to lose their distinctive form and hence their usefulness. To some extent the same thing is true of the verb. This leveling of inflectional endings was due partly to phonetic changes, partly to the operation of analogy. The phonetic changes were simple but far-reaching. The earliest seems to have been the change of final *-m* to *-n* wherever it occurred, i.e., in the dative plural of nouns and adjectives and in the dative singular (masculine and neuter) of adjectives when inflected according to the strong declension. Thus *mûðum* (to the mouths) >*mûðun, gôdum>gôdun.* This *-n,* along with the *-n* of the other inflectional endings, was then dropped *(*mûðu, *gôdu).* At the same time,[2] the vowels *a, o, u, e* in inflectional endings were obscured to a sound, the so-called "indeterminate vowel," which came to be written *e* (less often *i, y, u,* depending on place and date). As a result, a number of originally distinct endings such as *-a, -u, -e, -an, -um* were reduced generally to a uniform *-e,* and such grammatical distinctions as they formerly expressed were no longer conveyed. Traces of these changes have been found in Old English manuscripts as early as the tenth century.[3] By the end of the twelfth century they seem to have been generally carried out. The leveling is somewhat obscured in the written language by the tendency of scribes to preserve the traditional spelling, and in some places the final *n* was retained even in the spoken language, especially as a sign of the plural. The effect of these changes on the inflection of the noun and the adjective, and the further simplification that was brought about by the operation of analogy, may be readily shown.

The Noun

A glance at the few examples of common noun declensions in Old English given in § 41 will show how seriously the inflectional endings were disturbed. For example, in the London

English of Chaucer in the strong masculine declension the forms *mûð, mûðes, mûðe, mûð* in the singular, and *mûðas, mûða and mûðum, mûðas* in the plural were reduced to three: *mûð, mûðes,* and *mûðe.* In such words the *-e,* which was organic in the dative singular and the genitive and dative plural (i.e., stood for an ending in the Old English paradigm), was extended by analogy to the nominative and accusative singular, so that forms like *stône, mûðe* appear, and the only distinctive termination is the *-s* of the possessive singular and of the nominative and accusative plural. Because these two cases of the plural were those most frequently used, the -s came to be thought of as the sign of the plural and was extended to all plural forms. We get thus an inflection of the noun identical with that which we have today.[4] Other declensions suffered even more, so that in many words *(giefu, sunu,* etc.) the distinctions of case and even of number were completely obliterated.

In early Middle English only two methods of indicating the plural remained fairly distinctive: the *-s* or *-es* from the strong masculine declension and the *-en* (as in *oxen)* from the weak (see § 41). And for a time, at least in southern England, it would have been difftcult to predict that the *-s* would become the almost universal sign of the plural that it has become. Until the thirteenth century the *-en* plural enjoyed great favor in the south, being often added to nouns which had not belonged to the weak declension in Old English. But in the rest of England the *-s* plural (and genitive singular) of the old first declension (masculine) was apparently felt to be so distinctive that it spread rapidly. Its extension took place most quickly in the north. Even in Old English many nouns originally of other declensions had gone over to this declension in the Northumbrian dialect. By 1200 -s was the standard plural ending in the north and north Midland areas; other forms were exceptional. Fifty years later it had conquered the rest of the Midlands, and in the course of the fourteenth century it had definitely been accepted all over England as the normal sign of the plural in English nouns. Its spread may have been helped by the early extension of *-s* throughout the plural in

Anglo-Norman, but in general it may be considered as an example of the survival of the fittest in language.

The Adjective

In the adjective the leveling of forms had even greater consequences. Partly as a result of the sound-changes already described, partly through the extensive working of analogy, the form of the nominative singular was early extended to all cases of the singular, and that of the nominative plural to all cases of the plural, both in the strong and the weak declensions. The result was that in the weak declension there was no longer any distinction between the singular and the plural: both ended in *-e (blinda> blinde* and *blindan>blinde).* This was also true of those adjectives under the strong declension whose singular ended in *-e.* By about 1250 the strong declension had distinctive forms for the singular and plural only in certain monosyllabic adjectives which ended in a consonant in Old English (sing. *glad,* plur. *glade).* Under the circumstances the only ending which remained to the adjective was often without distinctive grammatical meaning and its use was not governed by any strong sense of adjectival inflection. Although it is clear that the *-e* ending of the weak and plural forms was available for use in poetry in both the East and West Midlands until the end of the fourteenth century, it is impossible to know the most usual status of the form in the spoken language. Certainly adjectival inflections other than *-e,* such as Chaucer's *oure aller cok,* were archaic survivals by the close of the Middle English period.[5]

The Pronoun

The decay of inflections that brought about such a simplification of the noun and the adjective as has just been described made it necessary to depend less upon formal indications of gender, case, and (in adjectives) number, and to rely more upon juxtaposition, word order, and the use of prepositions to make clear the relation of words in a sentence. This is apparent from the corresponding decay of pronominal inflections, where the simplification of forms was due in only a slight measure to the weakening of final syllables that played so large a part in the reduction of endings in the noun and the adjective. The loss was greatest in the demonstratives. Of the numerous forms of *sç, sço, þæt* (cf. § 44) we have only *the* and *that* surviving through Middle English and continuing in use today. A plural *tho* (those) survived to Elizabethan times. All the other forms indicative of different gender, number, and case disappeared in most dialects early in the Middle English period. The same may be said of the demonstrative *þçs, þços, þis*[6] (this). Everywhere but in the south the neuter form *þis* came to be used early in Middle English for all genders and cases of the singular, while the forms of the nominative plural were similarly extended to all cases of the plural, appearing in Modern English as *those* and *these.*

In the personal pronoun the losses were not so great. Most of the distinctions that existed in Old English were retained. However the forms of the dtive and accusative cases were early combined, generally under that of the dative *(him, her, [t]hem).* In the neuter the form of the accusative *(h)it* became the general objective case, partly because it was like the nominative, and partly because the dative him would have been subject to confusion with the corresponding case of the masculine. One other general simplification is to be noted: the loss of the dual number. A language can get along without a distinction in pronouns for two persons and more than two; the forms *wit,* and their oblique cases did not survive beyond the thirteenth century, and English lost the dual number.

It will be observed that the pronoun *she* had the form *hço* in Old English. The modern form could have developed from the Old English *hço,* but it is believed by some that it is due in part at least to the influence of the demonstrative *sço.* A similar reinforcing influence of the demonstrative is perhaps to be seen in the forms of the third person plural, *they, their, them,* but here the source of the modern developments was undoubtedly Scandinavian. The normal development of the Old English pronouns would have been *hi (he), here, hem,* and these are very common. In the districts, however, where Scandinavian influence was strong, the nominative *hi* began early to be replaced by the Scandinavian form *þei* (ON *þeir),* and somewhat later a similar replacement occurred in the other cases, *their* and them. The new forms were adopted more slowly farther south, and the usual inflection in Chaucer is thei, *here, hem.* But by the end of the Middle English period the forms *they, their, them* may be regarded as the normal English plurals.

The Verb

Apart from some leveling of inflections and the weakening of endings in accordance with the general tendency,[7] the principal changes in the verb during the Middle English period were the serious losses suffered by the strong conjugation (see §§ 117-18). This conjugation, although including some of the most important verbs in the language, was relatively small[8] as compared with the large and steadily growing body of weak verbs.

While an occasional verb developed a strong past tense or past participle by analogy with similar strong verbs, new verbs formed from nouns and adjectives or borrowed from other languages were regularly conjugated as weak. Thus the minority position of the strong conjugation was becoming constantly more appreciable. After the Norman Conquest the loss of native words further depleted the ranks of the strong verbs. Those that survived were exposed to the influence of the majority, and many have changed over in the course of time to the weak inflection.

Losses among the Strong Verbs

Nearly a third of the strong verbs in Old English seem to have died out early in the Middle English period. In any case about ninety of them have left no traces in written records after 1150. Some of them may have been current for a time in the spoken language, but except where an occasional verb survives in a modern dialect they are not recorded. Some were rare in Old English and others were in competition with weak verbs of similar derivation and meaning which superseded them. In addition to verbs that are not found at all after the Old English period there are about a dozen more that appear only in Layamon (c. 1200) or in certain twelfth-century texts based directly on the homilies of Ælfric and other Old English works. In other words, more than a hundred of the Old English strong verbs were lost at the beginning of the Middle English period.

But this was not all. The loss has continued in subsequent periods. Some thirty more became obsolete in the course of Middle English, and an equal number, which were still in use in the sixteenth and seventeenth centuries, finally died out except in the dialects, often after they had passed over to the weak conjugation or had developed weak forms alongside the strong. Today more than half of the Old English strong verbs have disappeared completely from the standard language.

Strong Verbs That Became Weak

The principle of analogy—the tendency of language to follow certain patterns and adapt a less common form to a more familiar one—is well exemplified in the further history of the strong verbs. The weak conjugation offered a fairly consistent pattern for the past tense and the past participle, whereas there was much variety in the different classes of the strong verb. We say *sing—sang—sung,* but *drive—drove—driven, fall—fell—fallen,* etc. At a time when English was the language chiefly of the lower classes and largely removed from the restraining influences of education and a literary standard, it was natural that many speakers should apply the pattern of weak verbs to some which were historically strong. The tendency was not unknown even in Old English. Thus ***F(EdClft*** (to advise) and *sceððan* (to injure) had already become weak in Old English, while other verbs show occasional weak forms.[9] In the thirteenth century the trend becomes clear in the written literature. Such verbs as *bow, brew, burn, climb, flee, flow, help, mourn, row, step, walk, weep* were then undergoing change. By the fourteenth century the movement was at its height. No less than thirty-two verbs in addition to those already mentioned now show weak forms. After this there are fewer changes. The impulse seems to have been checked, possibly by the steady rise of English in the social scale and later by the stabilizing effect of printing. At all events the fifteenth century shows only about a dozen new weak formations and in the whole modern period there are only about as many more.

In none of the many verbs which have thus become weak was the change from the strong conjugation a sudden one. Strong forms continued to be used while the weak ones were growing up, and in many cases they continued in use long after the weak inflection had become well established. Thus *oke* as the past tense of *ache* was still written throughout the fifteenth century although the weak form *ached* had been current for a hundred years. In the same way we find *stope* beside *stepped, rewe* beside *rowed, clew* beside *clawed.* In a good many cases the strong forms remained in the language well into modern times. *Climb,* which was conjugated as a weak verb as early as the thirteenth century, still has an alternative past tense *clomb* not only in Chaucer and Spenser but in Dryden, and the strong past tense *crope* was more common than *crept* down to Shakespeare's day. *Low* for *laughed, shove* for *shaved, yold* for *yielded,* etc., were still used in the sixteenth century although these verbs were already passing over to the weak conjugation two centuries before. While the weak forms commonly won out, this was not always the case. Many strong verbs also had weak forms *(blowed* for *blew, knowed* for *knew, teared* for *tore)* that did not survive in the standard speech, while in other cases both forms have continued in use *(cleft—clove, crowed—crew, heaved—hove, sheared— shore, shrived—shrove).*

Survival of Strong Participles

For some reason the past participle of strong verbs seems to have been more tenacious than the past tense. In a number of verbs weak participles are later in appearing and the strong form often continued in use after the verb had definitely become weak. In the verb *beat* the principle *beaten* has remained the standard form, while in a number of other verbs the strong participle *(cloven, graven, hewn, laden, molten, mown, (mis)shapen, shaven, sodden, swollen)* are still used, especially as adjectives.

Surviving Strong Verbs

When we subtract the verbs that have been lost completely

and the eighty-one that have become weak, there remain just sixty-eight of the Old English strong verbs in the language today. To this number may be added thirteen verbs that are conjugated in both ways or have kept one strong form. These figures indicate how extensive the loss of strong verbs in the language has been. Beside this loss the number of new strong formations has been negligible.[10] Since the irregularity of such verbs constitutes a difficulty in language, the loss in this case must be considered a gain.

The surviving strong verbs have seldom come down to the present day in the form that would represent the normal development of their principal parts in Old English. In all periods of the language they have been subjected to various forms of leveling and analogical influence from one class to another. For example, the verb *to slay had* in Old English the forms *slçan—slôg—slôgon—slægen.* These would normally have become *slea* (pronounced *slee)—slough—slain,* and the present tense *slea* actually existed down to the seventeenth century. The modern *slay*is reformed from the past participle. The past tense *slew* is due to the analogy of preterites like *blew, grew.* In Old English the past tense commonly had a different form in the singular and the plural,[11] and in two large classes of verbs the vowel of the plural was also like that of the past participle (e.g., *bindan—band—bundon—bunden).* Consequently, although normally the singular form survived in Modern English, in many cases the vowel of the plural or of the past participle has taken its place. Thus *cling, sting, spin,* etc., should have had a past tense *clang, stang, span* (like *sing)*, but these forms have been replaced by *clung, stung, spun* from the plural and the past participle. The past tense of *slide* should have been *slode,* but the plural and the past participle had i and we now say *slide—slid—slid.* Sometimes a verb has changed from one class to another. *Break* belonged originally to the fifth class of strong verbs, and had it remained there, would have had a past participle *breken.* But in Old English it was confused with verbs of the fourth class, which had *o* in the past participle, whence our form *broken.* This form has now spread to the past tense. We should be saying *brack* or *brake,* and the latter is still used in the Bible, but except in biblical language the current form is now *broke. Speak* has had a similar development. Almost every strong verb in the language has an interesting formhistory, but our present purpose will be sufficiently served by these few examples of the sort of fluctuation and change that was going on all through the Middle English period and which has not yet ended.

Loss of Grammatical Gender

One of the consequences of the decay of inflections described above was the elimination of that troublesome feature of language, grammatical gender. As explained in § 42, the gender of Old English nouns was not often determined by meaning. Sometimes it was in direct contradiction with the meaning. Thus *woman* (OE *wîf-mann)* was masculine, because the second element in the compound was masculine; *wife* and *child,* like German *Weib* and *Kind,* were neuter. Moreover, the gender of nouns in Old English was not so generally indicated by the declension as it is in a language like Latin. Instead it was revealed chiefly by the concord of the strong adjective and the demonstratives. These by their distinctive endings generally showed, at least in the singular, whether a noun was masculine, feminine, or neuter. When the inflections of these gender-distinguishing words were reduced to a single ending for the adjective, and the fixed forms of *the, this, that, these,* and *those* for the demonstratives, the support for grammatical gender was removed. The weakening of inflections and the confusion and loss of the old gender proceeded in a remarkably parallel course. In the north, where inflections weakened earliest, grammatical gender disappeared first. In the south it lingered longer because there the decay of inflections was slower.

Our present method of determining gender was no sudden invention of Middle English times. The recognition of sex that lies at the root of natural gender is shown in Old English by the noticeable tendency to use the personal pronouns in accordance with natural gender, even when such use involves a clear conflict with the grammatical gender of the antecedent. For example, the pronoun *it* i$_n$ *Etað þisne hlâf* (masculine), *hit is mîm lîchama* (Ælfric's Homilies) is exactly in accordance with modern usage when we say, *Eat this bread, it is my body.* Such a use of the personal pronouns is clearly indicative of the feeling for natural gender even while grammatical gender was in full force. With the disappearance of grammatical gender sex became the only factor in determining the gender of English nouns.

Middle English Syntax

As a result of the leveling of inflections, syntactic and semantic relationships that had been signaled by the endings on words now became ambiguous. Whereas in Old English the grammatical functions of two consecutive nouns were clear from their endings in, say, the nominative and dative cases, in Middle English their functions might be uncertain. The most direct way to avoid this kind of ambiguity is through limiting the possible patterns of word order. The process of development from the highly synthetic stage of Old English to the highly analytic stages of Late Middle English and Modern English can be seen in the *Peterborough Chronicle.* Written in installments between 1070 and 1154, this text of the *Anglo-Saxon Chronide* spans the period from Old English to Early Middle English. Within the continuations of the text it is possible to trace first a significant loss of inflections and afterwards a corresponding rigidity of word order, making clear the direction of cause and effect.[12] This process of development and the reality of Middle English as a separate stage of the language grammatically (as well as phonologically and lexically) can be seen in the patterns of subject and verb. In addition to the Modern English order SV, Old English had VS and, in subordinate clauses, S...V (with the finite verb in final position). All of these patterns are still possible even in the last years of the *Peterborough Chronicle.* Thus, the word order looked much like that of Old English at a time when the inflectional system looked much like that of Modern English. As Bruce Mitchell writes, "the language of the *Peterborough Chronide* 1122-1154 is Middle, not

Modern, English. It is transitional."[13] And as its most recent editor puts it: "before our eyes English is beginning to change from a synthetic language to an analytic one."[14]

It is important to emphasize that these changes which affected the grammatical structure of English after the Norman Conquest were not the result of contact with the French language. Certain idioms and syntactic usages that appear in Middle English are clearly the result of such contact.[15] But the decay of inflections and the confusion of forms that constitute the truly significant development in Middle English grammar are the result of the Norman Conquest only insofar as that event brought about conditions favorable to such changes. By removing the authority that a standard variety of English would have, the Norman Conquest made it easier for grammatical changes to go forward unchecked. Beyond this it is not considered a factor in syntactic changes.

French Influence on the Vocabulary

While the loss of inflections and the consequent simplification of English grammar were thus only indirectly due to the use of French in England, French influence is much more direct and observable upon the vocabulary. Where two languages exist side by side for a long time and the relations between the people speaking them are as intimate as they were in England, a considerable transference of words from one language to the other is inevitable. As is generally the case, the interchange was to some extent mutual. A good many English words found their way into the French spoken in England. We are naturally less interested in them here, because they concern rather the history of the Anglo-Norman language. Their number was not so large as that of the French words introduced into English. English, representing a culture that was regarded as inferior, had more to gain from French, and there were other factors involved. The number of French words that poured into English was unbelievably great. There is nothing comparable to it in the previous or subsequent history of the language.

Although this influx of French words was brought about by the victory of the Conqueror and by the political and social consequences of that victory, it was neither sudden nor immediately apparent. Rather it began slowly and continued with varying tempo for a long time. Indeed it can hardly be said to have ever stopped. The large number of French words borrowed during the Middle Ages has made it easy for us to go on borrowing, and the close cultural relations between France and England in all subsequent periods have furnished a constant opportunity for the transfer of words. But there was a time in the centuries following the Conquest when this movement had its start and a stream of French words poured into English with a momentum that continued until toward the end of the Middle English period.

In this movement two stages can be observed, an earlier and a later, with the year 1250 as the approximate dividing line. The borrowings of the first stage differ from those of the second in being much less numerous, in being more likely to show peculiarities of Anglo-Norman phonology, and, especially, in the circumstances that brought about their introduction. When we study the French words appearing in English before 1250, roughly 900 in number, we find that many of them were such as the lower classes would become familiar with through contact with a French-speaking nobility *(baron, noble, dame, servant, messenger, feast, minstrel, juggler, largess)*. Others, such as *story, rime, lay, douzepers* (the twelve peers of the Charlemagne romances), obviously owed their introduction into English to literary channels. The largest single group among the words that came in early was associated with the church, where the necessity for the prompt transference of doctrine and belief from the clergy to the people is sufficient to account for the frequent transfer of words. In the period after 1250 the conditions under which French words had been making their way into English were supplemented by a new and powerful factor: those who had been accustomed to speak French were turning increasingly to the use of English. Whether to supply deficiencies in the English vocabulary or in their own imperfect command of that vocabulary, or perhaps merely yielding to a natural impulse to use a word long familiar to them and to those they addressed, the upper classes carried over into English an astonishing number of common French words. In changing from French to English they transferred much of their governmental and administrative vocabulary, their ecclesiastical, legal, and military terms, their familiar words of fashion, food, and social life, the vocabulary of art, learning, and medicine. In general we may say that in the earlier Middle English period

the French words introduced into English were such as people speaking one language often learn from those speaking another; in the century and a half following 1250, when all classes were speaking or learning to speak English, they were also such words as people who had been accustomed to speak French would carry over with them into the language of their adoption. Only in this way can we understand the nature and extent of the French importations in this period.

Governmental and Administrative Words

We should expect that English would owe many of its words dealing with government and administration to the language of those who for more than 200 years made public affairs their chief concern. The words *government, govern, administer* might appropriately introduce a list of such words. It would include such fundamental terms as *crown, state, empire, realm, reign, royal, prerogative, authority, sovereign, majesty, scepter, tyrant, usurp, oppress, court, council, parliament, assembly, statute, treaty, alliance, record, repeal, adjourn, tax, subsidy, revenue, tally, exchequer.* Intimately associated with the idea of government are also words like *subject, allegiance, rebel, traitor, treason, exile, public, liberty.* The word *office* and the titles of many offices are likewise French: *chancellor, treasurer, chamberlain, marshal, governor, councilor, minister, viscount, warden, castellan, mayor, constable, coroner,* and even the humble *crier.* Except for the words *king* and *queen, lord, lady,* and *earl,* most designations of rank are French: *noble, nobility, peer, prince, princess, duke, duchess, count, countess, marquis, baron, squire, page,* as well as such words as *courtier, retinue,* and titles of respect like *sir, madam, mistress.* The list might well be extended to include words relating to the economic organization of society—*manor, demesne, bailiff, vassal, homage, peasant, bondman, slave, servant,* and *caitiff—since* they often have a political or administrative aspect.

Ecclesiastical Words

The church was scarcely second to the government as an object of Norman interest and ambition. The higher clergy, occupying positions of wealth and power, were, as we have seen, practically all Normans. Ecclesiastical preferment opened the way to a career that often led to the highest political offices at court. In monasteries and religious houses French was for a long time the usual language. Accordingly we find in English such French words as *religion, theology, sermon, homily, sacrament, baptism, communion, confession, penance, prayer, orison, lesson, passion, psalmody;* such indications of rank or class as *clergy, clerk, prelate, cardinal, legate, dean, chaplain, parson, pastor, vicar, sexton, abbess, novice, friar, hermit;* the names of objects associated with the service or with the religious life, such as *crucifix, crosier, miter, surplice, censer, incense, lectern, image, chancel, chantry, chapter, abbey, convent, priory, hermitage, cloister, sanctuary;* words expressing such fundamental religious or theological concepts as *creator, savior, trinity, virgin, saint, miracle, mystery, faith, heresy, schism, reverence, devotion, sacrilege, simony, temptation, damnation, penitence, contrition, remission, absolution, redemption, salvation, immortality,* and the more general virtues of *piety, sanctity, charity, mercy, pity, obedience,* as well as the word *virtue* itself. We should include also a number of adjectives, like *solemn, divine, reverend, devout,* and verbs, such as *preach, pray, chant, repent, confess, adore, sacrifice, convert, anoint, ordain.*

Law

French was so long the language of the law courts in England that the greater part of the English legal vocabulary comes from the language of the conquerors. The fact that we speak of *justice* and *equity* instead of *gerihte, judgment* rather than *dom* (doom), *crime* in place of *synn, gylt, undæd,* etc., shows how completely we have adopted the terminology of French law. Even where the Old English word survives it has lost its technical sense. In the same way we say *bar, assize, eyre, plea, suit, plaintiff, defendant, judge, advocate, attorney, bill, petition, complaint, inquest, summons, hue and cry, indictment, jury, juror, panel, felon, evidence, proof, bail, ransom, mainpernor, judgment, verdict, sentence, decree, award, fine, forfeit, punishment, prison, gaol, pillory.* We have likewise a rich array of verbs associated with legal processes: *sue, plead, implead, accuse, indict, arraign, depose, blame, arrest, seize, pledge, warrant, assail, assign, judge, condemn, convict, award, amerce, distrain, imprison, banish, acquit, pardon.* The names of many crimes and misdemeanors are French: *felony, trespass, assault, arson, larceny, fraud, libel, slander, perjury, adultery,* and many others. Suits involving property brought into use such words as *property, estate, tenement, chattels, appurtenances, encumbrance, bounds, seisin, tenant, dower, legacy, patrimony, heritage, heir, executor, entail.* Common adjectives like *just, innocent, culpable* have obvious legal import though they are also of wider application.

Army and Navy

The large part that war played in English affairs in the Middle Ages, the fact that the control of the army and navy was in the hands of those who spoke French, and the circumstance that much of English fighting was done in France all resulted in the introduction into English of a number of French military terms. The art of war has undergone such changes since the days of Hastings and Lewes and Agincourt that many words once common are now obsolete or only in historical use. Their places have been taken by later borrowings, often likewise from French, many of them being words acquired by the French in the course of their wars in Italy during the sixteenth century. Nevertheless, we still use medieval French words when we speak of the *army* and the *navy,* of *peace, enemy, arms, battle, combat, skirmish, siege, defense, ambush, stratagem, retreat, soldier, garrison, guard, spy,* and we have kept the names of officers such as *captain, lieutenant, sergeant.* We recognize as once having had greater significance words like *dart, lance, banner, mail, buckler, hauberk, archer, chieftain, portcullis, barbican,* and *moat.* Sometimes we have retained a word while forgetting its original military significance. The word *"Havoc!"* was originally an order giving an army the signal to commence plundering and seizing spoil. Verbs like *to arm, array, harness,*

brandish, vanquish, besiege, defend, among many, suffice to remind us of this important French element in our vocabulary.

Fashion, Meals, and Social Life

That the upper classes should have set the standard in fashion and dress is so obvious an assumption that the number of French words belonging to this class occasions no surprise. The words *fashion* and *dress* are themselves French, as are *apparel, habit, gown, robe, garment, attire, cape, cloak, coat, frock, collar, veil, train, chemise, petticoat.* So too are *lace, embroidery, pleat, gusset, buckle, button, tassel, plume,* and the names of such articles as *kerchief, mitten, garter, galoshes,* and *boots.* Verbs like *embellish* and *adorn* often occur in contexts which suggest the word *luxury,* and this in turn carries with it *satin, taffeta, fur, sable, beaver, ermine.* The colors *blue, brown, vermilion, scarlet, saffron, russet,* and *tawny*are French borrowings of this period. *Jewel, ornament, brooch, chaplet, ivory,* and *enamel* point to the luxuries of the wealthy, and it is significant that the names of all the more familiar precious stones are French: *turquoise, amethyst, topaz, garnet, ruby, emerald, sapphire, pearl, diamond,* not to mention *crystal, coral,* and *beryl.*

The French-speaking classes, it would seem, must also be credited with a considerable adornment of the English table. Not only are the words *dinner* and *supper* French, but also the words *feast, repast, collation,* and *mess* (now military). So, too, are *appetite, taste, victuals, viand,* and *sustenance.* One could have found on the medieval menu, had there been one, among the fish, *mackerel, sole, perch, bream, sturgeon, salmon, sardine, oyster, porpoise;* among meats, *venison, beef, veal, mutton, pork, bacon, sausage, tripe,* with a choice of *loin, chine, haunch,* or *brawn,* and with *gravy* included; among fowl, *poultry, pullet, pigeon,* and various game birds mentioned below. One could have *pottage, gruel, toast, biscuit, cream, sugar, olives, salad, lettuce, endive,* and for dessert *almonds,* and many *fruits,* including *raisin, fig, date, grape, orange, lemon, pomegranate, cherry,*[16] *peach,* or a *confection, pasty, tart, jelly, treacle.* Among seasoning and condiments we find *spice, clove, thyme, herb, mustard, vinegar, marjoram, cinnamon, nutmeg.* The verbs *roast, boil, parboil, stew, fry, broach, blanch, grate,* and *mince* describe various culinary processes, and *goblet, saucer, cruet, plate, platter* suggest French refinements in the serving of meals. It is melancholy to think what the English dinner table would have been like had there been no Norman Conquest.

A variety of new words suggests the innovations made by the French in domestic economy and social life. *Arras, curtain, couch, chair, cushion, screen, lamp, lantern, sconce, chandelier, blanket, quilt, coverlet, counterpane, towel,* and *basin* indicate articles of comfort or convenience, while *dais, parlor, wardrobe, closet, pantry, scullery,* and *garner* (storehouse) imply improvements in domestic arrangements. *Recreation, solace, jollity, leisure, dance, carol, revel, minstrel, juggler, fool, ribald, lute, tabor, melody, music, chess, checkers, dalliance,* and *conversation* reveal various aspects of entertainment in a baronial hall, while numerous words associated with hunting and riding are a reflection of the principal outdoor pastime of the nobility: *ambler, courser, hackney, palfrey, rouncy, stallion* for various types of horse, together with *rein, curb, crupper, rowel, curry, trot, stable, harness; mastiff, terrier, spaniel, leash, kennel, scent, retrieve; falcon, merlin, tercelet, mallard, partridge, pheasant, quail, plover, heron, squirrel; forest, park, covert, warren.* One might extend the list to include other activities, with terms like *joust, tournament, pavilion,* but those given are sufficient to show how much the English vocabulary owes to French in matters of domestic and social life.

Art, Learning, Medicine

The cultural and intellectual interests of the ruling class are reflected in words pertaining to the arts, architecture, literature, learning, and science, especially medicine. Such words as *art, painting, sculpture, music, beauty, color, figure, image, tone* are typical of the first class, while architecture and building have given us *cathedral, palace, mansion, chamber, ceiling, joist, cellar, garret, chimney, lintel, latch, lattice, wicket, tower, pinnacle, turret, porch, bay, choir, cloister, baptistry, column, pillar, base,* and many similar words. Literature is represented by the word itself and by *poet, rime, prose, romance, lay, story, chronicle, tragedy, prologue, preface, title, volume, chapter, quire, parchment, vellum, paper,* and *pen,* and learning by *treatise, compilation, study, logic, geometry, grammar, noun, clause, gender,* together with verbs like *copy, expound,* and *compile.* Among the sciences, medicine has brought in the largest number of early French words still in common use, among them the word *medicine* itself, *chirurgy, physician, surgeon, apothecary, malady, debility, distemper, pain, ague, palsy, pleurisy, gout, jaundice, leper, paralytic, plague, pestilence, contagion, anatomy, stomach, pulse, remedy, ointment, balm, pellet, alum, arsenic, niter, sulphur, alkali, poison.* It is clear that the arts and sciences, being largely cultivated or patronized by the higher classes, owe an important part of their vocabulary to French.

Breadth of the French Influence

Such classes of words as have been illustrated in the foregoing paragraphs indicate important departments in which the French language altered the English vocabulary in the Middle Ages. But they do not sufficiently indicate how very general was the adoption of French words in every province of life and thought. One has only to glance over a miscellaneous list of words—nouns, adjectives, verbs—to realize how universal was the French contribution. In the noun we may consider the range of ideas in the following list, made up of words that were already in English by 1300: *action, adventure, affection, age, air, bucket, bushel, calendar, carpenter, cheer, city, coast, comfort, cost, country, courage, courtesy, coward, crocodile, cruelty, damage, debt, deceit, dozen, ease, envy, error, face, faggot, fame, fault, flower, folly, force, gibbet, glutton, grain, grief, gum, harlot, honor, hour, jest, joy, labor, leopard, malice, manner, marriage, mason, metal, mischief, mountain, noise, number, ocean, odor, opinion, order, pair, people, peril, person, pewter, piece, point, poverty, powder, power, quality, quart, rage, rancor, reason, river, scandal, seal, season, sign, sound, sphere, spirit, square, strife, stubble, substance, sum, tailor, task, tavern, tempest, unity, use, vision, waste.* The same universality is shown in the adjective. Here the additions were of special importance since Old English was not very well provided with adjective distinctions. From nearly a thousand French adjectives in Middle English we may consider the following selection, all the words in this list being in use in Chaucer's time: *able, abundant, active, actual, amiable, amorous, barren, blank, brief, calm, certain, chaste, chief, clear, common, contrary, courageous, courteous, covetous, coy, cruel, curious, debonair, double, eager, easy, faint, feeble, fierce, final, firm, foreign, frail, frank, gay, gentle, gracious, hardy, hasty, honest, horrible, innocent, jolly, large, liberal, luxurious, malicious, mean, moist, natural, nice, obedient, original, perfect, pertinent, plain, pliant, poor, precious, principal, probable, proper, pure, quaint, real, rude, safe, sage, savage, scarce, second, secret, simple, single, sober, solid, special, stable, stout, strange, sturdy, subtle, sudden, supple, sure, tender, treacherous, universal, usual* A list of the verbs borrowed at the same time shows equal diversity. Examples are: *advance, advise, aim, allow, apply, approach, arrange, arrive, betray, butt, carry, chafe, change, chase, close, comfort, commence, complain, conceal, consider, continue, count, cover, covet, cry, cull, deceive, declare, defeat, defer, defy, delay, desire, destroy, embrace, enclose, endure, enjoy, enter, err, excuse, flatter, flourish, force, forge, form, furnish, grant, increase, nform, inquire, join, languish, launch, marry, mount, move, murmur, muse, nourish, obey, oblige, observe, pass, pay, pierce, pinch, please, practise, praise, prefer, proceed, propose, prove, purify, pursue, push, quash, quit, receive, refuse, rejoice, relieve, remember, reply, rinse, rob, satisfy, save, scald, serve, spoil, strangle, strive, stun, succeed, summon, suppose, surprise, tax, tempt, trace, travel, tremble, trip, wait, waive, waste, wince.* Finally, the influence of French may be seen in numerous phrases and turns of expression, such as *to take leave, to draw near, to hold one's peace, to come to a head, to do justice,* or *make believe, hand to hand, on the point of, according to, subject to, at large, by heart, in vain, without fail.* In these and other phrases, even when the words are English the pattern is French.[17]

These four lists have been presented for the general impression which they create and as the basis for an inference which they clearly justify. This is, that so far as the vocabulary is concerned, what we have in the influence of the Norman Conquest is a merging of the resources of two languages, a merger in which thousands of words in common use in each language became partners in a reorganized concern. English retains a controlling interest, but French as a large minority stockholder supplements and rounds out the major organization in almost every department.

Anglo-Norman and Central French

It will be observed that the French words introduced into English as a result of the Norman Conquest often present an appearance quite different from that which they have in Modern French. This is due first of all to subsequent developments that have taken place in the two languages. Thus the OF *feste* passed into Middle English as *feste,* whence it has become *feast* in Modern English, while in French the *s* disappeared before other consonants at the end of the twelfth century and we have in Modern French the form *fête.* The same difference appears in *forest—*

A second cause of difference between English words and their French counterparts is the fact that the Anglo-Norman or Anglo-French dialect spoken in England differed from the language of Paris (Central French) in numerous respects. A few examples will make this clear. In Anglo-Norman[18] initial *ca-* was often retained, whereas it became *cha-, chie-* in Central French.[19] For example, our word *caitiff* represents the AN *caitif,* whereas the Central French form was *chaitif.* In the same way are explained words like *carry, carriage, case* (box), *cauldron, carrion,* etc., since the corresponding words in the dialect of Paris were pronounced with *ch (charrier, chaudron,* etc.). In some cases English has taken over the same word in both its Norman and its Central French form. Thus AN *catel* corresponds to Central French *chatel:* one gives us our word *cattle,* the other *chattel(s).* The English verb *catch* represents the Anglo-Norman *cachier,* while the Central French *chacier* (Modern French *chasser)* appears in the English *chase.* Or we may take another peculiarity of Anglo-Norman which appears in English. It is a well-known fact that Central French showed an early avoidance of the wsound, both separately and in combination with other consonants, and whether found in Latin or in words borrowed from the Germanic languages. But the dialects of northern and especially northeastern France, possibly because of their proximity to Flemish and Dutch, showed less hostility to this sound and it accordingly is found in Anglo-Norman. And so we have English *wicket* representing the old Norman French *wiket,* which became in the Paris dialect *guichet,* the form which it has in Modern French. In the same way *waste* (AN *waster)* was in Central French *guaster* or *gaster* (Mod. F. *gâter).* Other examples are *wasp (F.guêpe), warmnt (F.garantir), reward (F.regarder), wardrobe, wait, warden* (cf. *guardian,* from Central French), *wage, warren, wince.* In the combination *qu-* Central French likewise dropped the labial element while it was retained for a time in Anglo-Norman. For this reason we say *quit, quarter, quality, question, require,* etc., all with the sound of [kw], where French has a simple [k] *(quitter, quartier, qualité,* etc.).

The consonants were not alone in showing special developments in England. The vowels also at times developed differently, and these differences are likewise reflected in the words borrowed by English. One or two illustrations will have to suffice. In Old French the diphthong *ui* was originally accented on the first element *(úi)*. This accentuation was retained in Anglo-Norman and the i disappeared, leaving a simple *u* [y]. In Middle English this [y] became [u] or [iu], written *u, ui, ew,* etc. Hence the English word *fruit.* In Central French, on the other hand, the accentuation of this diphthong was shifted in the twelfth century from *úi* to *uí,* and as a consequence we have in Modern French the form *fruit* with a quite different pronunciation. Again, the diphthong *ei* was retained in Anglo-Norman, but early in the twelfth century it had become *oi* in Central French. Thus we have in English *leal, real* (AN *leial, reial)* as compared with French *loyal, royal* (which we have also subsequently adopted). The Latin endings *-ârius, -ôrius* appear in AngloNorman as *-arie,*[20] *-orie,* but in Central French they developed into *-aire, -oire.* Hence we have English *salary, victory,* but in French *salaire, victoire.* Of course, in many respects the French spoken in England was identical in its forms with that of Paris, but the cases in which it differed are sufficient to establish the conclusion that until well into the fourteenth century English borrowed its French words generally in the form which they had in the spoken French of England.

While this statement is in accordance with inherent probability and is supported by abundant evidence so far as that evidence enables us to recognize dialectal differences, it must be qualified in one way. We have already seen (§ 101) that by the thirteenth century the preeminence of the Paris dialect was making itself felt outside the capital and it is probable that the French of England was gradually modified in the direction of conformity with that dialect. In spite of Chaucer's jest about the French of Stratford-at-Bow and the undoubted fact that the French of England was ridiculed by those who spoke the dialect of the Ile-de-France, we know that English children were at times sent abroad to correct their accent and that there was much travel to the continent. All this could not have been without some effect in making the forms of Central French more familiar in England. There was moreover the constant influence of French literature. It is reasonable to suppose, therefore, that as time went on and the use of French in

England became more artificial, a larger share of the English borrowing was from Central French. This was more particularly the case in the fifteenth century when the less popular character of many of the words borrowed suggests that they came more often through literary than through colloquial channels.[21]

Popular and Literary Borrowings

There can be little doubt that a large proportion of the words borrowed from French were thoroughly popular in character, that is, words current in the everyday French spoken in England. At the same time the importance of literature is not to be underestimated as a means of transfer. So much of Middle English literature was based directly on French originals that it would have been rather exceptional if English writers had consistently resisted the temptation to carry French words over into their adaptations. Layamon resisted, but most others did not, and when in the thirteenth and fourteenth centuries French words were being taken by the hundreds into the popular speech, the way was made easier for the entrance of literary words as well. Although literature was one of the channels by which French words entered English all through the Middle English period, in the fifteenth century it became the principal source. Words like *adolescence, affability, appellation, cohort, combustion, destitution, harangue, immensity, ingenious, pacification, representation, sumptuous* betray their learned or bookish origin, and in the works of Caxton at the end of the century new words like *aggravation, diversify, furtive, prolongation,* and *ravishment* abound. The number of such words entering the language at this time is probably no greater than in the preceding century, but they are more prominent because the adoption of popular words was now greatly curtailed by the practical disappearance of French as a spoken language in England.

The Period of Greatest Influence

Some time elapsed after the Norman Conquest before its effects were felt to any appreciable degree by the English vocabulary. This fact has long been recognized in a general way, but it is only within this century that the materials have been available which enable us to speak with any assurance as to the exact period when the greatest number of French words came into the language. These materials are the dated quotations in the *Oxford English Dictionary.* In 1905 Otto Jespersen made a statistical study of one thousand words borrowed from French, classifying them according to the dates when they were first recorded in English and grouping them by half centuries.[22] The result is highly illuminating. For a hundred years after the Conquest there is no increase in the number of French words being adopted. In the last half of the twelfth century the number increases slightly and in the period from 1200 to 1250 somewhat more rapidly. But it does not become really great until after 1250. Then the full tide sets in, rising to a climax at the end of the fourteenth century. By 1400 the movement has spent its force. A sharp drop in the fifteenth century has been followed by a gradual tapering off ever since.

Although there is no way of knowing how long a word had been in the language before the earliest recorded instance, it is a striking fact that so far as surviving records show, the introduction of French words into English follows closely the progressive adoption of English by the upper classes (cf. § 95). As we have seen, the years from 1250 to 1400 mark the period when English was everywhere replacing French. During these 150 years 40 percent of all the French words in the English language came in.[23]

A further calculation shows that the total number of French words adopted during the Middle English period was slightly over 10,000. Of these about 75 percent are still in current use.

Assimilation

The rapidity with which the new French words were assimilated is evidenced by the promptness with which many of them became the basis of derivatives. English endings were apparently added to them with as much freedom as to English words. For example, the adjective *gentle* is recorded in 1225 and within five years we have it compounded with an English noun to make *gentlewoman* (1230). A little later we find *gentleman* (1275), gentleness (1300), and gently (1330). These compounds and derivatives all occur within about a century of the time when the original adjective was adopted. In the same way we have *faith* (1250) giving *faithless* and *faithful* (both by 1300), *faithfully* (1362), and *faithfulness* (1388), as well as the obsolete *faithly* (1325). The adverbial ending *-ly* seems to have been added to adjectives almost as soon as they appeared in the language. The adverbs *commonly, courteously, eagerly, feebly, fiercely, justly, peacefully,* and many more occur almost as early as the adjectives from which they are derived, while *faintly* by mere chance has been preserved in writing from a slightly earlier date than *faint.* Hybrid forms (French root with English prefix or suffix) like chasthed (chastity), lecherness, debonairship, poorness, *spusbruche* (spousebreach, adultery), becatch, ungracious, overpraising, forscald[24] occur quite early (mostly before 1250), while *common* (1297) has been made into *commonweal* (OE *wela)* by 1330, *battle* (1297) combined with *ax* (OE *æx)* by 1380, and so on. It is clear that the new French words were quickly assimilated, and entered into an easy and natural fusion with the native element in English.

Loss of Native Words

Language often seems lavish, if not wasteful, in having many words that appear to duplicate each other. And yet it has been said that there are no exact synonyms in English. There are usually certain peculiarities of meaning or use that distinguish a word from others with which it has much in common. This seems to indicate that a certain sense of economy characterizes people in their use of language and causes them to get rid of a word when its function is fully performed by some other word. After the Norman Conquest, duplications frequently resulted, for many of the French words that came into use bore meanings already expressed by a native word. In such cases one of two things happened: of the two words one was eventually lost, or, where both survived, they were differentiated in meaning. In some cases the French word disappeared, but in a great many cases it was the Old English word that died out. The substitution was not always immediate; often both words continued in use for a longer or shorter time, and the English word occasionally survives in the dialects today. Thus the OE *çam,* which has been replaced in the standard speech by the French word *uncle,* is still in use *(eme)* in Scotland. The OE *anda* contested its position with the French *envy* until the time of Chaucer, but eventually lost out and with it went the adjective *andig* (envious) and the verb *andian* (to envy). In this way many common Old English words succumbed. The OE *æþele* yielded to F. *noble,* and *æþeling* became *nobleman. Dryhten* and *frça* were displaced by the French *prince,* although the English word *lord,* which survived as a synonym, helped in the elimination. At the same time leod was being ousted by *people.* The OE *dçma* (judge), *dçman* (to judge), and *dôm* (judgment) gave way before French influence in matters of law, but we still use *deem* in the sense of to think or hold an opinion, and *dôm* has survived in special senses, as in *the day of doom, or to meet* one's *doom.* OE (witness),*firen* (crime), and *scyldig* (guilty) have likewise disappeared, as have *here* (army), *cempa* (warrior), and *sibb* (peace). OE *OitGtl* lived on beside *flower* from French until the thirteenth century, and *blço* (color) survives dialectally as *blee.* Other common words that were lost may be illustrated by *âdl* (disease), *ieldu* (age), *lof* (praise), *lyft* (air), *hold* (gracious), *earm* (poor), *slîþe* (cruel), *gecynde* (natural), although it survived as *kind* with this meaning until the sixteenth century, *wuldor* (glory) with its adjective *wuldrig* (glorious), and *wlite* (beauty), *wlitig* (beautiful). In all these cases the place of the English word was taken by the word in parentheses, introduced from French. Many common verbs died out in the same way, such as *andettan* (confess), *beorgan* (preserve, defend), *bieldan* and *elnian* (encourage), *dihtan* (composo), *flîtan* (contend; flite [dialect]), *gôdian* (improve), *healsian* (implore), *herian* (praise), *lçanian* (reward), *belîfan* (remain), *miltsian* (pity). Here likewise the words in parentheses are the French verbs that replaced the native word. Not all the Old English words that have disappeared were driven out by French equivalents. Some gave way to other more or less synonymous words in Old English. Many independently fell into disuse. Nevertheless the enormous invasion of French words not only took the place of many English words that had been lost but itself accounts for a great many of the losses from the Old English vocabulary.

Differentiation in Meaning

Where both the English and the French words survived they were generally differentiated in meaning. The words *doom* and *judgment, to deem* and *to judge* are examples that have already been mentioned. In the fifteenth century *hearty* and *cordial* came to be used for feelings which were supposed to spring from the heart. Etymologiscally they are alike, coming respectively from the Old English and the Latin words for heart. But we have kept them both because we use them with a slight difference in meaning, *hearty* implying a certain physical vigor and downrightness, as in *a hearty dinner, cordial a* more quiet or conventional manifestation, as in *a cordial reception.* In the same way we have kept a number of words for *smell.* The common word in Old English was *stench.* During the Middle English period this was supplemented by the word *smell* (of unknown origin) and the French words *aroma, odor,* and *scent.* To these we have since added *stink* (from the verb) and *perfume* and *fragrance,* from French. Most of these have special connotations and *smell* has become the general word. *Stench* now always means an unpleasant smell. An interesting group of words illustrating the principle is *ox, sheep, swine,* and *calf* beside the French equivalents *beef, mutton, pork,* and *veal.* The French words primarily denoted the animal, as they still do, but in English they were used from the beginning to distinguish the meat from the living beast.[25] Other cases of differentiation are English *house* beside *mansion* from French, *might* beside *power,* and the pairs *ask—demand, shun—avoid, seethe—boil, wish—desire.* In most of these cases where duplication occurred, the French word, when it came into English, was a close synonym of the corresponding English word. The discrimination between them has been a matter of gradual growth, but it justifies the retention of both words in the language.

Curtailment of OE Processes of Derivation

Because language is a form of human activity, it often displays habits or tendencies that one recognizes as characteristic of the speech of a given people at a given time. These habits may be altered by circumstances. As we have already seen (§§ 49-50), Old English, like other Indo-European languages, enlarged its vocabulary chiefly by a liberal use of prefixes and suffixes and an easy power of combining native elements into self-interpreting compounds. In this way the existing resources of the language were expanded at will and any new needs were met. In the centuries following the Norman Conquest, however, there is a visible decline in the use of these old methods of word formation.

Prefixes

This is first of all apparent in the matter of prefixes. Many of the Old English prefixes gradually lost their vitality, their ability to enter into new combinations. The Old English prefix *for-* (corresponding to German *ver-)* was often used to intensify the meaning of a verb or to add the idea of something destructive or prejudicial. For a while during the Middle English period it continued to be used occasionally in new formations. Thus at about 1300 we find *forhang* (put to death by hanging), *forcleave* (cut to pieces), and *forshake* (shake off). It was even combined with words borrowed from French: *forcover, forbar, forgab* (deride), *fortmvail* (tire). But while these occasional instances show that the prefix was not dead, it seems to have had no real vitality. None of these new formations lived long, and the prefix is now entirely obsolete. The only verbs in which it occurs in Modern English are *forbear, forbid, fordo, forget, forgive, forgo, forsake, forswear,* and the participle *forlorn.* All of them had their origin in Old English. The prefix *to-* (German *zer-)* has disappeared even more completely. Although the 1611 Bible tells us that the woman who cast a millstone upon Abimelech's head "all tobrake his skull," and expressions like *tomelt* and *toburst* lived on for a time, there is no trace of the prefix in current use. *With-* (meaning *against)* gave a few new words in Middle English such as *withdraw, withgo, withsake,* and others. *Withdraw* and *withhold* survive, together with the Old English *withstand,* but other equally useful words have been replaced by later borrowings from Latin: *withsay* by *renounce, withspeak* by *contradict, withset* by *resist,* etc. Some prefixes which are still productive today, like *over-* and *under-,* fell into comparative disuse for a time after the Norman Conquest. Most compounds of *over-* that are not of Old English origin have arisen in the modern period. The prefix *on-* (now *un-)* which was used to reverse the action of a verb as in *unbind, undo, unfold, unwind,* and which in Middle English gave us *unfasten, unbuckle, uncover,* and *unwrap,* seems to owe such life as it still enjoys to association with the negative prefix *un-.* The productive power which these formative elements once enjoyed has in many cases been transferred to prefixes like *counter-, dis-, re-, trans-,* and others of Latin origin. It is possible that some of them would have gone out of use had there been no Norman Conquest, but when we see their disuse keeping pace with the increase of the French element in the language and find them in many cases disappearing at the end of the Middle English period, at a time when French borrowings have reached their maximum, it is impossible to doubt that the wealth of easily acquired new words had weakened English habits of word formation.

Suffixes

A similar decline is observable in the formative power of certain suffixes that were widely used in Old English. The loss here is perhaps less distinctly felt because some important endings have remained in full force. Such are the noun suffix *-ness* and the adjective endings *-ful, -less, -some,* and *-ish.* But others equally important were either lost or greatly diminished in vitality. Thus the abstract suffix *-lock* (OE *lâc)* survives only in *wedlock, -red* (OE*)* only in *hatred* and *kindred.* The ending *-dom* was used in Old English to form abstract nouns from other nouns *(kingdom, earldom, martyrdom)* and from adjectives *(freedom, wisdom).* In Middle English there are some new formations such as *dukedom* and *thralldom,* but most of the formations from adjectives, like *falsedom* and *richdom,* did not prove permanent, and the suffix is to all intents and purposes now dead. When used today it is for the most part employed in half serious coinages, such as *fandom, stardom, topsy-turvydom.* The endings *-hood* and *-ship* have had a similar history. *Manhood, womanhood, likelihood* are new formations in Middle English, showing that the suffix retained its power for a while. In fact it occasionally reasserts itself in modern times. *Boyhood* and *girlhood* date from the eighteenth century, while *hardihood* is apparently a creation of Milton's that was revived by Macaulay. Many of the Old English abstracts in *-ship* were lost. We have kept *friendship* but not *fiendship,* and of those formed from adjectives in Old English the only one still in use is *worship* (worthship). Most of the new formations in Middle English had a short life. We have retained *hardship* but not *boldship, busiship, cleanship, kindship,* etc. In all these instances the ending *-ness* was preferred. As in the case of prefixes, we can see here a gradual change in English habits of word formation resulting from the available supply of French words with which to fill the needs formerly met by the native resources of the language.

Self-explaining Compounds

One further habit that was somewhat weakened, although by no means broken, was that of combining native words into self-interpreting compounds. The extent to which words like *bookhouse or boatswain* entered into Old English has been pointed out above. The practice was not abandoned in Middle English, but in many cases where a new word could have been easily formed on the native model, a ready-made French word was borrowed instead. Today self-explaining compounds are still formed by a sure instinct *(picture tube, driver's-side air bag, four-wheel disc brakes),* but the method is much less universal than it once was because of new habits introduced after the Norman Conquest.

The Language Still English

It must not be thought that the extensive modification of the

English language caused by the Norman Conquest had made of it something else than English. The language had undergone much simplification of its inflections, but its grammar was still English. It had absorbed several thousand French words as a natural consequence of a situation in which large numbers of people were for a time bilingual and then gradually turned from the habitual use of French to the habitual use of English. It had lost a great many native words and abandoned some of its most characteristic habits of word formation. But great and basic elements of the vocabulary were still English. No matter what class of society they belonged to, the English *ate, drank,* and *slept,* so to speak, in English, *worked* and *played, spoke* and *sang, walked, ran, rode, leaped,* and *swam* in the same language. The *house* they lived in, with its *hall, bower, rooms, windows, doors, floor, steps, gate,* etc., reminds us that their language was basically Germanic. Their *meat* and *drink, bread, butter, fish, milk, cheese, salt, pepper, wine, ale,* and *beer* were inherited from pre-Conquest days, while they could not refer to their *arms, legs, feet, hands, eyes, ears, head, nose, mouth,* or any common part of the body without using English words for the purpose. While we are under the necessity of paying considerable attention to the large French element that the Norman Conquest brought directly and indirectly into the language, we must see it in proper perspective. The language that the Normans and their successors finally adopted was English, and although it was an English changed in many important particulars from the language of King Alfred, its predominant features were those inherited from the Germanic tribes that settled in England in the fifth century.

Latin Borrowings in Middle English

The influence of the Norman Conquest is generally known as the Latin Influence of the Third Period in recognition of the ultimate source of the new French words. But it is right to include also under this designation the large number of words borrowed directly from Latin in Middle English. These differed from the French borrowings in being less popular and in gaining admission generally through the written language. Of course, it must not be forgotten that Latin was a spoken language among ecclesiastics and men of learning, and a certain number of Latin words could well have passed directly into spoken English. Their number, however, is small in comparison with those that we can observe entering by way of literature. In a single work like Trevisa's translation of the *De Proprietatibus Rerum* of Bartholomew Anglicus we meet with several hundred words taken over from the Latin original. Since they are not found before this in English, we can hardly doubt that we have here a typical instance of the way such words first came to be used. The fourteenth and fifteenth centuries were especially prolific in Latin borrowings. An anonymous writer of the first half of the fifteenth century complains that it is not easy to translate from Latin into English, for "there ys many wordes in Latyn that we have no propre Englysh accordynge therto."[26] Wycliffe and his associates are credited with more than a thousand Latin words not previously found in English.[27] Since many of them occur in the so-called Wycliffe translation of the Bible and have been retained in subsequent translations, they have passed into common use. The innovations of other writers were not always so fortunate. Many of them, like the inkhorn terms of the Renaissance, were but passing experiments. Nevertheless the permanent additions from Latin to the English vocabulary in this period are much larger than has generally been realized.

It is unnecessary to attempt a formal classification of these borrowings. Some idea of their range and character may be gained from a selected but miscellaneous list of examples: *abject, adjacent, allegory, conspiracy, contempt, custody, distract, frustrate, genius, gesture, history, homicide, immune, incarnate, include, incredible, incubus, incumbent, index, individual, infancy, inferior, infinite, innate, innumemble, intellect, interrupt, juniper, lapidary, legal, limbo, lucrative, lunatic, magnify, malefactor, mechanical, minor, missal, moderate, necessary, nervous, notary, ornate, picture, polite, popular, prevent, private, project, promote, prosecute, prosody, pulpit, quiet, rational, reject, remit, reprehend, rosary, script, scripture, scrutiny, secular, solar, solitary, spacious, stupor, subdivide, subjugate, submit, subordinate, subscribe, substitute, summary, superabundance, supplicate, suppress, temperate, temporal, testify, testimony, tincture, tract, tributary, ulcer, zenith, zephyr.* Here we have terms relating to law, medicine, theology, science, and literature, words often justified in the beginning by technical or professional use and later acquiring a wider application. Among them may be noticed several with endings like *-able, -ible, -ent, -al, -ous, -ive,* and others, which thus became familiar in English and, reinforced often by French, now form common elements in English derivatives. All the words in the above list are accepted by the *Oxford English Dictionary* as direct borrowings from Latin. But in many cases Latin words were being borrowed by French at the same time, and the adoption of a word in English may often have been due to the impact of both languages.

Aureate Terms

The introduction of unusual words from Latin (and occasionally elsewhere) became a conscious stylistic device in the fifteenth century, extensively used by poets and occasionally by writers of prose. By means of such words as *abusion, dispone, diurne, equipolent, palestral,* and *tenebrous,* poets attempted what has been described as a kind of stylistic gilding, and this feature of their language is accordingly known as "aureate diction."[28] The beginnings of this tendency have been traced back to the fourteenth century. It occurs in moderation in the poetry of Chaucer, becomes a distinct mannerism in the work of Lydgate, and runs riot in the productions of the Scottish Chaucerians—James I, Henryson, Dunbar, and the rest. How far this affectation went may be seen in the opening lines of Dunbar's *Ballad of Our Lady:*

Hale, sterne superne! Hale, in eterne,
In Godis sicht to schyne!

Lucerne in derne,[29] for to discerne
Be glory and grace devyne;

Hodiern, modern, sempitern,

Angelicallregyne!

Our tern[30] infern for to dispern

Helpe, rialest Rosyne![31]

The use of such "halff chongyd Latyne," as a contemporary poet describes it,[32] was quite artificial. The poets who affected aureate terms have been described as tearing up words from Latin "which never took root in the language, like children making a mock garden with flowers and branches stuck in the ground, which speedily wither."[33] This is essentially true, but not wholly so. The novelty that was sought after, and that such words had in the beginning, wore off with use; and words which were "aureate" in Chaucer, like *laureate, mediation, oriental, prolixity,* have sometimes become part of the common speech. These innovations are of considerable interest in the history of style; in the history of language they appear as a minor current in the stream of Latin words flowing into English in the course of the Middle Ages.

Synonyms at Three Levels

Much nonsense has been written on the relative merits of the Germanic and Romance elements in the English vocabulary.[34] The Latinized diction of many seventeenth- and eighteenth-century writers brought up in the tradition of the classics provoked a reaction in which the "Saxon" element of the language was glorified as the strong, simple, and direct component in contrast with the many abstract and literary words derived from Latin and French. It is easy to select pairs like *deed—exploit, spell—enchantment, take-apprehend, weariness—lassitude* and on the basis of such examples make generalizations about the superior directness, the homely force and concreteness of the Old English words. But such contrasts ignore the many hundreds of words from French which are equally simple and as capable of conveying a vivid image, idea, or emotion—nouns like *bar, beak, cell, cry, fool, frown, fury, glory, guile, gullet, horror, humor, isle, pity, river, rock, ruin, stain, stuff, touch, wreck,* or adjectives such as *calm, clear, cruel, eager, fierce,, gay, mean, rude, safe, tender,* to take examples almost at random. The truth is that many of the most vivid and forceful words in English are French, and even where the French and Latin words are more literary or learned, as indeed they often are, they are no less valuable and important. Language has need for the simple, the polished, and even the recondite word. The richness of English in synonyms is largely due to the happy mingling of Latin, French, and native elements. It has been said that we have a synonym at each level—popular, literary, and learned. Although this statement must not be pressed too hard, a difference is often apparent, as in *rise—mount—ascend, ask—question-interrogate, goodness—virtue—probity, fast—firm—secure, fire—flame—conflagration, fear—terror—trepidation, holy—sacred—consecrated, time—age—epoch.* In each of these sets of three words the first is English, the second is from French, and the third from Latin. The difference in tone between the English and the French words is often slight; the Latin word is generally more bookish. However, it is more important to recognize the distinctive uses of each than to form prejudices in favor of one group above another.

Words from the Low Countries

The importance of the Romance element in English has overshadowed and caused to be neglected another source of foreign words in the vocabulary, the languages of the Low Countries—Flemish, Dutch, and Low German. The similarity of these languages to English makes it difftcult often to tell whether a word has been adopted from one of them or is of native origin. Moreover, the influence was not the result of some single cause, like the introduction of Christianity or the Norman Conquest, confined more or less to a given period of time, but was rather a gradual infiltration due to the constant and close relations between England and the people of Flanders, Holland, and northern Germany. This intercourse extends from the days of William the Conqueror, whose wife was Flemish, down to the eighteenth century. All through the Middle Ages Flemings came to England in considerable numbers. In the English wars at home and abroad we repeatedly find Flemish mercenaries fighting with the English forces. Others came for more peaceful purposes and settled in the country. The wool industry was the major industry of England in the Middle Ages. Most of the wool exported from England went to supply Flemish and Dutch looms. On the other hand, weavers from the Low Countries, noted for their superior cloths, were encouraged to come to England and at various times came in large numbers. They were sufficiently numerous to arouse at intervals the antagonism of the native population. In the Peasants' Revolt of 1381 we are told that "many fflemmynges loste here heedes...and namely they that koude nat say Breede and Chese, But Case and Brode."[35] Trade between these countries and England was responsible for much travel to and fro. Flemish and German merchants had their hanse at London, Boston, Lynn, and elsewhere. The English wool staple was at different times at Dordrecht, Louvain, Bruges, and other towns near the coast. Add to this the fact that the carrying trade was largely in the hands of the Dutch until the Navigation Act of 1651, and we see that there were many favorable conditions for the introduction of Low German words into English. At the end of the Middle Ages we find entering the language such words as *nap* (of cloth), *deck, bowsprit, lighter, dock, freight, rover, mart, groat, guilder.* Later borrowings include *cambric, duck* (cloth), *boom* (of a boat), *beleaguer, furlough, commodore, gin, gherkin, dollar.* Dutch eminence in art is responsible for *easel, etching, landscape,* while Dutch settlers in America seem to have caused the adoption of *cruller, cookie, cranberry, bowery, boodle,* and other words. The latest study of the Low Dutch element in English considers some 2,500 words. Many of these are admittedly doubtful, but one must grant the possibility of more influence from the Low Countries upon English than can be proved by phonological or other direct evidence.[36]

Dialectal Diversity of Middle English

One of the striking characteristics of Middle English is its great variety in the different parts of England. This variety was not confined to the forms of the spoken language, as it is to a great extent today, but appears equally in the written literature. In the absence of any recognized literary standard before the close of the period, writers naturally wrote in the dialect of that part of the country to which they belonged. And they did so not through any lack of awareness of the diversity that existed. Giraldus Cambrensis in the twelfth century remarked that the language of the southern parts of England, and particularly of Devonshire, was more archaic and seemed less agreeable than that of other parts with which he was familiar;[37] and at a slightly earlier date (c. 1125) William of Malmesbury had complained of the harshness of the speech of Yorkshire, saying that southerners could not understand it.[38] Such observations continue in subsequent censturies.[39] The author of the *Cursor Mundi,* a northern poem of about 1300, notes that he found the story of the Assumption of Our Lady in Southern English and turned it into his own dialect for "northern people who can read no other English."[40] Even Chaucer, by whose time a literary standard was in process of creation, sends off his *Troilus and Criseyde with* the famous "Go, little book," adding,

And for ther is so gret diversite In Englissh, and in writyng of oure tonge, So prey I god that non myswrite the, Ne the mysmetre for defaute of tonge.

The Middle English Dialects

The language differed almost from county to county, and noticeable variations are sometimes observable between different parts of the same county. The features characteristic of a given dialect do not all cover the same territory; some extend into adjoining districts or may be characteristic also of another dialect. Consequently it is rather difftcult to decide how many dialectal divisions should be recognized and to mark off with any exactness their respective boundaries. In a rough way, however, it is customary to distinguish four principal dialects of Middle English: Northern, East Midland, West Midland, and Southern. Generally speaking, the Northern dialect extends as far south as the Humber; East Mid-land and West Midland together cover the area between the Humber and the Thames; and Southern occupies the district south of the Thames, together with Gloucestershire and parts of the counties of Worcester and Hereford, thus taking in the West

Saxon and Kentish districts of Old English. Throughout the Middle English period and later, Kentish preserves individual features marking it off as a distinct variety of Southern English.[41]

The peculiarities that distinguish these dialects are of such a character that their adequate enumeration would carry us beyond our present purpose. They are partly matters of pronunciation, partly of vocabulary, partly of inflection. A few illustrations will give some idea of the nature and extent of the differences. The feature most easily recognized is the ending of the plural, present indicative, of verbs. In Old English this form always ended in *-th* with some variation of the preceding vowel. In Middle English this ending was preserved as *-eth* in the Southern dialect. In the Midland district, however, it was replaced by *-en,* probably taken over from the corresponding forms of the subjunctive or from preterite-present verbs and the verb *to be,*[42] while in the north it was altered to *-es,* an ending that makes its appearance in Old English times. Thus we have *loves* in the north, *loven* in the Midlands, and *loveth* in the south. Another fairly distinctive form is the present participle before the spread of the ending *-ing.* In the north we have *lovande,* in the Midlands *lovende,* and in the south *lovinde.* In later Middle English the ending *-ing* appears in the Midlands and the south, thus obscuring the dialectal distinction. Dialectal differences are more noticeable between Northern and Southern; the Midland dialect often occupies an intermediate position, tending toward the one or the other in those districts lying nearer to the adjacent dialects. Thus the characteristic forms of the pronoun *they* in the south were *hi, here (hire, hure), hem,* while in the north forms with *th-* (modern *they, their, them)* early became predominant. In matters of pronunciation the Northern and Southern dialects sometimes presented notable differences. Thus OE *â,* which developed into an V south of the Humber, was retained in the north, giving us such characteristic forms as Southern *stone* and *home,* beside *stane* and *hame* in Scotland today. Initial f and *s* were often voiced in the south to v and *z.* In Southern Middle English we find *vor, vrom, vox, vorzoþe* instead of *for, from, fox, forsope* (forsooth). This dialectal difference is preserved in Modern English *fox* and *vixen,* where the former represents the Northern and Midland pronunciation and the latter the Southern. Similarly *ch* in the south often corresponds to a *k* in the north: *bench* beside *benk,* or *church* beside *kirk.* Such variety was fortunately lessened toward the end of the Middle English period by the general adoption of a standard written (and later spoken) English.[43]

The Rise of Standard English

Out of this variety of local dialects there emerged toward the end of the fourteenth century a written language that in the course of the fifteenth won general recognition and has since become the recognized standard in both speech and writing. The part of England that contributed most to the formation of this standard was the East Midland district, and it was the East Midland type of English that became its basis, particularly the dialect of the metropolis, London. Several causes contributed to the attainment of this result.

In the first place, as a Midland dialect the English of this region occupied a middle position between the extreme divergences of the north and south. It was less conservative than the Southern dialect, less radical than the Northern. In its sounds and inflections it represents a kind of compromise, sharing some of the characteristics of both its neighbors. Its intermediate position was recognized in the fourteenth century by Ranulph Higden. A well-known passage in Trevisa's translation of Higden's *Polychronicon* (c. 1385) reads:

> for men of þe est wiþ men of þe west, as it were vnder þe same partie of heuene, acordeþ more in sownynge of speche þan men of þe norþ wiþ men of þe souþ; þerfore it is þat Mercii, þat beeþ men of myddel Engelond, as it were parteners of þe endes, vnderstondeþ bettre þe side langages, Norþerne and Souþerne, þan Norþerne and Souþerne vnderstondeþ eiþer oþer.

In the second place, the East Midland district was the largest and most populous of the major dialect areas. The land was more valuable than the hilly country to the north and west, and in an agricultural age this advantage was reflected in both the number and the prosperity of the inhabitants. As Maitland remarks, "If we leave Lincolnshire, Norfolk and Suffolk out of account we are to all appearances leaving out of account not much less than a quarter of the whole nation.... No doubt all inferences drawn from medieval statistics are exceedingly precarious; but, unless a good many figures have conspired to deceive us, Lincolnshire, Norfolk and Suffolk were at the time of the Conquest and for three centuries afterwards vastly richer and more populous than any tract of equal area in the West."[44] Only the southern counties possessed natural advantages at all comparable, and they were much smaller. The prominence of Middlesex, Oxford, Norfolk, and the East Midlands generally in political affairs all through the later Middle Ages is but another evidence of the importance of the district and of the extent to which its influence was likely to be felt.

A third factor, more difficult to evaluate, was the presence of the universities, Oxford and Cambridge, in this region. In the fourteenth century the monasteries were playing a less important role in the dissemination of learning than they had once played, while the two universities had developed into important intellectual centers. So far as Cambridge is concerned any influence that it had would be exerted in support of the East Midland dialect. That of Oxford is less certain because Oxfordshire is on the border between Midland and Southern and its dialect shows certain characteristic Southern features. Moreover, we can no longer attribute to Wycliffe an important part in the establishment of a written standard.[45] Though he spent much of his life at Oxford, he seems not to have conformed fully to the Oxford dialect. All we can say is that the dialect of Oxford had no apparent influence on the form of London English, which was ultimately adopted as standard. Such support as the East Midland type of English received from the universities must have been largely confined to that furnished by Cambridge.

Much the same uncertainty attaches to the influence of Chaucer. It was once thought that Chaucer's importance was paramount among the influences bringing about the adoption of a written standard. And, indeed, it is unbelievable that the language of the greatest English poet before Shakespeare was not spread by the popularity of his works and, through the use of that language, by subsequent poets who looked upon him as their master and model. But it is nevertheless unlikely that the English used in official records and in letters and papers by men of affairs was greatly influenced by the language of his poetry. Yet it is the language found in such documents rather than the language of Chaucer that is at the basis of Standard English. Chaucer's dialect is not in all respects the same as the language of these documents, presumably identical with the ordinary speech of the city. It is slightly more conservative and shows a greater number of Southern characteristics. Chaucer was a court poet, and his usage may reflect the speech of the court and to a certain extent literary tradition. His influence must be thought of as lending support in a general way to the dialect of the region to which he belonged rather than as determining the precise form which Standard English was to take in the century following his death.

The Importance of London English

By far the most influential factor in the rise of Standard English was the importance of London as the capital of England. Indeed, it is altogether likely that the language of the city would have become the prevailing dialect without the help of any of the factors previously discussed. In doing so it would have been following the course of other national tongues—French as the dialect of Paris, Spanish as that of Castile, and others. London was, and still is, the political and commercial center of England. It was the seat of the court, of the highest judicial tribunals, the focus of the social and intellectual activities of the country. In the practicalities of commerce the London economy was especially important as "an engine of communication and exchange which enabled ideas and information to be distributed and business to be done across an increasingly extensive, complex and varied field."[46] Patterns of migration at this time cannot be fully reconstructed, but clearly London drew in a constant stream those whose affairs took them beyond the limits of their provincial homes. They brought to it traits of their local speech, there to mingle with the London idiom and to survive or die as the silent forces of amalgamation and standardization determined. They took back with them the forms and usages of the great city by which their own speech had been modified. The influence was reciprocal. London English took as well as gave. It began as a Southern and ended as a Midland dialect. By the fifteenth century there had come to prevail in the East Midlands a fairly uniform dialect, and the language of London agrees in all important respects with it. We can hardly doubt that the importance of the eastern counties, pointed out above, is largely responsible for this change. Even such Northern characteristics as are found in the standard speech seem to have entered by way of these counties. The history of Standard English is almost a history of London English.

The Spread of the London Standard

In the latter part of the fifteenth century the London standard had been accepted, at least in writing, in most parts of the country. Its prestige may possibly be reflected in the fact that Mak the sheep-stealer in the *Towneley Plays* attempts to impose upon the Yorkshire shepherds by masquerading as a person of some importance and affects a "Southern tooth." Considerable diversity still existed in the spoken dialects, as will be apparent from what is said in the next paragraph. But in literary works after 1450 it becomes almost impossible, except in distinctly northern texts, to determine with any precision the region in which a given work was written. And in correspondence and local records there is a widespread tendency to conform in matters of language to the London standard. This influence emanating from London can be seen in the variety of English used in documents of the national bureaucracy as written by the clerks of Chancery. By the middle of the century a fairly consistent variety of written English in both spelling and grammar had developed, and as the language of official use it was likely to have influence in similar situations elsewhere.[47] With the introduction of printing in 1476 a new influence of great importance in the dissemination of London

English came into play. From the beginning London has been the center of book publishing in England. Caxton, the first English printer, used the current speech of London in his numerous translations, and the books that issued from his press and from the presses of his successors gave a currency to London English that assured more than anything else its rapid adoption. In the sixteenth century the use of London English had become a matter of precept as well as practice. The author of *The Arte of English Poesie* (attributed to Puttenham) advises the poet: "ye shall therefore take the usuall speach of the Court, and that of London and the shires lying about London within 1x. myles, and not much above."

Complete Uniformity Still Unattained

It would be a mistake to think that complete uniformity was attained within the space of a few generations. Even in matters of vocabulary dialectal differences have persisted in cultivated speech down to the present day, and they were no less noticeable in the period during which London English was gaining general acceptance. Then, too, there were many French and Latin words, such as the aureate stylists were indulging in, that had not been assimilated. It was not easy for a writer at the end of the fifteenth century to choose his words so that his language would find favor with all people. How difftcult it was may be seen from the remarks that Caxton prefixed to his *Eneydos,* a paraphrase of Virgil's *Aeneid that* he translated from French and published in 1490:

> After dyverse werkes made, translated, and achieved, havyng noo werke in hande, I, sittyng in my studye where as laye many dyverse paunflettis and bookys, happened that to my hande came a lytyl booke in frenshe, whiche late was translated oute of latyn by some noble clerke of fraunce, whiche booke is named Eneydos.... And whan I had advysed me in this sayd boke, I delybered and concluded to translate it into englysshe, and forthwyth toke a penne & ynke, and wrote a leef or tweyne, whyche I oversawe agayn to corecte it. And whan I sawe the fayr & straunge termes therin I

doubted that it sholde not please some gentylmen whiche late blamed me, sayeng that in my translacyons I had over curyous termes whiche coude not be understande of comyn peple, and desired me to use olde and homely termes in my translacyons. And fayn wolde I satysfye every man, and so to doo, toke an olde boke and redde therin; and certaynly the englysshe was so rude and brood that I coude not wele understande it. And also my lorde abbot of westmynster ded do shewe to me late, certayn evydences wryton in olde englysshe, for to reduce it in-to our englysshe now usid. And certaynly it was wreton in suche wyse that it was more lyke to dutche than englysshe; I coude not reduce ne brynge it to be understonden. And certaynly our langage now used varyeth ferre from that whiche was used and spoken whan I was borne. For we englysshe men ben borne under the domynacyon of the mone, whiche is never stedfaste, but ever waverynge, wexynge one season, and waneth & dyscreaseth another season. And that comyn englysshe that is spoken in one shyre varyeth from a nother. In so moche that in my dayes happened that certayn marchauntes were in a shippe in tamyse, for to have sayled over the see into zelande, and for lacke of wynde, thei taryed atte forlond, and wente to lande for to refreshe them. And one of theym named Sheffelde, a mercer, cam in-to an hows and axed for mete; and specyally he axyd after eggys. And the goode wyf answerde, that she coude speke no frenshe. And the marchaunt was angry, for he also coude speke no frenshe, but wolde have hadde egges, and she understode hym not. And thenne at laste a nother sayd that he wolde have eyren. Then the good wyf sayd that she understod hym wel. Loo, what sholde a man in thyse dayes now wryte, egges or eyren? Certaynly it is harde to playse every man by cause of dyversite & chaunge of langage. For in these dayes every man that is in ony reputacyon in his countre, wyll utter his commynycacyon and maters in suche maners & termes that fewe men shall understonde theym. And som honest and grete clerkes have ben wyth me, and desired me to wryte the moste curyous termes that I could fynde. And thus bytwene playn, rude, & curyous, I stande abasshed. But in my judgemente the comyn termes that be dayli used ben lyghter to be understonde than the olde and auncyent englysshe. And for as moche as this present booke is not for a rude uplondyssh man to laboure therin, ne rede it, but onely for a clerke & a noble gentylman that feleth and understondeth in faytes of armes, in love, & in noble chyvalrye, therfor in a meane bytwene bothe I have reduced & translated this sayd booke in to our englysshe, not ouer rude ne curyous, but in suche termes as shall be understanden, by goddys grace, accordynge to my copye.

REFERENCES

1. That the change was complete by 1500 has been shown with convincing statistics by Charles C.Fries, "On the Development of the Structural Use of Word-Order in Modern English," *Language,* 16(1940), 199-208.
2. The chronology of these changes has been worked out by Samuel Moore in two articles: "Loss of Final n in Inflectional Syllables of Middle English," *Language,* 3 (1927), 232-59; "Earliest Morphological Changes in Middle English," *Language,* 4 (1928), 238-66.
3. Kemp Malone, "When Did Middle English Begin?" *Curme Volume of Linguistic Studies* (Philadelphia, 1930), pp. 110-17.
4. For the use of the apostrophe in the possessive, see § 180.
5. In context *oure aller cok* is translated 'the cock who wakened us all,' where the r of *aller* '*of* us all' indicates the genitive plural of *al.* Today we have what may be considered an inflected adjective in such combinations as *men students, women soldiers.*
6. *Ibid.*
7. For example, the *-an* of the Old English infinitive became *-en* and later *-e:* OE *drîfan*> M.E. *drîven*> *drive.*
8. The facts stated in this section are based upon collections for 333 strong verbs in Old English. This number includes a few verbs for which only isolated forms occur and one *(*stecan)* that is not recorded at all, although its existence is to be inferred from its surviving forms in Middle English.
9. For example, *dwînan* (to disappear), *rçocan* (to smoke). Ten strong verbs had developed weak forms by the twelfth century. Doubtless most

of these weak forms were of occasional occurrence in Old English though they have not been recorded.

10 There are fifteen such verbs. *Strive* (from French) has been inflected on the pattern of *drive,* as have *thrive* and *rive* (both from Old Norse). In some varieties of English *dive* has developed a past tense *dove.* Since the eighteenth century *stave* has had a strong form *stove.* So, too, has *reeve,* a *nautical term. Wear—wore—worn,* a weak verb in Old English, has been reformed on the analogy of verbs like *bear* and *swear. Spat* has been the past tense of *spit* since the sixteenth century, and the strong forms of *stick* date from the same time. An analogous formation *dug* appears as a past participle at this date and since the eighteenth century has been used as the past tense. *Fling, ring,* and *string are* conjugated like *cling, sting,* and *swing. Hide* and occasionally *chide* have strong past participles like *ride—ridden. Tug and drug* (like *dug)* are sometimes heard for *tagged and dragged* but are not in standard use. A few verbs like *show have* developed past participles on the analogy of *know.*

11. The second person singular had the vowel of the plural.

12. Although some earlier scholars believe the loss of inflections to have resulted from a fixed word order, the sequence of development is clearly the reverse. See Cecily Clark, ed., *The Peterborough Chronicle, 1070-1154* (2nd ed., Oxford, 1970), p. lxix; and Bruce Mitchell, *Old English Syntax (2* vols., Oxford, 1985), § 3950.

13. Mitchell, "Syntax and Word-Order in *The Peterborough Chronicle," Neuphilologische Mitteilungen,* 65 (1964), 143.

14. Clark, p. lxxiii.

15. F.H.Sykes, *French Elements in Middle English* (Oxford, 1899) makes an attempt to support this view. The most extensive treatment of the subject is A. A.Prins, *French Influence in English Phrasing* (Leiden, Nether lands, 1952), supplemented by articles in *English Studies,* vols. 40-41. A striking array of instances in which English reflects the use of prepositions and adverbs in French, Latin, and Danish is given in H.T.Price, *Foreign Influences on Middle English* (Ann Arbor, MI, 1947; *Univ. of Michigan Contributions in Modern Philology,* no. 10). The standard work on Middle English syntax is Tauno F.Mustanoja, *A Middle English Syntax,* part 1 (Helsinki, 1960).

16. *Ibid.*

17. *Ibid*

18. There is still considerable difference of opinion as to whether this

dialect was in any real sense a unified speech. It shows great diversity of forms and this diversity may reflect the variety of the French people who settled in England. Many others besides Normans took part in William's invasion, and among those who came later every part of France was represented. In this mixture, however, it is certain that Normans predominated, and the Anglo-Norman dialect agrees in its most characteristic features with the dialects of northern France and especially with that of Normandy. Some features of the Norman dialect were characteristic also of its neighbor, Picard, and such features would be reinforced in England by the speech of those who came from the Picard area.

19. This distinction as it appears in Middle English has been studied by S.H.Bush, "Old Northern French Loan-words in Middle English," *PQ,* 1 (1922), 161-72.

20. Also as *-er,* as in *carpenter, danger.*

21. There is a discussion of the Central French element in English in Skeat, *Principles of English Etymology,* Second Series (Oxford, 1891), chap. 8.

22. *Growth and Structure of the English Language* (10th ed., 1982), p. 94. The following table differs somewhat from his. It represents an independent calculation based upon the completed dictionary.

    For statistics based on the letter A only, see F.Mossé, "On the Chronology of French Loan-Words in English," *English Studies,* 25 (1943), 33-40. See also Xavier Dekeyser, "Romance Loans in Middle English: A Re-assessment," in *Linguistics across Historical and Geographical Boundaries: In Honour of Jacek Fisiak,* ed. Dieter Kastovsky and Aleksander Szwedek (2 vols., Berlin, 1986), I, 253-65.

23. As indicated in the text, a word may have been in use some time before the date at which it is first recorded in the *Oxford English Dictionary,* but such a circumstance can hardly invalidate the conclusion here stated.

24. Behrens, *Beiträge zur Geschichte der französischen Sprache in England* (Heilbronn, Germany, 1886), p. 9.

25. The well-known passage in Scott's *Ivanhoe* in which this distinction is entertainingly introduced into a conversation between Wamba and Gurth (chap. 1) is open to criticism only because the episode occurs about a century too early. *Beef is* first found in English at about 1300.

26. *The Myroure of Oure Ladye, EETSES,* 19, p. 7.

27. Otto Dellit, *Über lateinische Elemente im Mittelenglischen* (Marburg, Germany, 1905), p. 38.

28. The standard treatment of the subject is John C.Mendenhall, *Aureate Terms* (Lancaster, PA, 1919).

29 lamp in darkness

30. woe

31. rose

32. John Metham, Cf. P.H.Nichols, "Lydgate's Influence on the Aureate Terms of the Scottish Chaucerians," *PMLA,* 47 (1932), 516-22.

33. Thomas Campbell, *Essay on English Poetry* (London, 1848), p. 39.

34. Even so sensible a scholar as Freeman could write: "This abiding corruption of our language I believe to have been the one result of the Norman Conquest which has been purely evil." *(Norman Conquest,* V, 547.)

35. C.L.Kingsford, *Chronicles of London* (Oxford, 1905), p. 15.

36. The fullest discussion of the Flemings in England and English relations with the Low Countries generally is J.F.Bense, *Anglo-Dutch Relations from the Earliest Times to the Death of William the Third* (London, 1925). J.A.Fleming, *Flemish Influence in Britain* (2 vols., Glasgow, 1930), is rather discursive and concerned mostly with Scotland. The Low German influence on English has been treated by Wilhelm Heuser, "Festländische Einflüsse im Mittelenglischen," *Bonner Beiträge zur Anglistik,* 12 (1902), 173-82; J.M.Toll, *Niederländisches Lehngut im Mittelenglischen* (Halle, Germany, 1926); J.F.Bense, *A Dictionary of the Low-Dutch Element in the English Vocabulary* (The Hague, 1939); H.Logeman, "Low-Dutch Elements in English," *Neophilologus,* 16 (1930- 1931), 31-46, 103-16 (a commentary on Bense); T.de Vries, *Holland's Influence on English Language and Literature* (Chicago, 1916), a work of slighter value; and E.Ekwall, *Shakspere's Vocabulary* (Uppsala, Sweden, 1903), pp. 92 ff.

37. *Description of Wales,* Bk. I, chap. 6.

38. *Gesta Pontificum,* Bk. III. The remark is repeated in Higden, and in Trevisa's translation of Higden.

39. "Our language is also so dyverse in yt selfe, that the commen maner of spekyng in Englysshe of some contre [i.e., county] can skante be understonded in some other contre of the same londe." *The Myroure of Oure Ladye* (first half of the fifteenth century), EETSES, 19, pp. 7-8.

40. In sotherin englis was it draun,
And turnd it haue I till our aun
Langage o northrin lede
Pat can nan oiþer englis rede. (II. 20,061-64)

41. A pioneering attempt to define significant dialect features was "Middle English Dialect Characteristics and Dialect Boundaries," by Samuel Moore, Sanford B.Meech, and Harold Whitehall, in *Univ. of Michigan Pubns in Lang. and Lit.*, vol. 13 (1935). It was based primarily on localized documents, which are not sufficiently numerous. The limitations of this study are pointed out in A.McIntosh, "A New Approach to Middle English Dialectology," *English Studies, 44* (1963), 1-11. See also M.L.Samuels, "Some Applications of Middle English Dialectology," *ibid.*, pp. 81-94. The results of several decades of research by McIntosh and Samuels are published in *A Linguistic Atlas of Late Mediaeval English* by Angus McIntosh, M.L.Samuels, and Michael Benskin with the assistance of Margaret Laing and Keith Williamson (4 vols., Aberdeen, 1986).

42. W.F.Bryan, "The Midland Present Plural Indicative Ending *-e(n),*" *MP,* 18 (1921), 457-73.

43. For further illustration see Appendix A.

44. *Domesday Book and Beyond*, pp. 20–22.

45. Wycliffe was credited with the chief part in the establishment of Standard English by Koch, as Chaucer was by Ten Brink. Later Dibelius *(Anglia,* 23-24) argued for the existence of an Oxford standard, recognized for a time beside the language of London. This view has now generally been abandoned.

46. Derek Keene, "Metropolitan Values: Migration, Mobility and Cultural Norms, London 1100-1700," in *The Development of Standard English 1300-1800: Theories, Descriptions, Conflicts,* ed. Laura Wright (Cambridge, UK, 2000), p. 111.

47. See John H.Fisher, *The Emergence of Standard English* (Lexington, KY, 1996).

7

Changing Conditions in the Modern Age

In the development of languages particular events often have recognizable and at times far-reaching effects. The Norman Conquest and the Black Death are typical instances that we have already seen. But there are also more general conditions that come into being and are no less influential. In the Modern English period, the beginning of which is conveniently placed at 1500, certain of these new conditions come into play, conditions that previously either had not existed at all or were present in only a limited way, and they cause English to develop along somewhat different lines from those that had characterized its history in the Middle Ages. The new factors were the printing press, the rapid spread of popular education, the increased communication and means of communication, the growth of specialized knowledge, and the emergence of various forms of self-consciousness about language.

The invention of the process of printing from movable type, which occurred in Germany about the middle of the fifteenth century, was destined to exercise a far-reaching influence on all the vernacular languages of Europe. Introduced into England about 1476 by William Caxton, who had learned the art on the continent, printing made such rapid progress that a scant century later it was observed that manuscript books were seldom to be seen and almost never used. Some idea of the rapidity with which the new process swept forward may be had from the fact that in Europe the number of books printed before the year 1500 reaches the surprising figure of 35,000. The majority of these, it is true, were in Latin, whereas it is in the modern languages that the effect of the printing press was chiefly to be felt. But in England over 20,000 titles in English had appeared by 1640, ranging all the way from mere pamphlets to massive folios. The result was to bring books, which had formerly been the expensive luxury of the few, within the reach of many. More important, however, was the fact, so obvious today, that it was possible to reproduce a book in a thousand copies or a hundred thousand, every one exactly like the other. A powerful force thus existed for promoting a standard, uniform language, and the means were now available for spreading that language throughout the territory in which it was understood.

Such a widespread influence would not have been possible were it not for the fact that education was making rapid progress among the people and literacy was becoming much more common. In the later Middle Ages a surprising number of people of the middle class could read and write, as the Paston Letters abundantly show. In Shakespeare's London, though we have no accurate means of measurement, it is probable that not less than a third and probably as many as half of the people could at least read. In the seventeenth and eighteenth centuries there arose a prosperous trades class with the means to obtain an education and the leisure to enjoy it, attested to, for example, by the great increase in the number of schools, the tremendous journalistic output of a man like Defoe, and the rapid rise of the novel. Nowadays, when practically everyone goes to school, we witness the phenomenon of newspapers with circulations of several hundred thousand copies daily, even up to 2 million, and magazines that in an exceptional case reach a total of 80 million copies per month. As a result of popular education the printing press has been able to exert its influence upon language as upon thought.

A third factor of great importance to language in modern times is the way in which the different parts of the world have been brought together through commerce, transportation, and the rapid means of communication we have developed. The exchange of commodities and the exchange of ideas are both stimulating to language. We shall see later how the expansion of the British Empire and the extension of trade enlarged the English vocabulary by words drawn from every part of the world, besides spreading the language over vast areas whose existence was undreamed of in the Middle Ages. But while diversification has been one of the results of transportation, unification has also resulted from ease of travel and communication. The steamship and the railroad, the automobile, and the airplane have brought people into contact with one another and joined communities hitherto isolated, while the post office sand the telegraph, the telephone, the radio, the movies, television, and electronic data transmission have been influential in the intermingling of language and the lessening of the more easily altered local idiosyncrasies.

The fourth factor, the growth of specialized knowledge, has been important not only because new knowledge often requires new vocabulary but also because, in the early centuries of the modern period, Latin became less and less the vehicle for learned discourse. Both trends accelerated strongly during the seventeenth century. As we shall see in the next chapter, the rapid accumulation of new knowledge was matched by a rapid trend away from publishing specialized and learned works in Latin.

Finally, there is the factor which we have referred to as self-consciousness about language. This has two aspects, one individual, one public. At the individual level we may observe a phenomenon that has become intensely important in modern times: as people lift themselves into a different economic or intellectual or social level, they are likely to make an effort to adopt the standards of grammar and pronunciation of the people with whom they have identified, just as they try to conform to fashions and tastes in dress and amusements. However superficial such conformity might be, people are as careful of their speech as of their manners. Awareness that there are standards of language is a part of their social consciousness. Most people are less aware that such standards are largely accidental rather than absolute, having developed through the historical contingencies of economics, culture, and class. At the public level a similar self-consciousness has driven issues of language policy over the past four centuries, long before "language policy" acquired its modern meaning. The beginnings of this public discussion are evident in the sixteenth-century defense of English and debates about orthography and the enrichment of the vocabulary. As we shall see in the next chapter, anxiety about language policy reached a new urgency in the second half of the seventeenth century. From that time, through eighteenth-century proposals for an academy to twentieth-century efforts at language planning in former colonies of European powers, a self-consciousness about the shape that English ought to take has been an endless source of concern. This concern has been no less passionate for often being fueled by naive beliefs about the nature of language and the determinants of linguistic change.[1]

Effect upon Grammar and Vocabulary

The forces here mentioned may be described as both radical and conservative—radical in matters of vocabulary, conservative in matters of grammar. By a radical force is meant anything that promotes change in language; by conservative, what tends to preserve the existing status. Now it is obvious that the printing press, the reading habit, the advances of learning and science, and all forms of communica tion are favorable to the spread of ideas and stimulating to the growth of the vocabulary, while these same agencies, together with social consciousness as we have described it, work actively toward the promotion and maintenance of a standard, especially in grammar and usage. They operate both singly and in combination. Education, for example, exerts its influence not only through formal instruction in language—grammar, spelling, pronunciation, etc.—but also by making possible something more important, the unconscious absorption of a more or less standard English through books, magazines, and newspapers. We shall accordingly be prepared to find that in modern times changes in grammar have been relatively slight and changes in vocabulary extensive. This is just the reverse of what was true in the Middle English period. Then the changes in grammar were revolutionary, but, apart from the special effects of the Norman Conquest, those in vocabulary were not so great.

The Problems of the Vernaculars

In the Middle Ages the development of English took place under conditions that, because of the Norman Conquest, were largely peculiar to England. None of the other modern languages of Europe had had to endure the consequences of a foreign conquest that temporarily imposed an outside tongue upon the dominant social class and left the native speech chiefly in the hands of the lower social classes. But by the close of the Middle English period English had passed through this experience and, though bearing deep and abiding marks of what it had gone through, had made a remarkable recovery. From this time on the course of its history runs in many ways parallel with that of the other important European languages. In the sixteenth century the modern languages faced three great problems: (1) recognition in the fields where Latin had for centuries been supreme, (2) the establishment of a more uniform orthography, and (3) the enrichment of the vocabulary so that it would be adequate to meet the demands that would be made upon it in its wider use. Each of these problems received extensive consideration in the England of the Renaissance, but it is interesting to note that they were likewise being discussed in much the same way in France and Italy, and to some extent in Germany and Spain. Italy had the additional task of deciding upon the basis of its literary dialect, a matter that in France and England had been largely taken care of by the ascendancy of Paris and London.

The Struggle for Recognition

Although English, along with the other vernaculars, had attained an established position as the language of popular literature, a strong tradition still sanctioned the use of Latin in all the fields of knowledge. This tradition was strengthened by the "revival of learning," in which the records of Greek civilization became once more available in the original. Latin and Greek were not only the key to the world's knowledge but also the languages in which much highly esteemed poetry, oratory, and philosophy were to be read. And Latin, at least, had the advantage of universal currency, so that the educated all over Europe could freely communicate with each other, both in speech and writing, in a common idiom. Beside the classical languages, which seemingly had attained perfection, the vulgar tongues seemed immature, unpolished, and limited in resource. It was felt that they could not express the abstract ideas and the range of thought embodied in the ancient languages. Scholars alone had access to this treasure; they could cultivate the things of the spirit and enrich their lives. It would seem at times as though they felt their superiority to the less educated and were jealous of a prerogative that belonged to them alone. The defenders of the classical tradition were at no loss for arguments in support of their position. It was feared that the study of the classical languages, and even learning itself, would suffer if the use of the vernaculars were carried too far. And there were many who felt that it would be dangerous if matters like the disputes of theology and discussions in medicine fell into the hands of the indiscreet.

Against this tradition the modern languages now had their champions. In Italy as early as 1434 Alberti, himself a humanist whose reputation was secured by numerous works in Latin, defends his use of the vernacular also, saying: "I confess that the ancient Latin language is very copious and highly adorned; but I do not see why our Tuscan of today should be held in so little esteem that whatever is written in it, however excellent, should be displeasing to us.... And if it is true, as they say, that this ancient language is full of authority among all people, only because many of the learned have written in it, it will certainly be the same with ours if scholars will only refine and polish it with zeal and care."[2] His position had strong supporters in Speroni and Cardinal Bembo. In France Du Bellay wrote his vigorous *Deffence et Illustration de la Langue Françoyse* (1549) "in order to show that our language did not have at its birth such enemies in the gods and the stars that it cannot arrive one day at the same state of excellence and of perfection as others, inasmuch as all sciences can be faithfully and copiously treated in it." Du Bellay's point of view was expressed many times by other members of the Pléiade. And in England likewise there were many defenders of English against those who wished to discriminate against it, among them influential names like Elyot and Ascham, Wilson, Puttenham, and Mulcaster. Of those champions none was more enthusiastic than Richard Mulcaster, Head Master of the Merchant Taylors' School: "But why not all in English, a tung of it self both depe in conceit, and frank in deliverie? I do not think that anie language, be it whatsoever, is better able to utter all arguments, either with more pith, or greater planesse, then our English tung is, if the English utterer be as skilfull in the matter, which he is to utter: as the foren utterer is." He expresses his opinion many times, but perhaps nowhere more eloquently than in the words: "For is it not in dede a mervellous bondage, to becom servants to one tung for learning sake, the most of our time, with losse of most time, whereas we maie have the verie same treasur in our own tung, with the gain of most time? our own bearing the joyfull title of our libertie and fredom, the Latin tung remembring us of our thraldom and bondage? I love Rome, but London better, I favor Italie, but England more, I honor the Latin, but I worship the English."

Influential as utterances such as these were, their importance lies in the fact that they voiced a widespread feeling. The real force behind the use of English was a popular demand, the demand of all sorts of men in practical life to share in the fruits of the Renaissance. The Revival of Learning had revealed how rich was the store of knowledge and experience preserved from the civilizations of Greece and Rome. The ancients not only had lived but had thought about life and drawn practical conclusions from experience. Much was to be learned from their discussion of conduct and ethics, their ideas of government and the state, their political precepts, their theories of education, their knowledge of military science, and the like. The Renaissance would have had but a limited effect if these ideas had remained the property solely of academicians. If the diplomat, the courtier, and the man of affairs were to profit by them, they had to be expressed in the language that everybody read.

The demand was soon met. Translations (and, it might be added, original works generated by the same intellectual ferment) virtually poured from the press in the course of the sixteenth century. The historians were great favorites, probably because their works, as so often described on the title pages, were "very delectable and profitable to read." Thucydides and Xenophon had been Englished before Shakespeare started school, and Herodotus appeared before the dramatist had begun his career. Caesar was translated by Arthur Golding in 1565, Livy and Sallust and Tacitus before the close of the century, and one of the great translations of the age, Plutarch's *Lives of the Noble Grecians and Romans,* in the version of Sir Thomas North, was published in 1579. Works dealing with politics and morals were equally popular. *The Doctrinal of Princes, made by the noble oratour Isocrates* was translated from the Greek as early as 1534 by Sir Thomas Elyot, who had already given the English a taste of Plato in *The Knowledge Which Maketh a Wise Man.* Aristotle, Cicero, Seneca, Epictetus, and Marcus Aurelius appeared in whole or in part, while the poets and dramatists included Virgil, Ovid (1567), Horace (1566-1567), Terence, Theocritus, and most of the lesser names. Various partial translations of Homer were printed before Chapman's version began to appear in 1598. The translators did not stop with the great works of antiquity but drew also upon medieval and contemporary sources. Saint Augustine, Boethius, Peter Martyr, Erasmus, Calvin, and Martin Luther were among those rendered into English. It would seem that while scholars were debating the merits of Latin and English, the issue was being decided by the translators.

Other factors, however, contributed to the victory. One was the overzeal of the humanists themselves. Not content with the vigorous and independent Latin that was written in the Middle Ages, they attempted to reform Latin prose on the style and vocabulary of Cicero. Ciceronianism substituted slavish imitation for what had been a natural and spontaneous form of expression. Not only was the vocabulary of Cicero inadequate for the conveyance of modern ideas, but there was no hope of being able to surpass one's model. As Ascham confessed in his *Toxophilus,* "as for ye Latin or greke tonge, every thyng is so excellently done in them, that none can do better." Another factor was the Protestant Reformation, itself a phase of the Renaissance. From the time that Wycliffe refused to carry on his quarrel with the church in the language of the schools and took his cause directly to the people in their own tongue, one of the strongholds of Latin was lost. The amount of theological writing in English is almost unbelievable, for as one Elizabethan remarked, "The dissension in divinity is fierce beyond God's forbid." Finally, we must not overlook the fact that the contest between Latin and English had a commercial side. The market for English books was naturally greater than for Latin, and we cannot blame the Elizabethan printer if he sometimes thought, as one said to Thomas Drant in 1567, "Though, sir, your book be wise and full of learning, yet peradventure it will not be so saleable."

Although it is plain to us nowadays that from the beginning the recognition of English was assured, the victory was not lightly won. The use of English for purposes of scholarship was frankly experimental. Sir Thomas Elyot in his *Doctrinal of Princes* (1534) says: "This little book...I have translated out of greke ...to the intent onely that I wolde assaie, if our English tongue mought receive the quicke and proper sentences pronounced by the greekes." The statement is slightly apologetic. Certainly those who used English where they might have been expected to write in Latin often seem to anticipate possible criticism, and they attempt to justify their action. Ascham prefaces his *Toxophilus* with the statement: "And althoughe to have written this boke either in latin or Greke... had bene more easier and fit for mi trade in study, yet neverthelesse, I sup-posinge it no point of honestie, that mi commodite should stop and hinder ani parte either of the pleasure or profite of manie, have written this Englishe matter in the Englishe tongue, for Englishe men." In his *Castle of Health* (1534) Elyot is somewhat bolder in his attitude: "If physicians be angry, that I have written physicke in englische, let them remember that the grekes wrate in greke, the Romains in latine, Avicenna, and the other in Arabike, whiche were their own proper and maternall tongues. And if thei had bene as muche attached with envie and covetise, as some nowe seeme to be, they wolde have devised some particular language, with a strange cipher or forme of letters, wherin they wold have written their scyence, whiche language or letters no manne should have knowen that had not professed and practised physicke." All these attempts at self-justification had as their strongest motive the desire to reach the whole people in the language they understood best. This is stated with engaging frankness by Mulcaster: "I do write in my naturall English toungue, bycause though I make the learned my judges, which understand Latin, yet I meane good to the unlearned, which understand but English, and he that understands Latin very well, can understand English farre better, if he will confesse the trueth, though he thinks he have the habite and can Latin it exceeding well." Statements such as these, which could be multiplied many times from the literature of the period, show that the recognition of English was achieved in spite of a rather persistent opposition.

As we approach the end of the century and see that English has slowly won recognition as a language of serious thought, we detect a note of patriotic feeling in the attitude of many people. They seem to have grown tired of being told that English was crude and barbarous. This is apparent in the outburst of George Pettie in his book on *Civile Conversation* (1586): "There are some others yet who wyll set lyght by my labours, because I write in Englysh: and...the woorst is, they thinke that impossible to be doone in our Tongue: for they count it barren, they count it barbarous, they count it unworthy to be accounted of." "But," he adds, "how hardly soever you deale with your tongue, how barbarous soever you count it, how litle soever you esteeme it, I durst my selfe undertake (if I were furnished with Learnying otherwyse) to wryte in it as copiouslye for varietie, as compendiously for brevitie, as choycely for woordes, as pithily for sentences, as pleasauntly for figures, and every way as eloquently, as any writer should do in any vulgar tongue whatsoever." Mulcaster goes so far as to say: "I take this present period of our English tung to be the verie height therof, bycause I find it so excellentlie well fined, both for the bodie of the tung it self, and for the customarie writing thereof, as either foren workmanship can give it glosse, or as homewrought hanling can give it grace. When the age of our peple, which now use the tung so well, is dead and departed there will another succede, and with the peple the tung will alter and change. Which change in the full harvest thereof maie prove comparable to this, but sure for this which we now use, it semeth even now to be at the best for substance, and the bravest for circumstance, and whatsoever shall becom of the English state, the English tung cannot prove fairer, then it is at this daie, if it maie please our learned sort to esteme so of it, and to bestow their travell upon such a subject, so capable of ornament, so proper to themselves, and the more to be honored, bycause it is their own." In 1595 Richard Carew wrote a discourse on *The Excellency of the English Tongue,* and about 1583 Sir Philip Sidney could say, "But for the uttering sweetly and properly the conceit of the minde, which is the end of speech, that [English] hath it equally with any other tongue in the world."

The Problem of Orthography

Spelling is for most people a pedestrian subject, but for the English, as for the French and the Italians, in the sixteenth century the question of orthography or "right writing," as Mulcaster preferred to call it, was a matter of real importance and the subject of much discussion. The trouble was not merely that English spelling was bad, for it is still bad today, but that there was no generally accepted system that everyone could conform to. In short, it was neither phonetic nor fixed. Speaking generally, the spelling of the modern languages in the Middle Ages had attempted with fair success to represent the pronunciation of words, and this is true of English in spite of the fact that Norman scribes introduced considerable confusion when they tried to write a language that they imperfectly knew and carried over habits that they had formed in writing French. The confusion was increased when certain spellings gradually became conventional while the pronunciation slowly changed. In some cases a further discrepancy between sound and symbol arose when letters were inserted in words where they were not pronounced (like the *b* in *debt or doubt)* because the corresponding word in Latin was so spelled *(debitum, dubitare),* or in other cases (for example, the *gh* in *delight, tight)* by analogy with words similarly pronounced *(light, night)* where the *gh* had formerly represented an actual sound. The variability of English spelling was an important part of the instability that people felt characterized the English language in the sixteenth century, especially as compared with a language like Latin. To many it seemed that English spelling was chaotic.

In reality it was not so bad as that. There were limits to its variety and inconsistency. It varied more from writer to writer, according to education and temperament, than within the practice of the individual. Then as now, some people were more inclined than others to adopt a given way of doing a thing and to stick to it. Consistency in a matter like spelling often went with a scholarly temperament. Sir John Cheke, for example, has a system of spelling that he adheres to fairly closely. He doubles long vowels *(taak, haat, maad, mijn, thijn,* etc., for *take, hate, made, mine, thine),* discards final *-e (giv, belev),* always uses i for *y (mighti, dai),* and so forth. It is not our system or that of most of his contemporaries, but it is a system, and he observed it.[3] Some writers observed a system for a particular reason. Thus Richard Stanyhurst, attempting a translation of Virgil (1582) in quantitative verse after the model of Latin poetry, employs a special spelling to help bring out what he believes to be the length of English syllables. He is consistent about spellings like *thee* (for *the), too* (for *to), mee, neere, coonning, woorde, yeet,* but he writes *featlye, neatlie, aptly* within three lines. He is strictly speaking consistent only so far as it serves his purpose to be. On the other hand, it is clear from the letters of such a man as John Chamberlain, which begin toward the end of the century, that the average educated person in Shakespeare's day did not spell by mere whim or caprice but had formed fairly constant spelling habits.[4] Such habits were to some extent personal with each individual and differed in some particulars from one person to the next, but most writers show a fair degree of consistency within their own practice. It was somewhat different with the hastier writing of the more popular playwrights and pamphleteers. It is not always clear how much of their spelling is to be credited to them and how much to the printer. Most printers probably took advantage of the variability of English spelling to "justify" a line, with as little scruple about optional letters as about extra spaces. In any case a certain difference is to be noticed between the spelling of pamphlets like those of Robert Greene, which we can hardly believe were proofread, and a book like North's *Plutarch* or Holinshed's *Chronicles.* In one of Greene's coney-catching pamphlets, *A Notable Discovery of Coosnage* (1591), we find *coney* spelled *cony, conny, conye, conie, connie, coni, cuny, cunny, cunnie,* while in other words there are such variations as *coosnage, coosenage, cosenage, cosnage, been, beene, bin, fellow, felow, felowe, fallow, fallowe, neibor, neighbor, go, goe, their, theyr,* and others. But in spite of all the variety that Elizabethan spelling presents, there was by 1550 a nucleus of common practice, and many of the features of English spelling today were clearly becoming established.

That the problem of bringing about greater agreement in the writing of English was recognized in the sixteenth century is apparent from the attempts made to draw up rules and to devise new systems. The earliest of these, *An A.B.C. for Children* (before 1558), is almost negligible. It consists of only a few pages, and part of the space is devoted to "precepts of good lyvynge," but the author manages to formulate certain general mles such as the use of the final *e* to indicate vowel length *(made, ride, hope).* Certain more ambitious treatises attacked the problem in what their authors conceived to be its most fundamental aspect. This was the very imperfect way in which the spelling of words represented their sound. These writers were prepared to discard the current spelling entirely and respell the language phonetically with the use of additional symbols where needed. Thus in 1568 Thomas Smith published a *Dialogue concerning the Correct and Emended Writing of the English Language.* He increased the alphabet to thirty-four letters and marked the long vowels. Smith's reform did not win much favor. His work, moreover, was in Latin, and this would further limit its chance of popular influence. The next year another attempt at phonetic writing was made in a work by John Hart called *An Orthographie,* elaborated in the following year in *A Method or Comfortable Beginning for All Unlearned, Whereby They May Bee Taught to Read English* (1570).[5] Hart makes use of special characters for *ch, sh, th,* etc., but his system seems to have won no more favor than Smith's. A more considerable attempt at phonetic reform was made in 1580 by William Bullokar in his *Booke at Large, for the Amendment of Orthographie for English Speech.* He confesses that he has profited by the mistakes of Smith and Hart, whose works were "not received in use (the chiefe cause whereof, I thinke, was their differing so farre from the old)." So he says, "My chiefe regard (from the beginning) was to follow the figures of the old letters and the use of them...as much as possible." He accordingly invents few special characters but makes liberal use of accents, apostrophes, and numerous hooks above and below the letters, both vowels and consonants. If his innovations in this way had been more moderate, English spelling might have come to the use of accents such as were being adopted for French at this time, but one glance at a specimen page printed according to his system shows why it could not possibly win acceptance.[6] Attempts such as the foregoing continued well into the seventeenth century. Many of them represented mere exercises in ingenuity, as when Charles Butler, in *The English Grammar, or The Institution of Letters, Syllables, and Woords in the English Tung* (1634), substitutes an inverted apostrophe for final *e's* and for efforts at such a radical reform as these enthusiasts proposed were largely wasted.

This was clearly perceived by Richard Mulcaster, the teacher of Spenser, whose *Elementarie* (1582), "which entreateth chefelie of the right writing of our English tung," is the most extensive and the most important treatise on English spelling in the sixteenth century. Mulcaster's great virtue is his moderation. He saw the futility of trying to make English spelling phonetic in any scientific sense. He was therefore willing to compromise between the ideal and the practical. He did not believe that the faults of English spelling were so desperate that they could be removed only by desperate remedies. The way to correct an existing difftculty was not to substitute a new and greater one. This seemed to him to be the effect of all those proposals that took into consideration only the sound of words. Even at its best, he did not think that spelling could ever perfectly represent sound. The differences between one sound and another were often too subtle. "Letters," he says, "can expresse sounds withall their joynts & properties no fuller then the pencill can the form & lineaments of the face." It was inevitable, he thought, that the same letter must sometimes be used for different sounds, but this was no worse than to use the same word, as we often do, in very different senses. Another difficulty that he saw was that pronunciation constantly changes. These were his theoretical reasons for refusing to go along with the phonetic reformers. His practical reason was that their systems were too cumbersome ever to be accepted. "But sure I take the thing to be to combersom and inconvenient,...where no likeliehood of anie profit at all doth appear in sight." Every attempt to force people against established custom "hath alwaie mist, with losse of labor where it offered service."

The basis of his reform, therefore, was custom or usage. This he defines not as the practice of the ignorant, but that "wherein the skilfull and best learned do agre." "The use & custom of our cuntrie hath allredie chosen a kinde of penning wherein she hath set down hir relligion, hir lawes, hir privat and publik dealings." This cannot now be completely changed, although it can be pruned "so that the substance maie remain, and the change take place in such points onelie as maie please without noveltie and profit without forcing." "I will therefor do my best," he says, "to confirm our custom in his own right, which will be easilie obtained where men be acquainted with the matter allredie and wold be verie glad to se wherein the right of their writing standeth." In making usage his point of departure he does not ignore sound; he merely insists that it shall not be given an undue share of attention. We must use common sense and try to remove defects in the existing system, not substitute a new one. He thinks ease and convenience in writing should be considered, for popular approval is the final authority. Only a general goodness, not perfection in each detail, can be expected. No set of rules can cover all points; some things must be left to observation and daily practice.

We cannot enter into the details of his system here but must be content with a statement of his general aims. He would first of all get rid of superfluous letters. There is no use in writing *putt, grubb, ledd* for *put, grub, led,* "and a thowsand such ignorant superfluities." On the other hand, we must not omit necessary letters such as the t in *fetch* or *scratch.* He allows double consonants only where they belong to separate syllables *(wit-ting),* and almost never at the end of a word except in the case of *ll (tall, generall).* Words ending in *-ss* he writes *-sse (glasse, confesse).* Otherwise final *-e* is used regularly to indicate a preceding long vowel, distinguishing *made* from *mad, stripe* from *strip,* and at the end of words ending in the sound of *v* or *z (deceive, love, wise).* An *e* is added to words that end in a lightly pronounced *i: daie, maie, trewlie, safetie;* but when the i is sounded "loud and sharp" it is spelled *y: deny, cry, defy.* Analogy, or as he calls it, "proportion," plays a justly important part in his system. Since we write *hear,* we should therefore write *fear* and *dear.* This principle, he admits, is subject to exceptions that must be made in deference to "prerogative," that is, the right of language to continue a common custom, as in employing an analogous spelling for *where, here, there.* In such a case he becomes frankly the apologist, justifying the common practice. He is really more interested in having everyone adopt the same spelling for a given word than he is in phonetic consistency. It is not so much a question of whether one should write *where* as that one should adopt a single spelling and use it regularly instead of writing *where, wher, whear, wheare, were, whair,* etc. To this end he prints in the latter part of his book a *General Table* giving the recommended spelling for some 7,000 of the most common words. Mulcaster's spelling is not always the one that ultimately came to be adopted. In spite of his effort for the most part to follow current usage, he seems sometimes to have gone counter to the tendency of his own and later times. He advocates spelling *guise, guide, guest,* and the like without the *u* and writes *bãble, dãble,* indicating the length of the vowel by a short mark over it. But his book had the great merit—or demerit—of standardizing a large number of current spellings, justifying them, and advocating the consistent use of them.

It is impossible to say how influential Mulcaster's work was. The effect of his precepts seems to be evident in certain later writers. Ben Jonson quotes from him, often without acknowledgment. That English spelling developed along the lines laid down by him is certain, but this may have been due largely to the fact that it was already developing along these lines and would have done so even without the help of his book.

During the first half of the next century the tendency toward uniformity increased steadily. The fixation of English spelling is associated in most people's minds with the name of Dr. Johnson, and a statement in the preface of his dictionary, published in 1755, might lend color to this idea. In reality, however, our spelling in its modern form had been practically established by about 1650. In *The New World of English Words* published in 1658 by Milton's nephew Edward Phillips, the compiler says: "As for orthography, it will not be requisite to say any more of it then may conduce to the readers direction in the finding out of words," and he adds two or three remarks about Latin *prae-*being rendered in English by *pre-*, and the like. Otherwise he seemed to think that the subject did not call for any discussion. And in reality it did not. The only changes we should make in the sentence just quoted are in the spelling *then* (for *than)* and the addition of an apostrophe in *readers.* A closer scrutiny of the preface as a whole[7] would reveal a few other differences such as an occasional *e* where we have dropped it *(kin*de*)*, *ll* and *sse* at the end of words *(gratefull,* *harshnesse), -ick* for *-ic (logick),* and a contracted form of the past participle *(authoriz'd, chanc't).* Even these differences are not very noticeable. Spelling was one of the problems that the English language began consciously to face in the sixteenth century. During the period from 1500 to 1650 it was fairly settled.[8]

The Problem of Enrichment

In 1531 Sir Thomas Elyot, statesman as well as scholar, published what has been described as the first book on education printed in English. He called it *The Governour* because it had to do with the training of those who in the future would be occupied at court. The dedication to Henry the Eighth is couched in the following terms:

> I late consideringe (moste excellent prince and myne onely redoughted soveraigne lorde) my duetie that I owe to my naturall contray with my faythe also of aliegeaunce and othe...I am (as God juge me) violently stered to *devulgate* or sette fourth some part of my studie, trustynge therby tacquite me of my dueties to God, your hyghnesse, and this my contray. Wherfore takinge comfort and boldenesse, partly of your graces moste benevolent inclination towarde the universall weale of your subjectes, partly inflamed with zele, I have now enterprised to *describe* in our vulgare tunge the fourme of a juste publike weale:... Whiche *attemptate* is nat of presumption to teache any persone, I my selfe havinge moste nede of teachinge: but onely to the intent that men which wil be studious about the weale publike may fynde the thinge therto expedient compendiously writen.

I *dedicate* it unto your hyghnesse as the fyrste frutes of my studye, verely trustynge that your moste excellent wysedome wyll therein *esteme* my loyall harte and diligent endevour...Protestinge unto your excellent majestie that where I commende herin any one vertue or *dispraise* any one vice I meane the generall description of thone and thother without any other particular meanynge to the reproche of any one persone. To the whiche protestation I am nowe dryven throughe the malignite of this present tyme all disposed to malicious detraction...

In this passage we have an early example of the attempt to improve the English language. The words printed in italics were all new in Elyot's day; two of them *(education, dedicate)* are first found in the English language as he uses them in this dedication. Two others *(esteem* and *devulgate)* are found in the sense here employed only one year earlier. Several others could be instanced which, although recorded slightly earlier, were not yet in general use.[9] In so short a passage these new words are fairly numerous, but not more numerous than in the rest of his book, and, what is more important, they are not the innovations of a pedant or an extremist. Other writers who could be cited were less restrained in their enthusiasm for words drawn from Latin, Greek, and French. Nor are these new words in Elyot the result of chance. They are part of a conscious effort to enrich the English vocabulary.

We have already indicated that enlarging the vocabulary was one of the three major problems confronting the modern languages in the eyes of men in the sixteenth century. And it is not difftcult to see why this was so. The Renaissance was a period of increased activity in almost every field. It would have been strange if the spirit of inquiry and experiment that led to the discovery of America, the reform of the church, the Copernican theory, and the revolution of thought in many fields should have left only language untouched. The rediscovery of Latin and Greek literature led to new activity in the modern languages and directed attention to them as the medium of literary expression. The result was a healthy desire for improvement. The intellectual aspect of the Revival of Learning had a similar effect. The scholarly monopoly of Latin throughout the Middle Ages had left the vernaculars undeveloped along certain lines. Now that this monopoly was being broken, the deficiencies of English were at the same time revealed. English was undoubtedly inadequate, as compared with the classical languages, to express the thought that those languages embodied and that in England was now becoming part of a rapidly expanding civilization. The translations that appeared in such numbers convinced people of the truth of this fact. The very act of translation brings home to the translators the limitations of their medium and tempts them to borrow from other languages the terms whose lack they feel in their own. For writers to whom Latin was almost a second mother tongue the temptation to transfer and naturalize in English important Latin radicals was particularly great. This was so, too, with French and Italian. In this way many foreign words were introduced into English. One may say that the same impulse that led scholars to furnish the English mind with the great works of classical and other literatures led them to enrich the English language with words drawn from the same source. New words were particularly needed in various technical fields, where English was notably weak. The author of a *Discourse of Warre* justifies his introduction of numerous military terms by an argument that was unanswerable: "I knowe no other names than are given by strangers, because there are fewe or none at all in our language."

It is not always easy, however, to draw the line between a word that is needed because no equivalent term exists, and one that merely expresses more fully an idea that could be conveyed in some fashion with existing words. We can appreciate the feeling of scholars for whom a familiar Latin word had a wealth of associations and a rich connotation; we must admit the reasonableness of their desire to carry such a word over into their English writing. The transfer is all the more excusable when one is convinced that English would be better for having it and that it is a patriotic duty to employ one's knowledge in so worthy a cause as that of improving the national speech. This motive actuated many people who were both earnest and sincere in their desire to relieve English of the charge of inadequacy and inelegance. Thus Elyot apologizes for introducing the word *maturity:* "Wherfore I am constrained to usurpe a latine worde..., which worde, though it be strange and darke [obscure], yet...ones brought in custome, shall be facile to understande as other wordes late commen out of Italy and Fraunce... Therfore that worde *maturitie* is translated to the actis of man,...reservyng the wordes *ripe* and *redy* to frute and other thinges seperate from affaires, as we have nowe in usage.

And this do I nowe remembre for the necessary augmentation of our langage." In another place he says, "I intended to augment our Englyshe tongue, wherby men shulde as well expresse more abundantly the thynge that they conceyved in theyr hartis,...havyng wordes apte for the pourpose: as also interprete out of greke, latyn or any other tonge into Englysshe as sufficiently as out of any one of the said tongues into an other." In any case, whether "of pure necessitie in new matters, or of mere braverie to garnish it self withall"—to quote a phrase of Mulcaster's—English acquired in the sixteenth and early seventeenth centuries thousands of new and strange words.

The greater number of these new words were borrowed from Latin. But they were not exclusively drawn from that source. Some were taken from Greek, a great many from French, and not a few from Italian and Spanish. Even the older periods of English and occasionally the local dialects were drawn upon to embellish the language, in this case chiefly the language of poetry. We shall see more particularly in a moment the character of the additions made at this time, but before doing so we must consider the conflicting views that different people held concerning their desirability.

The Opposition to Inkhorn Terms

The wholesale borrowing of words from other languages did not meet with universal favor. The strangeness of the new words was an objection to some people. As Edward Phillips said in his *New World of Words,* "some people if they spy but a hard word are as much amazed as if they had met with a Hobgoblin." Even Elyot's prestige did not save him from criticism on this score. In a book published two years after *The Governour* he alludes to "divers men...[who] doo shewe them selfes offended (as they say) with my strange termes," and he attempts to justify his practice. Other men were purists by nature and took their stand on general principles. Such a man was Sir John Cheke. His attitude is interesting because he was himself a fine classical scholar and might have been expected to show sympathy for classical borrowings. In a letter to Sir Thomas Hoby, prefaced to Hoby's translation of *The Courtier* (1561), he wrote:

> I am of this opinion that our own tung shold be written cleane and pure, unmixt and unmangeled with borowing of other tunges, wherin if we take not heed by tijm, ever borowing and never payeng, she shall be fain to keep her house as bankrupt. For then doth our tung naturallie and praisablie utter her meaning, when she bouroweth no counterfeitness of other tunges to attire her self withall, but useth plainlie her own, with such shift, as nature, craft, experiens and folowing of other excellent doth lead her unto, and if she want at ani tijm (as being unperfight she must) yet let her borow with suche bashfulnes, that it mai appeer, that if either the mould of our own tung could serve us to fascion a woord of our own, or if the old denisoned wordes could content and ease this neede, we wold not boldly venture of unknowen wordes.

Ascham's admiration for Cheke led him to a similar attitude. Some considered the use of learned words mere pedantry and tried to drive them out by ridicule, calling them "inkhorn" terms. Sir Thomas Chaloner, who translated Erasmus' *Praise of Folly m* 1549, is an example:

> Such men therfore, that in deede are archdoltes, and woulde be taken yet for sages and philosophers, maie I not aptelie calle theim foolelosophers? For as in this behalfe I have thought good to borowe a littell of the Rethoriciens of these daies, who plainely thynke theim selfes demygods, if lyke horsleches thei can shew two tongues, I meane to mingle their writings with words sought out of strange langages, as if it were alonely thyng for theim to poudre theyr bokes with ynkehorne termes, although perchaunce as unaptly applied as a gold rynge in a sowes nose. That and if they want suche farre fetched vocables, than serche they out of some rotten Pamphlet foure or five disused woords of antiquitee, therewith to darken the sence unto the reader, to the ende that who so understandeth theim maie repute hym selfe for more cunnyng and litterate: and who so dooeth not, shall so muche the rather yet esteeme it to be some high mattier, because it passeth his learnyng.

The strongest objection to the new words, however, was on the score of their obscurity. The great exponent of this view was Thomas Wilson, whose *Arte of Rhetorique* (1553) was several times reprinted in the course of the century and was used by Shakespeare. In a classic passage on "Plainnesse, what it is" he makes a savage attack on inkhorn terms and illustrates the fault by a burlesque letter overloaded with them:

> Among all other lessons this should first be learned, that wee never affect any straunge ynkehorne termes, but to speake as is commonly received: neither seeking to be over fine, nor yet living over-carelesse, using our speeche as most men doe, and ordering our wittes as the fewest have done. Some seeke so far for outlandish English, that they forget altogether their mothers language. And I dare sweare this, if some of their mothers were alive, thei were not able to tell what they say: and yet these fine English clerkes will say, they speake in their mother tongue, if a man should charge them for counterfeiting the Kings English. Some farre journeyed gentlemen at their returne home, like as they love to goe in forraine apparell, so thei wil pouder their talke with oversea language. He that commeth lately out of Fraunce will talke French English and never blush at the matter. An other chops in with English Italienated, and applieth the Italian phrase to our English speaking, the which is, as if an Oratour that professeth to utter his mind in plaine Latine, would needes speake Poetrie, and farre fetched colours of straunge antiquitie....The unlearned or foolish phantasticall, that smelles but of learning (such fellowes as have seen learned men in their daies) wil so Latin their tongues, that the simple can not but wonder at their talke, and thinke surely they speake by some revelation. I know them that thinke *Rhetorique* to stande wholie upon darke wordes, and hee that can catche an ynke horne terme by the taile, him they coumpt to be a fine Englisheman, and a good *Rhetorician.* And the rather to set out this foly, I will adde suche a letter as William Sommer himselfe, could not make a better for that purpose. Some will thinke and sweare it too, that there was

never any such thing written: well, I will not force any man to beleeve it, but I will say thus much, and abide by it too, the like have been made heretofore, and praised above the Moone.

A letter devised by a Lincolneshire man, for a voyde benefice, to a gentleman that then waited upon the Lorde Chauncellour, for the time being.

Pondering, *expending,*[10] and *revoluting* with my selfe, your *ingent*[11] *affabilitie,* and *ingenious capacity* for *mundaine* affaires: I cannot but *celebrate, & extol* your *magnifical dexteritie* above all other. For how could you have *adepted*[12] such *illustrate* prerogative, and *dominicall superioritie,* if the fecunditie of your *ingenie*[13] had not been so *fertile* and wonderfull pregnant. Now therefore being *accersited*[14] to such *splendente* renoume and dignitie *splendidious:* I doubt not but you will *adjuvate*[15] such poore *adnichilate*[16] orphanes, as whilome ware *condisciples*[17] with you, and of *antique* familiaritie in Lincolneshire. Among whom I being a *scholasticall panion,*[18] *obtestate*[19] your *sublimitie,* to *extoll* mine infirmitie. There is a Sacerdotall dignitie in my *native* Countrey, *contiguate* to me, where I now *contemplate:* which your worshipfull benignitie could sone *impetrate*[20] for mee, if it would like you to extend your sedules, and *collaude*[21] me in them to the right honourable Lord Chauncellor, or rather *Archgrammacian* of Englande. You know my literature, you knowe the *pastorall* promotion. I *obtestate* your *clemencie,* to *invigilate*[22] thus much for me, according to my *confidence,* and as you knowe my condigne merites for such a *compendious* living. But now I *relinquish* to *fatigate* your intelligence, with any more *frivolous verbositie,* and therfore he that rules the climates, be evermore your beautreux, your fortresse, and your bulwarke. *Amen.*

Dated at my *Dome*[23] or rather Mansion place in Lincolnshire, the *penulte of* the moneth Sextile. *Anno Millimo, quillimo, trillimo.*

Per me Johannes Octo.

What wiseman reading this Letter, will not take him for a very Caulf that made it in good earnest, and thought by his ynke pot termes to get a good Parsonage?

In the letter included in the above passage the italicized words were new in Wilson's day and therefore somewhat strange and obscure—dark, as he says—to the ordinary reader. Of the forty-five, thirty are not found before the sixteenth century, and the remaining fifteen are of such infrequent occurrence as to be considered by him inkhorn terms. It is interesting to note in passing that many of them are in common use today.

The Defense of Borrowing

The attitude revealed in these utterances was apparently not the prevailing one. There were many more who in precept or practice approved of judicious importations. As Dryden wrote somewhat later, "I trade both with the living and the dead, for the enrichment of our native tongue. We have enough in England to supply our necessity, but if we will have things of magnificence and splendour, we must get them by commerce."[24] The innovators had precedent on their side. Not only had English borrowed much in the past, but, as they frequently pointed out, all other languages, including Latin and Greek, had enriched themselves in this way.[25] The strangeness of the new words, they argued, would soon wear off. As Mulcaster observed, we must first become acquainted with any new thing "and make the thing familiar if it seme to be strange. For all strange things seme great novelties, and hard of entertainment at their first arrivall, till theie be acquainted: but after acquaintance theie be verie familiar, and easie to entreat.... Familiaritie and acquaintance will cause facilitie, both in matter and in words." The charge of obscurity was also met. Elyot maintained that throughout *The Governour* "there was no terme new made by me of a latine or frenche worde, but it is there declared so playnly by one mene or other to a diligent reder that no sentence is therby made derke or harde to be understande." Not all men could say as much, but in theory this was their aim. The position of the defender was in general summed up by George Pettie, the translator of Guazzo's *Civile Conversation:*

> For the barbarousnesse[26] of our tongue, I must lykewyse say that it is much the worse for them [the objectors], and some such curious fellowes as they are: who if one chaunce to

derive any woord from the Latine, which is insolent to their eares (as perchaunce they wyll take that phrase to be) they foorthwith make a jest at it, and terme it an Inkehorne terme. And though for my part I use those woords as litle as any, yet I know no reason why I should not use them, and I finde it a fault in my selfe that I do not use them: for it is in deed the ready way to inrich our tongue, and make it copious, and it is the way which all tongues have taken to inrich them selves.... Wherefore I marveile how our English tongue hath crackt it credite,[27] that it may not borrow of the Latine as well as other tongues: and if it have broken, it is but of late, for it is not unknowen to all men how many woordes we have fetcht from thence within these fewe yeeres, which if they should be all counted inkepot termes, I know not how we should speake any thing without blacking our mouthes with inke: for what woord can be more plaine then this word *plaine,* and yet what can come more neere to the Latine? What more manifest then *manifest?* and yet in a maner Latine: What more commune then *rare,* or lesse rare then *commune,* and yet both of them comming of the Latine? But you wyll say, long use hath made these woords curraunt: and why may not use doo as much for these woords which we shall now derive? Why should not we doo as much for the posteritie as we have received of the antiquitie?[28]

A little later some sanction for the borrowings was derived from authority. Bullokar says (1616) "it is familiar among best writers to usurpe strange words."

Compromise

The opposition to inkhorn terms was at its height in the middle of the sixteenth century. At the end of Elizabeth's reign it had largely spent its force. By this time borrowing had gone so far that the attack was rather directed at the abuse of the procedure than at the procedure itself. The use of unfamiliar words could easily be overdone. It was the enthusiast and the pedant who brought down the criticism of reasonable people upon the practice and caused them to condemn it in more sweeping terms than they knew at heart were justified or were consistent with their own usage. Puttenham, for example, although issuing a warning against inkhorn terms, admits having to use some of them himself and seeks to justify them in particular instances. He defends the words *scientific, major domo, politien* (politician), *conduct* (verb), and others. The word *significative,* he says, "doth so well serve the turne, as it could not now be spared: and many more like usurped Latine and French words: as, *Methode, methodicall, placation, function, assubtiling, refining, compendious, prolixe, figurative, inveigle,* a term borrowed of our common lawyers,. *impression,* also a new terme, but well expressing the matter, and more than our English word.. Also ye finde these wordes, *penetrate, penetrable, indignitie,* which I cannot see how we may spare them, whatsoever fault wee finde with Ink-horne termes: for our speach wanteth wordes to such sence so well to be used." Even Wilson, after exercising his wit in the lively bit of burlesque quoted above, proceeds at once to qualify his disapproval: "Now whereas wordes be received, as well Greke as Latine, to set furthe our meanyng in thenglishe tongue, either for lacke of store, or els because wee would enriche the language: it is well doen to use them, and no man therin can be charged for any affectation when all other are agreed to folowe the same waie," and he cites some that meet with his approval. Each person who used a new word doubtless felt the justification of it and, in a matter about which only time could bring agreement, ran the risk of having their innovations disliked by others. As Ben Jonson remarked in his *Discoveries,* "A man coins not a new word without some peril and less fruit; for if it happen to be received, the praise is but moderate; if refused, the scorn is assured." Some of the words that Puttenham defends have not stood the test of time, and some of those he objects to, such as *audacious, egregious, compatible,* have won a permanent place in the language. One who used any considerable number of new words was in a way on the defensive. Chapman in presenting his translation of Homer says: "For my varietie of new wordes, I have none Inckepot I am sure you know, but such as I give pasport with such authoritie, so significant and not ill sounding, that if my countrey language were an usurer, or a man of this age speaking it, hee would thanke mee for enriching him." Obscurity is always a valid object of criti-cism, and if the word "inkhorn" could be hurled at an opponent, it was sure to strike him in a vulnerable spot. It was thus that Nash attacked Harvey,[29] who, it must be confessed, lent himself to such an attack. He replied in kind[30] and was able to convict Nash of *interfuseth, finicallitie, sillogistrie, disputative, hermaphrodite, declamatorie, censoriall moralizers, unlineall usurpers of judgement, infringement to destitute the inditement,* and a dozen similar expressions. Not the least interesting feature about the whole question of learned borrowings is the way it aroused popular interest. It even got into the playhouses. In the stage quarrel known as the "War of the Theatres"

Ben Jonson delivered a purge to Marston in the *Poetaster* (1601), relieving him of *retrograde, reciprocal, incubus, lubrical, defunct, magnificate, spurious, inflate, turgidous, ventosity, strenuous, obstupefact,* and a number of similar words. The attitude of most people seems to have been one of compromise. No Elizabethan could avoid wholly the use of the new words. Writers differed chiefly in the extent to which they allied themselves with the movement or resisted the tendency. As is so often the case, the safest course was a middle one, to borrow, but "without too manifest insolence and too wanton affectation."

Permanent Additions

From the exaggeration of a critic like Wilson one might get the impression that much of the effort to introduce new words into the language was pedantic and ill-advised. Some of the words Wilson ridicules seem forced and in individual cases were certainly unnecessary. But it would be a mistake to conclude that all or even a large part of the additions were of this sort. Indeed the surprising thing about the movement here described is the number of words that we owe to this period and that seem now to be indispensable. Many of them are in such common use today that it is hard for us to realize that to the Elizabethan they were so strange and difficult as to be a subject of controversy. When Elyot wished to describe a democracy he said, "This manner of governaunce was called in Greke *democratia,* in Latine *popularis potentia,* in Englisshe the rule of the comminaltie." If he were not to have to refer to "the rule of the commonalty" by this roundabout phrase, he could hardly do better than to try to naturalize the Greek word. Again he felt the need of a single word for "all maner of lerning, which of some is called the world of science, of other the circle of doctrine, which is in one word of Greke, *encyclopedia"* Though purists might object, the word *encydopedia* filled a need in English, and it has lived on. The words that were introduced at this time were often basic words—nouns, adjectives, verbs. Among nouns we may note as random examples *allurement, allusion, anachronism, atmosphere, autograph, capsule, denunciation, dexterity, disability, disrespect, emanation, excrescence, excursion, expectation, halo, inclemency, jurisprudence.* Among adjectives we find *abject* (in our sense of "down in spirit"), *agile, appropriate, conspicuous, dexterous, expensive, external, habitual, hereditary, impersonal, insane, jocular, malignant.* Few of these could we dispense with. But it is among the verbs, perhaps, that we find our most important acquisitions, words like *adapt, alienate, assassinate, benefit* (first used by Cheke, who thought "our language should be writ pure"!), *consolidate, disregard* (introduced by Milton), *emancipate, emdicate, erupt, excavate, exert, exhilarate, exist, extinguish, harass, meditate* (which Sidney apparently introduced). It is hard to exaggerate the importance of a movement that enriched the language with words such as these.

Most of the words in this list are Latin. But some of them were earlier acquired by Latin from Greek. Examples are *anachronism, atmosphere, autograph.* Others might be added, such as *antipathy, antithesis, caustic, chaos, chronology, climax, crisis, critic, dogma, emphasis, enthusiasm, epitome, parasite, parenthesis, pathetic, pneumonia, scheme, skeleton, system, tactics.* Indeed most of the Greek words in English until lately have come to us either through Latin or French. But in the Renaissance the renewed study of Greek led to the introduction of some Greek words at first hand. Such, for example, are *acme, anonymous, catastrophe, criterion, ephemeral, heterodox, idiosyncrasy, lexicon, misanthrope, ostracize, polemic, tantalize, thermometer,* and *tonic.*

Adaptation

Some words, in entering the language, retained their original form; others underwent change. Words like *climax, appendix, epitome, exterior, delirium,* and *axis* still have their Latin form. The adaptation of others to English was effected by the simple process of cutting off the Latin ending. *Conjectural* (L. *conjectural-is), consult* (L. *consult-are) exclusion* (L. *exclusion-em)*, and *exotic* (L. *exotic-us)* show how easily in many cases this could be done. But more often a further change was necessary to bring the word into accord with the usual English forms. Thus the Latin ending *-us* in adjectives was changed to *-ous (conspicu-us>conspicuous)* or was replaced by *-al* as in *external* (L. *externus).* Latin nouns ending in *-tas* were changed in English to *-ty (brevity<brevitas)* because English had so many words of this kind borrowed from French where the Latin *-tatem* regularly became *-té.* For the same reason nouns ending in *-antia, -entia* appear in English with the ending *-ance, -ence* or *-ancy, -ency,* while adjectives ending in *-bilis* take the usual English (or French) ending *-ble.* Examples are *consonance, concurrence, constancy, frequency, considerable, susceptible.* Many English verbs borrowed from Latin at this time end in *-ate (create, consolidate, eradicate).* These verbs were formed on the basis of the Latin past participle (e.g., *exterminatus,* whereas the French *exterminer* represents the Latin infinitive *exterminare).* The English practice arose from the fact that the Latin past participle was often equivalent to an adjective, and it was a common thing in English to make verbs out of adjectives *(busy, dry, darken).*

Reintroductions and New Meanings

Sometimes the same word has been borrowed more than once

in the course of time. The Latin words *episcopus* and *discus* appear in Old English as *bishop* and *dish* and were again borrowed later to make our words *episcopal* and *disc* (also *dais, desk,* and *discus).* In the same way *chaos* and *malignity* were apparently reintroduced in the sixteenth century. The word *intelligence* is used once in Gower and occasionally in the fifteenth century, but in *The Governour* Elyot remarks that "*intelligence* is nowe used for an elegant worde where there is mutuall treaties or appoyntementes, eyther by letters or message." A word when introduced a second time often carries a different meaning, and in estimating the importance of the Latin and other loanwords of the Renaissance it is just as essential to consider new meanings as new words. Indeed, the fact that a word had been borrowed once before and used in a different sense is of less significance than its reintroduction in a sense that has continued or been productive of new ones. Thus the word *fastidious* is found once in 1440 with the significance 'proud, scornful,' but this is of less importance than the fact that both More and Elyot use it a century later in its more usual Latin sense of 'distasteful, disgusting.' From this it was possible for the modern meaning to develop, aided no doubt by the frequent use of the word in Latin with the force of 'easily disgusted, hard to please, over nice.' Chaucer uses the words *artificial, declination, hemisphere* in astronomical senses, but their present use is due to the sixteenth century; and the word *abject,* although found earlier in the sense of 'cast off, rejected,' was reintroduced in its present meaning in the Renaissance.

Rejected Words

There are some things about language that we cannot explain. One of them is why certain words survive while others, apparently just as good, do not. Among the many new words that were introduced into English at this time there were a goodly number that we have not permanently retained. Some are found used a few times and then forgotten. Others enjoyed a rather longer life without becoming in any sense popular. A few were in sufficiently common use for a while to seem assured of a permanent place but later, for some reason, lost favor and dropped out of use.

Uncounsellable, for example, was very common in the seventeenth century but after that practically disappeared. Some of the new words were apparently too learned and smelled too much of the lamp. *Anacephalize,* a Greek word meaning "to sum up," was of this sort and the more unnecessary since we had already adopted the Latin *recapitulate. Deruncinate* (to weed) was another, although it was no worse than *eradicate* for which we had the English expression *to root out.* Elyot's *adminiculation* (aid) and *illecebrous* (delicate, alluring) are of the same sort. Some words might logically have survived but did not. *Expede* (to accomplish, expedite) would have been parallel to *impede. Cohibit* (to restrain) is like *inhibit* and *prohibit. Demit* (to send away) was common in the sixteenth and seventeenth centuries and would have been as natural as *commit* or *transmit,* but *dismiss* gradually replaced it. It is in fact not uncommon to find words discarded in favor of somewhat similar formations. Examples are *exsiccate* (to dry) alongside of *desiccate, emacerate* (emaciate), *discongruity* (incongruity), *appendance* (appendage). In some cases we have preferred a word in a shorter form: *cautionate* (caution), *consolate* (console), *attemptate* (attempt), *denunciate* (denounce). Often there seems to be no explanation but chance or caprice to account for a word's failure to survive. *Eximious* (excellent, distinguished) is frequently found in seventeenth-century literature and was used by Browning, but is now unknown or at least very rare. Similarly, *mansuetude* (mildness) has a history that extends from Chaucer to Browning, but it is no longer used. We have given up *disaccustom, disacquaint, disadorn,* etc., but we say *disabuse, disaffect, disagree.* Shakespeare used *disquantity* as a verb meaning 'to lessen in quantity' or 'diminish.' Sometimes we have kept one part of speech and discarded another. We say *exorbitant* but not *exorbitate* (to stray from the ordinary course), *approbation* but not *approbate, consternation* but not *consternate.* The most convincing reason for the failure of a new word to take hold is that it was not needed. *Aspectable* (visible), *assate* (to roast) and the noun *assation, exolete* (faded), *suppeditate* (furnish, supply), and many other rejected words were unnecessary, and there was certainly no need for *temulent when* we had *drunk, intoxicated,* and a score of other expressions of various degrees of respectability to express the idea. We must look upon the borrowings of this period as often experimental. New words were being freely introduced at the judgment or caprice of the individual. They were being tried out, sometimes in various forms. In Shakespeare's day no one could have told whether we should say *effectual, effectuous, effectful, effectuating,* or *effective.* Two of these five options have survived. It was necessary for time to do the sifting.

Reinforcement through French

It is not always possible to say whether a word borrowed at this time was taken over directly from Latin or indirectly through French, for the same wholesale enrichment was going on in French simultaneously and the same words were being introduced in both lan-guages. Often the two streams of influence must have merged. But that English borrowed many words from Latin firsthand is indicated in a number of ways. The word *fact* represents the Latin *factum* and not the French *fait,* which was taken into English earlier as *feat.* Many verbs like *confiscate, congratulate,* and *exonerate* are formed from the Latin participle *(confiscat-us,* etc.) and not from the French *confisquer, congratuler, exonerer,* which are derived from the infmitives *confiscare,* etc. Caxton has the form *confisk,* which is from French, but the word did not survive in this shape. The form *prejudicate* is from Latin while *prejudge* represents the French *prejuger.* In the same way *instruct* and *subtract* show their Latin ancestry *(instructus, subtractus)* since the French *instruire* and *subtraire* would have become in English *instroy* (like *destroy)* and *subtray* (which is found in the fifteenth century). Our word *conjugation* is probably a direct importation from Latin *(conjugation-em)* since the more usual form in French was *conjugaison.* Sometimes the occurrence of a word in English earlier than in French (e.g., *obtuse)* points to the direct adoption from Latin, as do words like *confidence, confident,* which are expressed in French by the forms *confiance, confiant,* but which in English are used in senses that the French forms do not have.

There still remain, however, a good many words that might equally well have come into English from Latin or French. Verbs like *consist* and *explore* could come either from the Latin *consistere* and *explorare* or the French *consister* and *explorer. Conformation, conflagration,* and many other similar nouns may represent either Latin *conformation-em, conflagration-em,* or French *conformation, conflagration.* It is so with words like *fidelity, ingenuity, proclivity,* where the Latin *fidelitat-em* developed into French *fidélité,* but English possessed so many words of this kind from French that it could easily have formed others on the same pattern. So adjectives like *affable, audible, jovial* may represent the Latin *affabilis* or the French *affable,* etc., and others like *consequent, modest, sublime* can have come equally well from the Latin or the French forms. It is really not important which language was the direct source of the English words because in either case they are ultimately of Latin origin. In many cases French may have offered a precedent for introducing the Latin words into English and may have assisted in their general adoption.

Words from the Romance Languages

Sixteenth-century purists objected to three classes of strange words, which they characterized as *inkhorn terms, oversea language,* and *Chaucerisms.* For the foreign borrowings in this period were by no means confined to learned words taken from Latin and Greek. The English vocabulary at this time shows words adopted from more than fifty languages,[31] the most important of which (besides Latin and Greek) were French, Italian, and Spanish. English travel in France and consumption of French books are reflected in such words as *alloy, ambuscade, baluster, bigot, bizarre, bombast, chocolate, comrade, detail, duel, entrance, equip, equipage, essay, explore, genteel, mustache, naturalize, probability, progress, retrenchment, shock, surpass, talisman, ticket, tomato, vogue,* and *volunteer.* But the English also traveled frequently in Italy, observed Italian architecture, and brought back not only Italian manners and styles of dress but also Italian words. Protests against the Italianate Englishman are frequent in

Elizabethan literature, and the objection is not only that the Englishmen came back corrupted in morals and affecting outlandish fashions, but that they "powdered their talk with oversea language."[32] Nevertheless, Italian words, like Italian fashions, were frequently adopted in England. Words like *algebra, argosy, balcony, cameo, capricio* (the common form of *caprice* until after the Restoration), *cupola, design, granite, grotto, piazza, portico, stanza, stucco, trill, violin, volcano* began to be heard on the lips of Englishmen or to be found in English books. Many other Italian words were introduced through French or adapted to French forms, words like *battalion, bankrupt, bastion, brigade, brusque, carat, cavalcade, charlatan, frigate, gala, gazette, grotesque, infantry, parakeet,* and *rebuff.* Many of these preserved for a time their Italian form. From Spanish and Portuguese, English adopted *alligator (el lagarto,* the lizard), *anchovy, apricot, armada, armadillo, banana, barricade* (often *barricado,* as in Shakespeare), *bastiment, bastinado, bilbo, bravado, brocade* (often employed in the form *brocado), cannibal, canoe, cedilla, cocoa, corral, desperado, embargo, hammock, hurricane, maize, mosquito, mulatto, negro, peccadillo, potato, renegado* (the original form of *renegade), rusk, sarsaparilla, sombrero, tobacco,* and *yam.* Many of these words reflect the Spanish enterprise on the sea and colonization of the American continent. Like Italian words, Spanish words sometimes entered English through French or took a French form. *Grenade, palisade, escalade,* and *cavalier* are examples, although commonly found in the sixteenth and seventeenth centuries in the form *grenado, palisado, escalado,* and *cavaliero,* even when the correct Spanish form would have been *granada, palisada, escalada,* and *caballero.* Sometimes the influence of all these languages combined to give us our English word, as in the case of *galleon, gallery, pistol, cochineal.*[33] Thus the cosmopolitan tendency, the spirit of exploration and adventure, and the interest in the New World that was being opened up show themselves in an interesting way in the growth of our vocabulary and contributed along with the more intellectual forms of activity to the enrichment of the English language.

The Method of Introducing New Words

The Latin words that form so important an element in the English vocabulary have generally entered the language through the medium of writing. Unlike the Scandinavian influence and to a large extent the French influence after the Norman Conquest, the various Latin influences, except the earliest, have been the work of churchmen and scholars. If the words themselves have not always been learned words, they have needed the help of learned people to become known. This was particularly true in the Renaissance. Even the words borrowed from the Romance languages in this period often came in through books, and the revivals and new formations from native material were due to the efforts of individual writers and their associates. It is impossible, of course, to say who was responsible for the introduction of each particular word, but in certain cases we can see individual writers at work—like Sir Thomas Elyot—conscious of their innovations and sometimes pausing to remark upon them. Another writer who introduced a large number of new words was Elyot's older contemporary Sir Thomas More. To More we owe the words *absurdity, acceptance, anticipate, combustible, compatible* (in our sense), *comprehensible, concomitance, congratulatory, contradictory, damnability, denunciation, detector, dissipate, endurable, eruditely, exact, exaggerate, exasperate, explain, extenuate, fact, frivolous, impenitent, implacable, incorporeal, indifference, insinuate, inveigh, inviolable, irrefragable, monopoly, monosyllable, necessitate, obstruction, paradox, pretext,* and others. Elyot, besides using some of these, gives us *accommodate, adumbrate, adumbration, analogy, animate, applicate* (as an alternative to the older *apply), beneficence, encyclopedia, exerp* (now spelled *excerpt), excogitate, excogitation, excrement, exhaust, exordium, experience* (verb), *exterminate, frugality, implacability, infrequent, inimitable, irritate, modesty, placability,* etc. at the risk of being wearisome, in order that they might be the more impressive. So far as we now know, these words had not been used in English previously. In addition both writers employ many words that are recorded from only a few years before. And so they either introduced or helped to establish many new words in the language. What More and Elyot were doing was being done by numerous others, and it is necessary to recognize the importance of individuals as "makers of English" in the sixteenth and early seventeenth century.

Enrichment from Native Sources

By far the greater part of the additions to the English vocabulary in the period of the Renaissance was drawn from sources outside of English. The popular favor shown to all kinds of foreign words seems to have implied a disparagement of English resources that was resented in some quarters. Gabriel Harvey remarked that "in Inglande... nothinge is reputid so contemptible, and so baselye and vilelye accountid of, as whatsoever is taken for Inglishe, whether it be handsum fasshions in apparrell, or seemely and honorable in behaviour, or choise wordes and phrases in speache, or anye notable thinge else...that savorith of our owne cuntrye and is not ether merely or mixtely outlandishe." But, as we have seen, there were purists like Cheke, and there were also others who believed that English could very well develop new words from old roots or revive expressions that had gone out of use. Cheke was so strongly opposed to the borrowing of Latin and Greek words that he sought wherever possible English equivalents. Thus, in his translation of the Gospel of St. Matthew, where the Authorized Version reads *lunatic he* wrote *mooned,* and in the same way he said *toller* for *publican, hundreder* for *centurion, foresayer* for *prophet, byword* for *parable, freshman* for *proselyte, crossed* for *crucified, gainrising* for *resurrection.* The poets, of course, were rather more given to the revival of old words, especially words that were familiar to them in Chaucer. For this reason their revivals and new formations that suggested an older period of English were sometimes referred to as "Chaucerisms." Among poets who consciously made use of old words to enlarge the poetical vocabulary the most important was Spenser, although there were also others, such as Thomas Drant, the translator of Horace, whose influence on Spenser has not been fully appreciated, and to a lesser degree Milton.

These poetical innovations were of several kinds. Some were old words revived, like *astound, blameful, displeasance, enroot, doom, forby* (hard by, past), *empight* (fixed, implanted), *natheless, nathemore, mickle, whilere* (a while before). Others were new, such as *askew, filch, flout, freak.* The origin of these is often uncertain; they may have been of dialectal provenience. Some were definitely coinages, such as Spenser's *bellibone* (a fair maid, possibly from *belle et bonne), blatant, braggadocio, chirrup, cosset* (lamb), *delve* (pit, den), dit (song), *scruze* (apparently a telescope word combining *screw* and *squeeze), squall* (to cry), and *wrizzled* (wrinkled, shriveled). Finally, many were simply adaptations and derivatives of old words, such as *baneful, briny, changeful, drear* (from *dreary), hapless, oaten, sunshiny,* or *wolfish.* Some of the innovations had a look much more rustic and strange than these, and, as in the case of inkhorn terms and oversea words, opinion varied as to their desirability. Sidney criticized Spenser for the "framing of his stile to an old rustick language," and Ben Jonson went so far as to say that "Spenser in affecting the ancients writ no language." But the poet also had his defenders. His friend "E.K." wrote,"...in my opinion it is one special prayse of many whych are dew to this poete, that he hath laboured to restore as to their rightfull heritage such good and naturall English words as have ben long time out of use and almost cleane disherited." The defenders, moreover, could have pointed to the fact that the same method of enriching the language was being urged in France. The words that English acquired in this way are not nearly so numerous as those obtained from outside, but when all is said the fact remains that to Spenser and others who shared his views we owe a great many useful words. *Belt, bevy, craggy, dapper, forthright, glen, glee, glance, surly, blandishment, birthright, changeling, elfin, endear, disrobe, don, enshrine, drizzling, fleecy, grovel, gaudy, gloomy, merriment, rancorous, shady, verdant, wakeful, wary,* and *witless* by no means exhaust the list. Many of these have passed from the language of poetry into common use, and, what is equally important, a vital principle of English word formation was being kept alive.

Methods of Interpreting the New Words

The diffculty for the reader presented by these new words of many different origins was met in various ways. In many cases the context or the reader's knowledge of Latin was expected to make the meaning clear. But the interpretation was not left entirely to chance. Explanations were sometimes added parenthetically. When Elyot uses the word *circumspection* he adds, "whiche signifieth as moche as beholdynge on every parte." In using the word *magnanimity* he says, "But nowe I remembre me, this worde *magnanimitie* beinge yet straunge, as late borowed out of the latyne, shall nat content all men"; he therefore explains what it means. Again, he says, "*Industrie* hath nat ben so longe tyme used in the englisshe tonge.... It is a qualitie procedying of witte and experience, by the whiche a man perceyveth quickly, inventeth fresshly, and consayleth spedily." This is not our way of using the word, but he also uses it in the sense of diligence in performance. A simpler way, where an equivalent word or expression existed, was to combine the new and the old in a self-interpreting pair. Thus he says "*animate or* give courage," "*devulgate or* set forth," "*explicating* or unfolding," "*difficile* or hard," "*education* or bringing up of children," "*adminiculation* or aid," "*ostent or* show," "*excerped or* gathered out of," "*obfuscate* or hid," and "*celerity*, commonly called speediness." Where no help like this was given, however, many a word must have remained troublesome to ordinary readers. Another means was therefore provided for their "adminiculation."

Dictionaries of Hard Words

As early as 1582 Mulcaster had written: "It were a thing verie praiseworthie in my opinion, and no lesse profitable than praiseworthie, if som one well learned and as laborious a man, wold gather all the words which we use in our English tung, whether naturall or incorporate, out of all professions, as well learned as not, into one dictionarie, and besides the right writing, which is incident to the alphabete, wold open unto us therein both their naturall force and their proper use." This statement shows another of the many ways in which Richard Mulcaster was in advance of his time. It was not until nearly 150 years later, when Nathaniel Bailey published his *Universal Etymological English Dictionary* (1721), that anyone attempted to list all the words in the language. The earliest dictionaries were those explaining the words in Latin or some other foreign language, and the earliest English dictionaries were dictionaries of hard words. The first of these was a little book of 120 pages by Robert Cawdrey, called *A Table Alphabeticall of Hard Words* (1604), explaining some 3,000 terms. It was followed in 1616 by John Bullokar's *English Expositor*and in 1623 by the *English Dictionarie of Henry* Cockeram, both of which passed through numerous editions. Blount's *Glossographia* (1656), Edward Philipps' *New World of Words* (1658), and other later compilations continued to treat only the more diffticult words until the time of Bailey, whose book held the field until the appearance of Dr. Johnson's. An interesting feature of Cockeram' s work and the later editions of Bullokar was a section "serving for the translation of ordinary English words into the more scholastick, or those derived from other languages." By means of this supplement a person might write in ordinary English and then, by making a few judicious substitutions, convey a fine impression of learning. The development of dictionaries was a consequence of the extensive additions that had been made to the language and in turn helped to facilitate their adoption into general use.

Nature and Extent of the Movement

In order to appreciate the importance of the Renaissance in enriching the English vocabulary it is worth-while to form some idea of the number of new words added at this time. A calculation based upon the data available in the *Oxford Dictionary* gives a figure somewhat above 12,000. This number is certain to be reduced somewhat when all of the materials assembled for the *Middle English Dictionary* are published; but it is likely to remain close to 10,000, since the calculation has been made conservatively, taking no account of minor variations of the same word, or of words which, while appearing before 1500, were reintroduced in the sixteenth century or first gained currency at that time. Many of the new words, of course, enjoyed but a short life. Some even appeared only once or twice and were forgotten. But about half of the total number have become a permanent part of the language. A very large majority were from Latin, and this accession from Latin is sometimes known as the Latin Influence of the Fourth Period. Not all of the additions filled gaps in the existing vocabulary, but they gave the language a wealth of synonyms. In the course of time these have often become differentiated, enabling us to express slight shades of meaning that would otherwise have been unattainable. Most of the new words entered English by way of the written language. They are a striking evidence of the new force exerted by the printing press. They also furnish a remarkable instance of the ease with which the printed word can pass into everyday speech. For although many of the new words were of a distinctly learned character in the beginning, they did not remain so very long, a fact that not only can be inferred from their widespread popular use today but also can be illustrated from the plays of Shakespeare or almost any of his contemporaries.

The Movement Illustrated in Shakespeare

It is a well-known fact that, except for a man like the Elizabethan translator Philemon Holland, Shakespeare had the largest vocabulary of any English writer. This is due not only to his daring and resourceful use of words but also in part to his ready acceptance of new words of every kind. It is true that he could make sport of the inkhorn terms of a pedant like Holofernes, who quotes Latin, affects words like *intimation, insinuation, explication,* and *replication,* and has a high scorn for anyone like the slow-witted Dull who, as another character remarks, "hath not eat paper." Shakespeare had not read Wilson in vain (see p. 218). But he was also not greatly impressed by Wilson's extreme views. Among Shakespearian words are found *agile, allurement, antipathy, catastrophe, consonancy, critical, demonstrate, dire.*

discountenance, emphasis, emulate, expostulation, extract, hereditary, horrid, impertinency, meditate, modest, pathetical, prodigious, vast, the Romance words *ambuscado, armada, barricade, bastinado, cavalier, mutiny, palisado, pell-mell, renegado*—all new to English in the latter half of the sixteenth century. Some of the words Shakespeare uses must have been very new indeed, because the earliest instance in which we find them at all is only a year or two before he uses them (*e.g., exist, initiate, jovial),* and in a number of cases his is the earliest occurrence of the word in English *(accommodation, apostrophe, assassination, dexterously, dislocate, frugal, indistinguishable, misanthrope, obscene, pedant, premeditated, reliance, submerged,* etc.). He would no doubt have been classed among the liberals in his attitude toward foreign borrowing. Shakespeare's use of the new words illustrates an important point in connection with them. This is the fact that they were often used, upon their first introduction, in a sense different from ours, closer to their etymological meaning in Latin. Thus, *to communicate* nowadays means to exchange information, but in Shakespeare's day it generally preserved its original meaning 'to share or make common to many'. This is its force when Adriana says in the *Comedy of Errors:*

> Thou art an elm, my husband, I a vine, Whose weakness married to thy stronger state Makes me with thy strength to *communicate,* that is, she shares his strength with him. When Lorenzo in the *Merchant of Venice* says "let's in and there *expect their* coming," he is using *expect* in its original sense of 'to await'. In the sixteenth century, when the verb to atone was first used, it did not have its modern meaning, 'to make amends' but simply 'to set at one, reconcile', as when Desdemona says, "I would do much to atone them." *Enlargement* meant freedom from confinement ("take this key, give *enlargement* to the swain") and *humorous* might mean 'damp' (as in "the *humorous* night" of *Romeo and Juliet)* or 'capricious', 'moody', 'peevish', that is, showing the effect of the various bodily humors which, according to medieval belief, determined one's disposition. The word did not acquire

its present meaning until the time of Addison. It would be easy to multiply examples from almost any page of Shakespeare. The few that have been given will suffice to show that the new words often remained close to their etymological meaning.

Shakespeare's Pronunciation

Shakespeare's pronunciation, though not ours, was much more like ours than has always been realized. He pronounced [e] for [i] in some words just as Pope could still say *tay*for tea.[36] The falling together of *er, ir, ur* (e.g., *herd, birth, hurt)* was under way but not yet completed. As explained in § 175, ME *ç* was sometimes open, sometimes close [å: e:] and the two sounds were still distinct in Shakespeare's day, [e:] and [i:] respectively. Consequently *sea* [se:] does not normally rhyme with see [si:], *heap* with *keep, speak* with *seek,* etc. Toward the close of the fifteenth century an attempt was made to distinguish between them by the spelling. The closer sound was often spelled with *ee* or *ie (deep, field)* while the more open sound was as often written *ea (sea, clean).* But the practice was not consistently carried out. Although the two sounds are now identical, this variation in spelling is a reminder of the difference in pronunciation that long existed. We should also probably notice considerable difference in the pronunciation of words containing a MEo. This regularly developed into [u:], as in *room, food, roof, root,* and it retains this sound in many words today. In some words the vowel was shortened in the fifteenth century and was unrounded to the sound in *blood, flood.* In still other words, however, it retained its length until about 1700 but was then shortened without being unrounded, giving us the sound in *good, stood, book, foot.* It is apparent that in Shakespeare's day there was much fluctuation in the pronunciation of words containing this Middle English vowel, both in the different parts of the country and in the usage of different individuals. Consequently we find in the poetry of the period a word like *flood* rhyming not only with *blood*but also with *mood and good.* In fact, as late as Dryden we find in the same rhyme *flood—mood—good,* the three developments of the sound at the present day. It is only in recent times that the pronunciation of these words has been standardized, and even today there is some vacillation between a long and short vowel in some of them, for example, in *broom, room,* and *roof.* In addition to such differences in the quality of vowels there were some differences of accent. Shakespeare said *perseVer, demonstrate,* and generally *aspect', de'testable,* while he has *character, com'mendable, envy', se'cure, welcome',* etc., in contrast to the accentuation that is customary in these words today. On the whole, however, we should probably have little more diffículty in understanding Shakespeare's pronunciation than we experience in listening to a broad Irish brogue. The situation would be very different with the language of Chaucer. And the reason is that in the course of the fifteenth and sixteenth centuries the vowels of Middle English, especially the long vowels, underwent a wholesale but quite regular shifting, about which something must be said.

The Importance of Sound-changes

The subject of sound-changes is just as important in the history of languages as the changes in grammar and vocabulary. But it lends itself less readily to generalization and brief presentation. Any treatment of even the vowels, if it would have value, must proceed by examining each of the vowel sounds individually, determining its character at a given time, tracing its source in the preceding period, and following its subsequent development both independently and under the influence of neighboring sounds and varying conditions of accent, often noting significant differences in its development in different dialects, and, sometimes, in individual words, its modification through the analogical influence of other words. It is obviously impossible to enter upon such a study here. Some sounds in English have been less subject to change than others and would offer little difficulty. For example, the short *e* under certain conditions has remained unchanged since Old English times: OE *bedd is* still *bed* today. On the other hand, to take a fairly simple case, the *â* in OE *stân* (stone) became about 1100 a sound like that in *law* (stc:n) central and southern England. In the great vowel shift that began to take place in all long vowels in the fifteenth century this sound underwent a further change so that in Shakespeare's pronunciation it has become a Ö close similar to its pronunciation at the present day *(stone).* Today the *o* is followed by a slight *u* glide [sto^{u}n] or [stoUn] which some authorities believe arose in the nineteenth century, while others trace it back as far as the seventeenth. On the other hand, the development here described did not take place in the north of England. There the OE *â* instead of being rounded to an *Q* developed into a sound that rhymes with *lane (stane),* and this is its pronunciation in Scotland today. For the detailed treatment of English sounds the student must be referred to the various historical grammars and works that make it their special concern.[37] Here we must confine ourselves to a few broad observations.

From Old to Middle English

In considering the changes in pronunciation that English words underwent in passing from Old to Middle English we may say that qualitatively they were slight, at least in comparison with those that occurred later. Changes in the consonants were rather insignificant, as they have always been in English. Some voiced consonants became voiceless, and vice versa, and consonants were occasionally lost. Thus *w* before a following *o* was lost when it followed another consonant: sô(OE *swâ), hô* (who, OE *kwâ). Sc* became *sh* (OE *scip>ME ship* or *schip)*, or had already done so in Old English. But we do not expect much change in the consonantal framework of words. Nor was there much alteration in the quality sof vowels in accented syllables. Most of the short vowels, unless lengthened, passed over into Middle English unaltered. But short æ became *a,* and *y* [y] was unrounded to i in most districts, either early or eventually (OE *crœft>ME craft; brycg>brigge).* The other short vowels, *ã, e, i, 6, m,* remained (OE *catte>cat, bedd>bed, scip>schip, folc> folk, full> ful).*

If the quality of Old English vowels did not change much in passing into Middle English, their quantity or length was subject to considerable alteration. For example, Old English long vowels were shortened late in the Old English period or early in Middle

English when followed by a double consonant or by most combinations of consonants *(gretter,* comparative of *grçt*< OE *grçat; ãsken*<*âxian,* ask). Conversely, short vowels in open syllables were lengthened in Middle English (OE *bãcan*>*ME bâken,* bake;

Such changes in length are little noticeable in the spelling, but they are of great importance because they determine the course which these vowels pursued in their subsequent development.

From Middle English to Modern

When we come to the vowel changes in Modern English we see the importance of the factors that determined the length of vowels in Middle English. All Middle English long vowels underwent extensive alteration in passing into Modern English, but the short vowels, in accented syllables, remained comparatively stable. If we compare Chaucer's pronunciation of the short vowels with ours, we note only two changes of importance, those of *a* and *u.* By Shakespeare's day (i.e., at the close of the sixteenth century) Chaucer's *a* had become an [æ] in pronunciation *(cat, thank, flax).* In some cases this ME *a* represented an OE *& (at, apple,. back),* and the new pronunciation was therefore a return to approximately the form that the word had had in Old English. It is the usual pronunciation in America and a considerable part of southern England today. The change the *u* underwent was what is known as unrounding. In Chaucer's pronunciation this vowel was like the *u* in *full.* By the sixteenth century it seems to have become in most words the sound we have in *but* (e.g., *cut, sun; love,* with the Anglo-Norman spelling of *o* for u). So far as the short vowels are concerned it is clear that a person today would have little difficulty in understanding the English of any period of the language.

The Great Vowel Shift

The situation is very different when we consider the long vowels. In Chaucer's pronunciation these had still their so-called "continental" value—that is, *a* was pronounced like the *a* in *father* and not as in *name, e* was pronounced either like the *e* in *there* or the *a* in *mate,* but not like the *ee* in *meet,* and so with the other vowels. But in the fifteenth century a great change is seen to be under way. All the long vowels gradually came to be pronounced with a greater elevation of the tongue and closing of the mouth,so that those that could be raised and those that could not without becoming consonantal (i, *u)* became diphthongs.

Such a diagram must be taken as only a very rough indication of what happened, especially in the breaking ofi and *u* into the diphthongs *ai* and *au.* Nor must the changes indicated by the arrows be thought of as taking place successively, but rather as all part of a general movement with slight differences in the speed with which the results were accomplished (or the date at which evidence for them can be found).

From this it is apparent that most of the long vowels had acquired at least by the sixteenth century (and probably earlier) approximately their present pronunciation. The most important development that has taken place since is the further raising of ME t to î. Whereas in Shakespeare *clean* was pronounced like our *lane,* it now rhymes with *lean.* The change occurred at the end of the seventeenth century and had become general by the middle of the eighteenth.[42] Such other changes as have occurred are slight and must be sought by the interested reader in the books devoted especially to the history of English sounds.

It will be noticed that the Great Vowel Shift is responsible for the unorthodox use of the vowel symbols in English spelling. The spelling of English had become fixed in a general way before the shift and therefore did not change when the quality of the long vowels changed. Consequently our vowel symbols no longer correspond to the sounds they once represented in English and still represent in the other modern languages.

Weakening of Unaccented Vowels

A little observation and reflection shows us that in unaccented syllables, too, the spelling does not accurately represent the pronunciation today. This is because in all periods of the language the vowels of unstressed syllables have had a tendency to weaken and then often to disappear. This is true of all parts of a word. For example, we do not distinguish in ordinary or rapid speech between the vowels at the beginning of *ago, upon, opinion.* The sound in all three words is [Y]; in other cases it is commonly [Y], or [I]. Consider the unstressed middle or final syllable in the words *introduce, elegant* [Y, I], *drama, color, kingdom, breakfast* (bråkfYst *or* bråkf'st), *Monday* [i]. The weakening is especially noticeable in words from French where an accented vowel came to be unaccented in English (cf. French *mouton, raisin, bonté* with English *mutton, raisin, bounty).* One must not be misled by the spelling. The original spelling was generally retained and in recent times has occasionally influenced the pronunciation so that the quality of the vowel has been restored to something like its earlier character. *Window* now has a fairly well-defined diphthong in the final syllable [oU] or [o^{u}], but the weakened vowel is evident in the dialectal pronunciation *winder.* Misguided purists often try to pronounce the final syllable of *Monday,* with the full quality of the diphthong in *day.* But even when the vowel has been restored in standard speech the weakened form is generally apparent in informal speech and in the dialects.

Grammatical Features

English grammar in the sixteenth and early seventeenth century is marked more by the survival of certain forms and usages that have since disappeared than by any fundamental developments. The great changes that reduced the inflections of Old English to their modern proportions had already taken place. In the few parts of speech that retain some of their original inflections, the reader of Shakespeare or the Authorized Version is conscious of minor differences of form and in the framing of sentences may note differences of syntax and idiom that, although they attract attention, are not sufficient to interfere seriously with understanding. The more important of these differences we may pass briefly in review.

The Noun

The only inflections retained in the noun were, as we have

seen above, those marking the plural and the possessive singular. In the former the s-plural had become so generalized that except for a few nouns like *sheep* and *swine* with unchanged plurals, and a few others like *mice* and *feet* with mutated vowels, we are scarcely conscious of any other forms. In the sixteenth century, however, there are certain survivals of the old weak plural in *-n*. Most of these had given way before the usual *s-* forms: *fon* (foes), *kneen* (knees), *fleen* (fleas). But beside the more modern forms Shakespeare occasionally has *eyen* (eyes), *shoon* (shoes), and *kine,* while the plural *hosen* is occasionally found in other writers. Today, except for the poetical *kine* and mixed plurals like *children* and *brethren,* the only plural of this type in general use is *oxen.*

An interesting peculiarity of this period, and indeed later, is the his-genitive. In Middle English the *-es* of the genitive, being unaccented, was frequently written and pronounced -is, *-ys*. The ending was thus often identical to the pronoun *his,* which commonly lost its *h* when unstressed. Thus there was no difference in pronunciation between *stonis* and *ston is* (his), and as early as the thirteenth century the ending was sometimes written separately as though the possessive case were a contraction of a noun and the pronoun *his.* This notion was long prevalent, and Shakespeare writes ' *Gainst the count his galleys I did some service* and *In characters as red as Mars his heart.* Until well into the eighteenth century people were troubled by the illogical consequences of this usage;[46] Dr. Johnson points out that one can hardly believe that the possessive ending is a contraction of *his* in such expressions as *a woman's beauty or a virgin's delicacy.* He, himself, seems to have been aware that its true source was the Old English genitive, but the error has left its trace in the apostrophe, which we still retain as a graphic convenience to mark the possessive.

One other construction affecting the noun becomes established during this period, the group possessive: *the Duke of Gloucester's niece, the King of England's nose, somebody else's hat.* The construction is perhaps illogical, since even a king may be considered to have some rights to his nose, and the earlier construction was *the Duke's niece of Gloucester,* etc. But the expressions *Duke of Gloucester, King of England,* and the like, occurred so commonly as a unit that in the fifteenth century we begin to get the sign of the possessive added to the group. Instances are not common before the sixteenth century, and the construction may be thought of properly as belonging to the modern expressions like *my sister her watch.*

The Adjective

Because the adjective had already lost all its endings, so that it no longer expressed distinctions of gender, number, and case, the chief interest of this part of speech in the modern period is in the forms of the comparative and superlative degrees. In the sixteenth century these were not always precisely those now in use. For example, comparatives such as *lenger, strenger* remind us that forms like our *elder were* once more common in the language. The two methods commonly used to form the comparative and superlative, with the endings *-er* and *-est* and with the adverbs *more* and *most,* had been customary since Old English times. But there was more variation in their use. Shakespearian comparisons like *honester, violentest* are now replaced by the analytical forms. A double comparative or superlative is also fairly frequent in the work of Shakespeare and his contemporaries: *more larger, most boldest,* or Mark Antony's *This was the most unkindest cut of all.* The chief development affecting the adjective in modern times has been the gradual settling down of usage so that monosyllables take *-er* and *-est* while most adjectives of two or more syllables (especially those with suffixes like those in *frugal,* learned, *careful,* poetic, active, famous) take *more* and *most.*

The Pronoun

The sixteenth century saw the establishment of the personal pronoun in the form that it has had ever since. In attaining this result three changes were involved: the disuse of *thou, thy, thee;* the substitution of *you* for *ye* as a nominative case; and the introduction of *its* as the possessive of *it.*

(1) In the earliest period of English the distinction between

thou and *ye* was simply one of number; *thou* was the singular and *ye* the plural form for the second person pronoun. In time, however, a quite different distinction grew up. In the thirteenth century the singular forms *(thou, thy, thee)* were used among familiars and in addressing children or persons of inferior rank, while the plural forms *(ye, your, you)* began to be used as a mark of respect in addressing a superior. In England the practice seems to have been suggested by French usage in court circles, but it finds a parallel in many other modern languages. In any case, the usage spread as a general concession to courtesy until *ye, your,* and *you* became the usual pronoun of direct address irrespective of rank or intimacy. By the sixteenth century the singular forms had all but disappeared from contexts in which the plural forms were deemed proper and were maintained into the twentieth century only among the Quakers.

Originally a clear distinction was made between the nominative *ye* and the objective *you.* But because both forms are so frequently unstressed, they were often pronounced alike [jY] A tendency to confuse the nominative and the accusative forms can be observed fairly early, and in the fourteenth century *you* began to be used as a nominative. By a similar substitution *ye* appears in the following century for the objective case, and from this time on the two forms seem to have been used pretty indiscriminately until *ye* finally disappeared. It is true that in the early part of the sixteenth century some writers (Lord Berners, for example) were careful to distinguish the two forms, and in the Authorized Version of the Bible (1611) they are often nicely differentiated: *No doubt but ye are the people, and wisdom shall die with you* (Job). On the other hand Ascham and Sir Thomas Elyot appear to make no distinction in the nominative, while Shakespeare says *A southwest wind blow on ye And blister you all* over! In *The Two Gentlemen of Verona* occurs the line *Stand, sirs, and throw us that you have about ye,* where the two pronouns represent the exact reverse of their historical use. Although in the latter instance, *ye* may owe something to its unemphatic position, as in similar cases it does in Milton, it is evident that there was very little feeling any more for the different functions of the two words, and in the course of the seventeenth century *you* becomes the regular form for both cases.

In some ways the most interesting development in the pronoun at this time was the formation of a new possessive neuter, *its.* As we have seen above, the neuter pronoun in Old English was declined *hit, his, him, hit,* which by the merging of the dative and accusative under *hit* in Middle English became *hit, his, hit.* In unstressed positions *hit* weakened to *it,* and at the beginning of the modern period *it* was the usual form for the subject and object. *His,* however, remained the proper form of the possessive. Although it was thus identical with the possessive case of *he,* its occurrence where we should now use *its* is very common in written English down to the middle of the seventeenth century. Thus Portia's words *How far that little candle throws his beams* are quite natural, as is the Biblical *if the salt have lost his savor, wherewith shall it be salted?*

If grammatical gender had survived in English the continued use of *his* when referring to neuter nouns wouldprobably never have seemed strange. But when, with the substitution of natural gender, meaning came to be the determining factor in the gender of nouns, and all lifeless objects were thought of as neuter, the situation was somewhat different. The personal pronouns of the third person singular, *he, she, it,* had a distinctive form for each gender in the nominative and objective cases, and a need seems to have been felt for some distinctive form in the possessive case as well. Various substitutes were tried, clearly indicating a desire, conscious or unconscious, to avoid the use of *his in* the neuter. Thus, we find frequently in the Bible expressions like *Two cubits and a half was the length of it* and *nine cubits was the length thereof.* Not infrequently the simple form it was used as a possessive, as when Horatio, describing the ghost in *Hamlet,* says *It lifted up it head,* or when the Fool in *Lear* says:

> The hedge-sparrow fed the cuckoo so long, That it had it head bit off by it young.

The same use of the pronoun *it is* seen in the combination *it own: We enjoin thee...that there thou leave it, Without more mercy, to it own protection (Winter's Tale).* Similarly, *the was* used in place of the pronoun: *growing of the own accord* (Holland's *Pliny,* 1601). Both of these makeshifts are as old as the fourteenth century.

It was perhaps inevitable that the possessive of nouns *(stone's, horse's)* should eventually suggest the analogical form *it's* for the possessive of *it.* (The word was spelled with an apostrophe down to about 1800.) The first recorded instance of this form is in *The Second Book of Madrigals,* published by Nicholas Yonge in 1597,[50] but, like most novelties of this kind in language, it had probably been in colloquial use for a time before it appeared in print. Nevertheless, it is not likely to have been common even at the end of the sixteenth century, considering the large amount of fairly colloquial English that has come down to us from this period with no trace of such a form. At the beginning of the seventeenth century it was clearly felt as a neologism not yet admitted to good use. There is no instance of it in the Bible (1611) or in any of the plays of Shakespeare printed during his lifetime. In the First Folio of 1623 there are only ten instances, and seven of these were in plays written near the end of the dramatist's career. Milton, although living until 1674, seems to have admitted it but grudgingly to his writings; there are only three occurrences of the word in all his poetry and not many in his prose. Yet so useful a word could hardly fail to win a place for itself among the rank and file of speakers. Toward the close of the seventeenth century its acceptance seems to have gained momentum rapidly, so that to Dryden (1631-1700) the older use of *his* as a neuter seemed an archaism worthy of comment.

Finally, mention should be made of one other noteworthy development of the pronoun in the sixteenth century. This is the use of *who* as a relative. Refinements in the use of subordinate clauses are a mark of maturity in style. As the loose association of clauses (parataxis) gives way to more precise indications of logical relationship and subordination (hypotaxis) there is need for a greater variety of words effecting the union. Old English had no relative pronoun proper.

It made use of the definite article *(sç, sço, þæf),* which, however it was felt in Old English times, strikes us as having more demonstrative force than relative. Sometimes the indeclinable particle *þe* was added *(sç, þe,* which that) and sometimes *þe* was used alone. At the end of the Old English period the particle *þe* had become the most usual relative pronoun, but it did not long retain its popularity. Early in the Middle English period its place was taken by *þæt* (that), and this was the almost universal relative pronoun, used for all genders, throughout the Middle English period. In the fifteenth century *which* begins to alternate fairly frequently with *that.* At first it referred mostly to neuter antecedents, although occasionally it was used for persons, a use that survives in *Our Father, which art in heaven.* But the tendency to employ *that* as a universal relative has never been lost in the language, and was so marked in the eighteenth century as to provoke Steele to address to the *Spectator* his well-known "Humble Petition of *Who and Which"* in protest. It was not until the sixteenth century that the pronoun *who* as a relative came into use. Occasional instances of such a use occur earlier, but they are quite exceptional. There is no example of the nominative case in Chaucer. Chaucer, however, does use the oblique cases *whose* and *whom* (infrequently) as relative pronouns, and it is clear that the use of *who* as a pure relative began with these forms. Two earlier uses of *who* are the sources of the new construction: *who* as an indefinite pronoun *(Who hath ears to hear, let him hear; Who steals my purse steals trash)* and as an interrogative in indirect questions. The latter appears to have been the more important. The sequence *Whom do you want?* (direct question), *They asked whom you wanted* (indirect question), I *know the man whom you wanted* (relative) is not a difftcult one to assume. In any case, our present-day widespread use of *who* as a relative pronoun is primarily a contribution of the sixteenth century to the language.

The Verb

Even the casual reader of Elizabethan English is aware of

certain differences of usage in the verb that distinguish this part of speech from its form in later times. These differences are sometimes so slight as to give only a mildly unfamiliar tinge to the construction. When Lennox asks in *Macbeth, Goes the King hence today?* we have merely an instance of the more common interrogative form without an auxiliary, where we should say *Does the king go?* or *Is the king leaving today?* Where we should say *has been* Shakespeare often says *is: Is execution done on Cawdor?* and ' *Tis unnatural, Even like the deed that's done;* or *Arthur, whom* [who] *they say is killed tonight.* A very noticeable difference is the scarcity of progressive forms. Polonius asks, *What do you read, my Lord?—that* is, *What are you reading?* The large increase in the use of the progressive is one of the important developments of later times. Likewise the compound participle, *having spoken thus, having decided to make the attempt,* etc., is conspicuous by its infrequency. There are only three instances in Shakespeare and less than threescore in the Bible. The construction arose in the sixteenth century. On the other hand, impersonal uses of the verb were much more common than they are today. *It yearns me not, it dislikes me, so please him come* are Shakespearian expressions which in more recent English have been replaced by personal constructions. In addition to such features of Elizabethan verbal usage, certain differences in inflection are more noticeable, particularly the ending of the third person singular of the present indicative, an occasional -s in the third person plural, and many forms of the past tense and past participle, especially of strong verbs.

The regular ending of the third person singular in the whole south and southeastern part of England—that is, the district most influential in the formation of the standard speech—was *-eth* all through the Middle English period. It is universal in Chaucer: *telleth, giveth, saith, doth,* etc. In the fifteenth century, forms with *-s* occasionally appear. These are difficult to account for, since it is not easy to see how the Northern dialect, where they were normal, could have exerted so important an influence upon the language of London and the south. But in the course of the sixteenth century their number increases, especially in writings that seem to reflect the colloquial usage. By the end of this century forms like *tells, gives, says* predominate, though in some words, such as *doth* and *hath,* the older usage may have been the more common. One was free to use either. In the famous plea for mercy in the *Merchant of Venice* Portia says:

> The quality of mercy is not strain'd, It droppeth as the gentle rain from heaven Upon the place beneath: it is twice bless'd; It blesseth him that gives and him that takes:...

It is worth noting, however, that in the trial scene as a whole, forms in *-s* outnumber those in *-eth* two to one. Certainly, during the first half of the next century *-s* had become universal in the spoken language. This is beyond doubt, even though *-eth* continued to be quite commonly written. A writer toward the middle of the century observes that "howsoever wee use to Write thus, *leadeth* it, *maketh* it, *noteth* it, *raketh* it, *per-fumeth* it, & c. Yet in our ordinary speech (which is best to bee understood) wee say, *leads* it, *makes* it, *notes* it, *rakes* it, *per-fumes* it." It is altogether probable that during Shakespeare's lifetime *-s* became the usual ending for this part of the verb in the spoken language.

Another feature of the English verb in the sixteenth century, more noticeable at the close than at the opening, is the occurrence of this -s as an ending also of the third person plural. Normally at this time the plural had no ending in the language of literature and the court, a circumstance resulting from the disappearance of the East Midland *-en, -e,* the characteristic endings of the plural in Chaucer. But alongside this predominant plural without ending, we find occasionally expressions like *troubled minds that wakes* in Shakespeare's *Lucrece,* or *Whose own hard dealings teaches them suspect the deeds of others* in the *Merchant of Venice.* These are not solecisms or misprints, as the reader might suppose. They represent forms in actual, if infrequent, use. Their occurrence is also often attributed to the influence of the Northern dialect, but this explanation has been quite justly questioned,[55] and it is suggested that they are due to analogy with the singular. While we are in some danger here of explaining *ignotum per ignotius,* we must admit that no better way of accounting for this peculiarity has been offered. And when we remember that a certain number of Southern plurals in *-eth* continued apparently in colloquial use, the alternation of *-s* with this *-eth* would be quite like the alternation of these endings in the singular. Only they were much less common. Plural forms in *-s* are occasionally found as late as the eighteenth century.

We have already seen that during the Middle English period extensive inroads were made in the ranks of the Old English strong verbs. Many of these verbs were lost, and many became weak. Moreover, those that remained were subject to considerable fluctuation and alteration in the past tense and past participle. Since all of these tendencies were still operative in the beginning of the modern period, we may expect to find them reflected in the language of Shakespeare and his contemporaries. Among verbs that developed weak forms in this period were *bide, crow, crowd, flay, mow, dread, sprout,* and *wade,* and we accordingly find corresponding strong forms that have since disappeared, still in common use. Strong forms also alternate with weak in verbs that had begun to change earlier. Some of these are mentioned in § 118. Others were *waxen,* more frequent in the Bible than *waxed, sew* beside *sowed, gnew* beside *gnawed, holp* beside *helped.* A number of weak forms like *blowed, growed, shined, shrinked, swinged were* in fairly common use, although these verbs ultimately remained strong. In certain common verbs the form of the past tense differed from that of today. Such preterites as *brake* and *spake, drave* and *clave, tare, bare,* and *sware* are familiar to us from the Bible. *Bote* as the past tense of *bite* (like *write—wrote)* was still in occasional use. The participle *baken* is more frequent in the Bible than *baked. Brent* and *brast* were common forms for *burnt* and *burst,* while *wesh* and *washen* were prevalent as the past tense and past participle of *wash* until the close of the sixteenth century. Because in all these cases the forms current today were also in use, it is apparent that in Shakespeare's day there was much more latitude in the inflection of the verb than is permitted today.

Usage and Idiom

Language isnotmerely a matter of words andinflections. We should neglect a very essential element if we failed to take account of the many conventional features—matters of idiom and usage—that often defy explanation or logical classification but are nevertheless characteristic of the language at a given time and, like other conventions, subject to change. Such a matter as the omission of the article where we customarily use it is an illustration in point. Shakespeare says *creeping like snail, with as big heart as thou, in number of our friends, within this mile and half, thy beauty's form in table of my heart,* where modern idiom requires an article in all these cases. On the other hand, where we say *at length, at last,* Shakespeare says *at the length, at the last.* Again, usage permitted a different placing of the negative—before the verb—as in such expressions as *I not doubt, it not appears to me, she not denies it.* For a long time English permitted the use of a double negative. We have now discarded it through a false application of mathematical logic to language; but in Elizabethan times it was felt merely as a stronger negative, as indeed it is today in the instinct of the uneducated. So Shakespeare could say *Thou hast spoken no word all this while—nor understood none neither; I know not, nor I greatly care not; Nor this is not my nose neither; First he denied you had in him no right; My father hath no child but I, nor none is like to have; Nor never none shall mistress be of it, save I alone.* It is a pity we have lost so useful an intensive.

Perhaps nothing illustrates so richly the idiomatic changes in a language from one age to another as the uses of prepositions. When Shakespeare says *I'll rent the fairest house in it after threepence a bay,* we should say *at:* in *Our fears in Banquo stick deep,* we should say *about.* The single preposition of shows how many changes in common idioms have come about since 1600: *One that I brought up* of (from) *a puppy; he came of*(on) *an errand to me; 'Tis pity of* (about) *him; your name. .I know not, nor by what wonder you do hit* of (upon) *mine; And not be seen to wink of* (during) *all the day; it was well done of* (by) *you; I wonder of* (at) *their being here together; I am provided of* (with) *a torch-bearer; I have no mind of* (for) *feasting forth tonight; I were better to be married of (by) him than of another; That did but show thee* of (as) *a fool.* Many more examples could be added. Although matters of idiom and usage generally claim less attention from students of the language than do sounds and inflections or additions to the vocabulary, no picture of Elizabethan English would be adequate that did not give them a fair measure of recognition.

General Characteristics of the Period

As we survey the period of the sixteenth and early seventeenth centuries—the period of early Modern English—we recognize certain general characteristics, some of which are exemplified in the foregoing discussion, while others concern the larger spirit of the age in linguistic matters.

First, a conscious interest in the English language and an attention to its problems are now widely manifested. The fifteenth century had witnessed sporadic attempts by individual writers to embellish their style with "aureate terms." These attempts show in a way a desire to improve the language, at least along certain limited lines. But in the sixteenth century we meet with a considerable body of literature—books and pamphlets, prefaces and incidental observations—defending the language against those who were disposed to compare it unfavorably to Latin or other modern tongues, patriotically recognizing its position as the national speech, and urging its fitness for learned and literary use. At the same time it is considered worthy of cultivation, and to be looked after in the education of the young. Whereas a century or two before, the upper classes seemed more interested in having their children acquire a correct French accent and sometimes sent them abroad for the purpose, we now find Elyot urging that noblemen's sons should be brought up by those who "speke none englisshe but that which is cleane, polite, perfectly and articulately pronounced, omittinge no lettre or sillable," and observing that he knew some children of noble birth who had "attained corrupte and foule pronunciation"[56] through the lack of such precautions. Numerous books attempt to describe the proper pronunciation of English, sometimes for foreigners but often presumably for those whose native dialect did not conform to the standard of London and the court. Along with this regard for English as an object of pride and cultivation went the desire to improve it in various ways—particularly to enlarge its vocabulary and to regulate its spelling. All of these efforts point clearly to a new attitude toward English, an attitude that makes it an object of conscious and in many ways fruitful consideration.

In the second place, we attain in this period to something in the nature of a standard, something moreover that is recognizably "modern." The effect of the Great Vowel Shift was to bring the pronunciation within measurable distance of that which prevails today. The influence of the printing press and the efforts of spelling reformers had resulted in a form of written English that offers little difficulty to the modern reader. And the many new words added by the methods already discussed had given us a vocabulary that has on the whole survived. Moreover, in the writings of Spenser and Shakespeare, and their contemporaries generally, we are aware of the existence of a standard literary language free from the variations of local dialect. Although Sir Walter Raleigh might speak with a broad Devonshire pronunciation, and for all we know Spenser and Shakespeare may have carried with them through life traces in their speech of their Lancashire and Warwickshire ancestry, yet when they wrote they wrote a common English without dialectal idiosyncrasies. This, as Puttenham (1589) reminds us, was to be the speech of London and the court. It is not without significance that he adds, "herein we are already ruled by th' English Dictionaries and other bookes written by learned men, and therefore it needeth none other direction in that behalfe." However subject to the variability characteristic of a language not yet completely settled, the written language in the latter part of the sixteenth century is fully entitled to be called Standard English. The regularization of spellings in this written standard can be seen as early as the mid-fifteenth century in the official documents of Chancery.

Thirdly, English in the Renaissance, at least as we see it in books, was much more plastic than now. People felt freer to mold it to their wills. Words had not always distributed themselves into rigid grammatical categories. Adjectives appear as adverbs or nouns or verbs, nouns appear as verbs—in fact, any part of speech as almost any other part. When Shakespeare wrote *stranger'd with an oath* he was fitting the language to his thought, rather than forcing his thought into the mold of conventional grammar. This was in keeping with the spirit of his age. It was in language, as in many other respects, an age with the characteristics of youth—vigor, a willingness to venture, and a disposition to attempt the untried. The spirit that animated Hawkins and Drake and Raleigh was not foreign to the language of their time.

Finally, we note that in spite of all the progress that had been made toward a uniform standard, a good many features of the language were still unsettled. There still existed a considerable variety of use—alternative forms in the grammar, experiments with new words, variations in pronunciation and spelling. A certain latitude was clearly permitted among speakers of education and social position, and the relation between the literary language and good colloquial English was so close that this latitude appears also in the written language. Where one might say *have wrote* or *have written* with equal propriety,[59] as well as *housen* or *houses, shoon* or *shoes,* one must often have been in doubt over which to use. One heard *service* also pronounced *sarvice,* and the same variation occurred in a number of other words *(certain—sartin, concern—consarn, divert—divart, clerk—clark, smert—smart,* etc.). These and many other matters were still unsettled at the close of the period. Their settlement, as we shall see, was one of the chief concerns of the next age.

REFERENCES

1. See the history of attitudes toward English traced by Richard W.Bailey, *Images of English: A Cultural History of the Language* (Ann Arbor, MI, 1991).

2. *Proemio* to Book III of his *Della Famiglia (Opera Volgari di Leon Batt. Alberti* (5 vols., Florence, 1843-1849), II, 221-22). Cf. G.Mancini, *Vita di Leon Battista Alberti* (2nd ed., rev., Florence, 1911),p. 198.

3. There were some spellings about which he had apparently not made up his mind. He writes *borrowing* in three ways within a single paragraph.

4. *Op.cit.*

5. On Hart see Bror Danielsson, *John Hart's Works on English Orthography and Pronunciation* (2 vols., Stockholm, 1955-1964), a model of scholarly editing.

6. Bullokar's *Booke at Large* has been reprinted in facsimile with an introduction by Diane Bornstein (Delmar, NY, 1977).

7. ibid.

8. For a comprehensive account of the English orthoepists see E.J.Dobson, *English Pronunciation 1500-1700* (2 vols., 2nd ed., Oxford, 1968), vol. 1.

9. *Benevolent, enterprise, studious, endeavor, protest, reproach, malignity.* The statements in the text are based upon the dated citations in the *OED.* An earlier occurrence of any word is always possible. For example, in a translation by Skelton (c. 1485) of the *History of the World by* Diodorus Siculus, more than 800 Latin innovations occur, many earlier than the first instance recorded in the *OED.* But the work exists in a unique MS and has never been published. While its influence on the English language was probably negligible, it shows that the attitude of the sixteenth-century innovators was not without precedent. See F.M.Salter, *John Skelton's Contribution to the English Language* (Ottawa, 1945; *Trans. Royal Soc. of Canada).* The purpose of this and the following paragraphs, of course, is to record the efforts of Elyot and others to enrich the English language by the conscious importation of words that they believed were needed.

10. Weighing mentally (L. *expendere)*

11. Huge (L. *ingens)*

12. Attained (L. *adeptus)*

13. Mind, intellect (L. *ingenium)*

14. Brought (L. *accersitus)*

15. Aid (L. *adjuvare)*

16. Reduced to nothing (L. *ad nihil)*

17. Fellow-students

18. Companion
19. Call upon (L. *obtestari,* to call upon as a witness)
20. Procure (L. impetrare)
21. Recommend
22. Be watchful
23. House (L. *domus)*
24. Dedication to his translation of the *Aeneid* (1697).
25. In France the same argument was being employed: "To wish to take away from a learned man who desires to enrich his language the freedom sometimes to adopt uncommon words would be to restrain our language, not yet rich enough, under a more rigorous law than that which the Greek and Romans gave themselves" (Du Bellay, *Deffence et Illustration,* chap. 6).
26. Corruption by foreign elements.
27. An allusion to Cheke's statement quoted on page 217.
28. Edited by Sir Edward Sullivan (2 vols., London, 1925), Pettie's Preface.
29. In *Strange Newes, or Four Letters Confuted* (1592).
30. *Pierce's Supererogation* (1593).

8

The Importanceof Language in the Ninteenth Century

Influences Affecting the Language

The events of the nineteenth and twentieth centuries affecting the English-speaking countries have been of great political and social importance, but in their effect on the language they have not been revolutionary. The success of the British on the sea in the course of the Napoleonic Wars, culminating in Nelson's famous victory at Trafalgar in 1805, left England in a position of undisputed naval supremacy and gave it control over most of the world's commerce. The war against Russia in the Crimea (1854-1856) and the contests with princes in India had the effect of again turning English attention to the East. The great reform measures—the reorganization of parliament, the revision of the penal code and the poor laws, the restrictions placed on child labor, and the other industrial reforms—were important factors in establishing English society on a more democratic basis. They lessened the distance between the upper and the lower classes and greatly increased the opportunities for the mass of the population to share in the economic and cultural advantages that became available in the course of the century. The establishment of the first cheap newspaper (1816) and of cheap postage (1840) and the improved means of travel and communication brought about by the railroad, the steamboat, and the telegraph had the effect of uniting more closely the different parts of Britain and of spreading the influence of the standard speech. During the first half of the twentieth century the world wars and the troubled periods following them affected the life of almost everyone and left their mark on the language. At the same time, the growth in importance of some of England's larger colonies, their eventual in-dependence, and the rapid development of the United States have given increased significance to the forms of English spoken in these territories and have led their populations to the belief that their use of the language is as entitled to be considered a standard as that of Great Britain.

Some of these events and changes are reflected in the English vocabulary. But more influential in this respect are the great developments in science and the rapid progress that has been made in every field of intellectual activity in the last 200 years. Periods of great enterprise and activity seem generally to be accompanied by a corresponding increase in new words. This is the more true when all classes of the people participate in such activity, both in work and play, and share in its benefits. Accordingly, the great developments in industry, the increased public interest in sports and amusements, and the many improvements in the mode of living, in which even the humblest worker has shared, have all contributed to the vocabulary. The last two centuries offer an excellent opportunity to observe the relation between a civilization and the language which is an expression of it.

The Growth of Science

The most striking thing about our present-day civilization is probably the part that science has played in bringing it to pass. We have only to think of the progress that has been made in medicine and the sciences auxiliary to it, such as bacteriology, biochemistry, and the like, to realize the difference that marks off our own day from that of only a few generations ago in the diagnosis, treatment, prevention, and cure of disease. Or we may pause to reflect upon the relatively short period that separates the

Wright brothers, making history's first powered and controlled airplane flight, from the landings of astronauts on the moon, the operation of a space shuttle, and the voyages of spacecraft past the outer planets of the solar system. In every field of science, pure and applied, there has been need in the last two centuries for thousands of new terms. The great majority of these are technical words known only to the specialist, but a certain number of them in time become familiar to the layperson and pass into general use.

In the field of medicine this is particularly apparent. We speak familiarly of *anemia, appendicitis, arteriosclerosis,* difficult as the word is, of *bronchitis, diphtheria,* and numerous other diseases and ailments. We use with some sense of their meaning words like *bacteriology, immunology, orthodontics,* and the acronym *AIDS (acquired immune deficiency syndrome).* We maintain *clinics,* administer an *antitoxin* or an *anesthetic,* and *vaccinate* for smallpox. We have learned the names of drugs like *aspirin, iodine, insulin, morphine,* and we acquire without effort the names of antibiotics, such as *penicillin, streptomycin,* and a whole family of *sulfa* compounds. We speak of *adenoids, endocrine glands,* and *hormones* and know the uses of the *stethoscope,* the *EKG (electrocardiogram),* and the *CAT scan (computerized axial tomography).* We refer to the combustion of food in the body as *metabolism,* distinguish between *proteins* and *carbohydrates,* know that a dog can digest bones because he has certain *enzymes* or digestive fluids in his stomach, and say that a person who has the idiosyncrasy of being made ill by certain foods has an *allergy. Cholesterol* is now a part of everyone's vocabulary, and there is an awareness that some fats are *polyunsaturated.* All of these words have come into use during the nineteenth and, in some cases, the twentieth century.

In almost every other field of science the same story could be told. In the field of electricity words like *dynamo, commutator, alternating current, arc light* have been in the language since about 1870. Physics has made us familiar with terms like *calorie, electron, ionization, ultraviolet rays, quantum mechanics,* and *relativity,* though we don't always have an exact idea of what they mean. The development of *atomic energy* and *nuclear weapons* has given us *radioactive, hydrogen bomb, chain reaction, fallout,* and *meltdown.* In recent years *laser, superconducting supercollider, quasar,* and *pulsar* have come into common use; and *black holes, quarks,* the *big bang model,* and *superstrings* have captured the popular imagination. Chemistry has contributed so many common words that it is difficult to make a selection—*alkali, benzine, creosote, cyanide, formaldehyde, nitroglycerine, radium,* to say nothing of such terms as *biochemical, petrochemical,* and the like. The psychologist has taught us to speak of *schizophrenia, extrovert* and *introvert, behaviorism, inhibition, defense mechanism, inferiority complex, bonding,* and *psychoanalysis.* Originally scientific words and expressions such as *ozone, natural selection, stratosphere, DNA* (for *deoxyribonudeic acid)* became familiar through the popularity of certain books or scientific reports in magazines and newspapers. Among the most publicized events since the 1960s have been the achievements of space and engineering in the exploration of space. In addition to *astronaut* and *cosmonaut,* space science has given us dozens of new words, especially compounds like *spacecraft, space shuttle, launch pad, countdown, blast off, flyby, command module.* Consciously or unconsciously, we have become scientifically minded in the last few generations, and our vocabularies reflect this extension of our consciousness and interest.

Automobile, Film, Broadcasting, Computer

Scientific discoveries and inventions do not always influence the language in proportion to their importance. It is doubtful whether the radio and motion pictures are more important than the telephone, but they have brought more new words into general use. Such additions to the vocabulary depend more upon the degree to which the discovery or invention enters into the life of the community. This can be seen especially in the many new words or new uses of old words that have re-sulted from the popularity of the automobile and the numerous activities associated with it.

Many an old word is now used in a special sense. Thus we *park* a car, and the verb *to park* scarcely suggests to the average driver anything except leaving his or her car along the side of a street or road or in a *parking space.* But the word is an old one, used as a military term *(to park cannon)* and later in reference to carriages. The word *automobile* is new, but such words as *sedan (saloon* in Britain) and *coupe* are terms adapted from earlier types of vehicles. The American *truck* is the British *lorry* to which we may attach a *trailer.* We have learned new words or new meanings in *carburetor, spark plug* (British *sparking plug), choke, clutch, gearshift* (British *gear lever), piston rings, differential, universal, steering wheel, shock absorber, radiator, hood* (British *bonnet), windshield* (in Britain *windscreen), bumper, chassis, hubcap, power steering, automatic transmission,* and *turbocharger.* We engage *cruise control,* have a *blowout,* use *radial tires,* carry a *spare,* drive a *convertible* or *station wagon* (British *estate car),* and put the car in a *garage.* We may *tune up* the engine or *stall* it, or we may *skid, cut in, sideswipe* another car and be fined for *speeding* or running a *traffic light.* We must buy *gas* in America and *petrol* in Britain. Many more examples could be added to terms familiar to every motorist, to illustrate further what is already sufficiently clear, the way in which a new thing that becomes genuinely popular makes demands upon and extends the resources of the language.

The same principle might be illustrated by film, radio, and television. The words *cinema* and *moving picture* date from 1899, whereas the alternative *motion picture* is somewhat later. *Screen, reel, film, scenario, projector, closeup, fade-out* are now common, and although the popularity of *three-D* (or *3-D)* as a cinematic effect was short-lived, the word is still used. The word *radio* in the sense of a receiving station dates from about 1925, and we get the first hint of *television* as early as 1904. Since many of the terms from radio broadcasting were applicable in the later development of television, it is not surprising to find a common vocabulary of broadcasting that includes *broadcast* itself, *aerial, antenna, lead-in, loudspeaker, stand by,* and *solid-state.* Words like *announcer, reception, microphone,* and *transmitter* have acquired special meanings sometimes more common than their more general senses. The abbreviations FM (for *frequency modulation)* and *AM* (for *amplitude modulation)* serve regularly in radio broadcasting for the identification of stations, while terms associated with television include *cable TV, teleprompter, videotape, VCR,* and *DVD.* The related development of increasingly refined equipment for the recording of sound since Thomas Edison's invention of the *phonograph* in 1877 has made the general consumer aware of *stereo* and *stereophonic, quad* and *quadraphonic, tweeter, woofer, tape deck, reel-to-reel,* and *compact disc* or *CD.*

The first electronic digital computers date from Word War II, and a few terms have been in general use since then. New meanings of *program, language, memory,* and *hardware* are familiar to people who have never used a computer. With the widespread manufacturing and marketing of personal computers during the 1980s, a much larger number of English speakers found the need for computer terms in their daily work: *PC* itself, *RAM (random-access memory), ROM (read-only memory), DOS (disk operating system), microprocessor, byte, cursor, modem, software, hacker, hard-wired, download,* and new meanings of *read, write, mouse, terminal, chip, network, workstation, windows,* and *virus.* The use of *bug* for a problem in running a computer program is sometimes traced in computer lore to an actual moth residing in the Mark II at Harvard in 1945. It was discovered by Grace Hopper and is taped in the logbook for September 9, 1945. As it turns out, however, the 1972 Supplement to the *OED* records *bug* for a problem in technology as early as 1889, by Thomas Edison working on his phonograph. Admiral Hopper may have a stronger claim to the first use of *debug.*

The World Wars

As another example of how great developments or events leave their mark upon language we may observe some of the words that came into English between 1914 and 1918 as a direct consequence of World War I. Some of these were military terms representing new methods of warfare, such as *air raid, antiaircraft gun, tank,* and *blimp. Gas mask* and *liaison officer* were new combinations with a military significance. *Camouflage* was borrowed from French, where it had formerly been a term of the scene-painter's craft, but it caught the popular fancy and was soon used half facetiously for various forms of disguise or misrepresentation. Old words were in some cases adapted to new uses. *Sector* was used in the sense of a specific portion of the fighting line; *barrage,* originally an artificial barrier like a dam in a river, designated a protective screen of heavy artillery or machine-gun fire; *dud,* a general word for any counterfeit thing, was specifically applied to a shell that did not explode; and *ace* acquired the meaning of a crack airman, especially one who had brought down five of the enemy's planes. In a number of cases a word that had had only limited circulation in the language now came into general use. Thus *hand grenade* goes back to 1661 but attained new currency during the war. Other expressions already in the language but popularized by the war were *dugout, machine gun, periscope, no man's land,* and even the popular designation of an American soldier, *doughboy,* which was in colloquial use in the United States as early as 1867. *Blighty was* a popular bit of British army slang, derived from India and signifying Britain or home, and was often applied to a wound that sent a man back to Britain. Other expressions such as *slacker, trench foot, cootie,* and *war bride* were either struck off in the heat of the moment or acquired a poignant significance from the circumstances under which they were used.

It would seem that World War II was less productive of memorable words, as it was of memorable songs. Nevertheless it made its contribution to the language in the form of certain new words, new meanings, or an increased currency for expressions that had been used before. In connection with the *air raid,* so prominent a feature of the war, we have the words and expressions *alert* (air-raid warning), *blackout, blitz* (German *Blitzkrieg,* literally 'lightning war'), *blockbuster, dive-bombing, evacuate,* air-raid *shelter.* The words *beachhead, parachutist, paratroop, landing strip, crash landing, roadblock, jeep, fox hole* (as a shelter for one or two men), *bulldozer* (an American word used in a new sense), *decontamination, task force* (a military or naval unit assigned to the carrying out of a particular operation), *resistance movement,* and *radar* are not in the first edition of the *OED* or its 1933 Supplement. *To spearhead* an attack, *to mop up,* and *to appease* were new verbs or old verbs with a new military or political significance. *Flak* (antiaircraft fire) was taken over from German, where it is an abbreviation of *Fliegerabwehrkanone,* 'antiaircraft gun'. *Commando,* a word that goes back to the Boer War, acquired a new and specialized meaning. Some words that were either new or that enjoyed great currency during the war—*priority, tooling up, bottleneck, ceiling* (upper limit), *backlog, stockpile*—have become a part of the vocabulary of civilian life, while *lend-lease* has passed into history. The aftermath of the war gave us such expressions as *iron curtain, cold war, fellow traveler, front organization, police state,* all with a very special connotation.

Language as a Mirror of Progress

Words, being but symbols by which people express their ideas, are an accurate measure of the range of their thoughts at any given time. Words obviously designate the things a culture knows, and just as obviously the vocabulary of a language must keep pace with the advance of the culture's knowledge. The date when a new word enters the language is in general the date when the object, experience, observation, or whatever it is that calls it forth has entered public consciousness. Thus with a work like the *OED,* which furnishes us with dated quotations showing when the different meanings of every word have arisen and when new words first appear in the language, we could almost write the history of civilization merely from linguistic evidence. When in the early part of the nineteenth century we find growing up a word like *horsepower* or *lithograph,* we may depend upon it that some form of mechanical power that needs to be measured in familiar terms or a new process of engraving has been devised. The appearance in the language of words like *railway, locomotive, turntable* about 1835 tells us that steam railways were then coming in. In 1839 the words *photograph* and *photography* first appear, and a beginning is made toward a considerable vocabulary of special words or senses of words such as *camera, film, enlargement, emulsion, focus, shutter, light meter. Concrete* in the sense of a mixture of crushed stone and cement dates from 1834, but *reinforced concrete* is an expression called forth only in the twentieth century. The word *cable* occurs but a few years before the laying of the first Atlantic cable in 1857-1858. *Refrigerator* is first found in English in an American quotation of 1841. The words *emancipation* and *abolitionist* have for every American specific meanings connected with the efforts to abolish slavery, efforts that culminated in the Civil War. In the last quarter of the nineteenth century an interesting story of progress is told by new words or new meanings such as *typewriter, telephone, apartment house, twist drill, drop-forging, blueprint, oilfield, motorcycle, feminist, fundamentalist, marathon* (introduced in 1896 as a result of the revival of the Olympic games at Athens in that year), *battery* and *bunt,* the last two indicating the growing popularity of professional baseball in America.

The twentieth century permits us to see the process of vocabulary growth going on under our eyes, sometimes, it would seem, at an accelerated rate. At the turn of the century we get the word *questionnaire,* and in 1906 *suffragette. Dictaphone, raincoat,* and *Thermos* became a part of the recorded vocabulary in 1907 and *free verse* in 1908. This is the period when many of the terms of aviation came in, some still current, some reflecting the aeronautics of the time—*airplane, aircraft, airman, monoplane, biplane, hydroplane, dirigible. Nose-dive* belongs to the period of the war. About 1910 we began talking about the *futurist* and the *postimpressionist* in art, and the *Freudian* in psychology. *Intelligentsia* as a designation for the class to which superior culture is attributed, and *bolshevik* for a holder of revolutionary political views were originally applied at the time of World War I to groups in Russia. At this time *profiteer* gained a specialized meaning. Meanwhile *foot fault, fairway, fox trot,* and *contract bridge* were indicative of popular interest in certain games and pastimes. The 1933 supplement to the *OED* records *Cellophane* (1921) and *rayon* (1924), but not *nylon, deep-freeze, air-conditioned,* or *transistor;* and it is not until the first volume of the new supplement in 1972 that the *OED* includes *credit card, ecosystem, existentialism* (1941, though in German a century earlier), *freeze-dried, convenience foods, bionics, electronic computer, automation, cybernetics, bikini, discotheque.* Only yesterday witnessed the birth of *biofeedback, power lunch, fractal, chaos theory,* and *cyberspace.* Tomorrow will witness others as the exigencies of the hour call them into being.

Sources of the New Words : Borrowings

Most of the new words coming into the language since 1800 have been derived from the same sources or created by the same methods as those that have long been familiar, but it will be convenient to examine them here as an illustration of the processes by which a language extends its vocabulary. It should be remembered that the principles are not new, that what has been going on in the last century and a half could be paralleled from almost any period of the language.

As is to be expected in the light of the English disposition to borrow words from other languages in the past, many of the new words have been taken over ready-made from the people from whom the idea or the thing designated has been obtained. Thus from the French come *apéritif, chauffeur, chiffon, consommé, garage;* from Italian come *ciao, confetti,* and *vendetta,* and from Spanish, *bonanza, canyon, patio, rodeo, barrio, machismo,* and *cantina.* In the Southwestern United States and increasingly throughout the country, the dinner table is enriched and spiced by borrowings from Mexican Spanish. Although *chili* has been in the language since the seventeenth century, most of the culinary terms date from the modern period: *enchilada, fajita, jalapeño, nachos, taco, tortilla, tostada;* and through Spanish from the Native American language Nahuatl, *guacamole* and *tamale.* German has given us *angst, festschrift, gestalt, schadenfreude, weltanschauung, zeitgeist,* and *zither.* From Russia have come *troika, vodka,* and, with momentous political and economic changes, *glasnost* and *perestroika*. *Goulash* is a Magyar word, and *robot* is from Czech. Asia is represented by *karma, loot,* and *thug* from India; *pajamas* (British *pyjamas)* from Persia; *yin, yang, t'ai chi,* and *chow mein* from China; and *geisha, haiku, Noh, sake, samurai, sayonara, shogun, sushi, soy,* and *yen* from Japan. The cosmopolitan character of the English vocabulary, already pointed out, is thus being maintained, and we shall see in the next chapter that America has added many other foreign words, particularly from Spanish and the languages of the Native Americans.

Self-explaining Compounds

A second source of new words is represented in the practice of making self-explaining compounds, one of the oldest methods of word formation in the language. In earlier editions of this book such words as *fingerprint* (in its technical sense), *fire extinguisher, hitchhike, jet propulsion,* the colloquial *know-how, lipstick, steamroller, steam shovel,* and *streamline* were mentioned as being rather new. They have now passed into such common use that they no longer carry any sense of novelty. This will probably happen, indeed has already happened, to some of the more recent formations that can be noted, such as *skydiving, jet lag, house sitter, lifestyle, hatchback, greenhouse effect, acid rain, roller blades, junk food, e-mail,* and the metaphorical *glass ceiling.* Many of these betray their newness by being written with a hyphen or as separate words, or by preserving a rather strong accent on each element. They give unmistakable testimony to the fact that the power to combine existing words into new ones expressing a single concept, a power that was so prominent a feature of Old English, still remains with us.

Compounds Formed from Greek and Latin Elements

The same method may be employed in forming words from elements derived from Latin and Greek. The large classical element already in the English vocabulary makes such formations seem quite congenial to the language, and this method has long been a favorite source of scientific terms. Thus *eugenics* is formed from two Greek roots, ευ)—meaning *well,* and γεν —meaning *to be born.* The word therefore means *well-born* and is applied to the efforts to bring about well-born offspring by the selection of healthy parents. The same root enters into *genetics*, the experimental study of heredity and allied topics. In the words *stethoscope, bronchoscope, fluoroscope,* and the like we have -*scope,* which appears in *telescope.* It is a Greek word σκοποζ meaning a *watcher.* Just as τηλε in Greek means *far* and enters into such words as *telephone, telescope, television,* and the like, so we have *stethoscope* with the first element from Greek στηθος (breast or chest), *bronchoscope* from Greek ßñóã÷oò (windpipe), and *fluoroscope* with the same

first element as in *fluorine* (from Latin *fluere,* to flow). *Panchromatic* comes from the Greek words παν (all) and χρωματικος; (relating to color), and is thus used in photography to describe a plate or film that is sensitive to all colors. An *automobile* is something that moves of itself (Greek αντος self +Latin *mobilis* 'movable'). *Orthodontia* is from Greek αντος'straight' and οδονς (οδοντ) thus describes the branch of dentistry that endeavors to straighten irregular teeth. A few minutes spent in looking up recent scientific words in any dictionary will supply abundant illustrations of this common method of English word formation.

Prefixes and Suffixes

Another method of enlarging the vocabulary is by appending familiar prefixes and suffixes to existing words on the pattern of similar words in the language. Several of the Latin prefixes seem to lend themselves readily to new combinations. Thus in the period under discussion we have formed *transoceanic, transcontinental, trans-Siberian, transliterate, transformer,* and several more or less technical terms such as *transfinite, transmarine, transpontine,* etc. We speak of *postimpressionists* in art, *postprandial* oratory, the *postclassical* period, and *postgraduate* study. In the same way we *use pre-* in such words as *prenatal, preschool* age, *prehistoric, pre-Raphaelite, preregistration:* we may *preheat* or *precool* in certain technical processes: and passengers who need more time may *preboard.* In film parlance we may have a *preview,* a *prerelease,* or even a *prequel.* From World War I came *counterattack* and from World War II *counterintelligence.* In his *Man and Superman* Bernard Shaw coined the word *superman* to translate the German *Übermensch* of Nietzschian philosophy. We *subirrigate* and build a *subcellar,* and foreign movies sometimes come to us with *subtitles.* We can *decode* a message, *defrost* a refrigerator, *deflate* the currency, and we may *debunk* a statement, *debug a* machine, and *decaffeinate* coffee. It is so also with suffixes. Twentieth-century popular creations on old patterns are *stardom, filmdom, fandom, gangster, pollster, profiteer, racketeer.* Familiar endings like *-some, -ful, -less* can be freely added in accordance with longstanding habits in the language.

Coinages

A considerable number of new words must be attributed to deliberate invention or coinage. There has probably never been a time when the creative impulse has not spent itself occasionally in inventing new words, but their chances of general adoption are nowadays often increased by a campaign of advertising as deliberate as the effort that created them. They are mostly the product of ingenuity and imitation, the two being blended in variable proportions. Thus the trademark *Kodak,* which seems to be pure invention, was popularly used for years to refer to cameras of any brand, and *Victrola* and *Frigidaire* enjoyed something of the same currency as synonyms for *phonograph* and *refrigerator. Kleenex* and *Xerox* are trade terms that are often treated as common nouns, and *Zipper,* a word coined by the B.F. Goodrich Company and registered in 1925 as the name for a boot fitted with a slide fastener, has become the universal name for the fastener itself. Words formed by combining the initial or first few letters of two or more words are known as acronyms. *Radar* (radio detecting and ranging) is an example, as are *scuba* (self-contained underwater breathing apparatus) and OPEC (Organization of Petroleum Exporting Countries).[1] In deliberate coinages there is often an analogy with some other word or words in the language. This is felt, consciously or unconsciously, to be desirable. It permits the meaning more easily to be guessed at, reveals a mild degree of ingenuity on the part of the inventor, and focuses the attention on the distinctive syllable or syllables. *Mazola* obviously refers to *maize* and *oil,* and *Sine-off* in addition to its reference to sinuses evokes associations with "signing off" in broadcasting or going to sleep. *Dictaphone* combines elements found in the words *dictate* and *telephone,* just as *travelogue* is a cross between *travel* and *dialogue. Bureaucrat* and *plutocrat* are obviously formed on the model of *aristocrat, autocrat,* etc., as *electrocute* is modeled after *execute.* Sometimes a Latin formative element is used and the new word has a rather specious classical air, as in *novocaine* from Latin *novus* (new) grafted upon the English word *cocaine.*

Words such as *electrocute* or *travelogue* are often called *portmanteau* words, or better, *blends.2* In them two words are, as it were, telescoped into one. This was a favorite pastime of the author of *Alice in Wonderland,* and to him we owe the words *chortle,* a blending of *snort* and *chuckle,* and *snark* (snake+shark). Similarly, the tunnel beneath the English Channel is called the *Chunnel.* Often such coinages are formed with a playful or humorous intent. The *OED* records *brunch* in the year 1900. Although it was originally used facetiously in speaking of those who get up too late for breakfast and therefore combine breakfast and lunch, it is now as likely to be used for the name of a social occasion. *Paradoxology, alcoholiday, revusical, yellocution, guestimate, condomania, ecopolypse,* and the like, often reveal flashes of wit. They carry a momentary appeal, like the coinages of *Time* magazine *(cinemactress, cinemaddict, cinemagnate),* but only a few of them—*socialite* for one—are likely to find a permanent place in the language. Like epigrams they lose their luster when passed about at second hand.

Common Words from Proper Names

Another source from which many English words have been derived in the past is the names of persons and places. For example, *sandwich* owes its use to the fact that the earl of Sandwich on one occasion put slices of meat between pieces of bread. Like other processes of English word derivation this can be well illustrated in the nineteenth century and later. Thus we get the word for *tabasco* sauce from the name of the Tabasco River in Mexico. *Camembert* comes from the village in France from which cheese of this type was originally exported. A *limousine* is so called from the name of a province in France, and during the 1920s the American city Charleston gave its name to a dance. The word *colt* for a certain kind of firearm is merely the name of the inventor. *Wistaria,* the vine whose most common variety is now known as *wisteria,* is named after Caspar Wistar, an American anatomist of the mid-1800s. In 1880 Captain Boycott, the agent of an Irish landowner, refused to accept rents at the figure set by the tenants. His life was threatened, his servants were forced to leave, and his figure was burnt in effigy. Hence from Ireland came the use of the verb *to boycott,* meaning to coerce a person by refusing to have, and preventing others from having, dealings with him. Similarly, *lynch law* owes its origin to Captain William Lynch of Virginia, about 1776, and in the early nineteenth century we find the verb *to lynch. Shrapnel* is from the name of the British general who invented the type of missile. More than 500 common words in English have been traced to proper names, and they must be considered as illustrating one of the sources from which new words are still being derived.

Old Words with New Meanings

The resources of the vocabulary are sometimes extended from within by employment of an old word in a new sense. We have already seen many examples of this in some of the paragraphs preceding, especially many of the words now applied to the automobile and the computer. But the process can be widely illustrated, for it is one of the commonest phenomena in language. *Skyline* formerly meant the horizon, but it is now more common in such an expression as the New York *skyline. Broadcast* originally had reference to seed, but its application to radio seems entirely appropriate. A *record may* be many other things than a phonograph disc, and *radiator was* used for anything that radiated heat or light before it was applied specifically to steam heat or the automobile. *Cabaret* is an old word meaning a booth or shed, and later a small drinking place. Today it signifies a certain type of nightclub. We *sign off or stand by*in broadcasting, *take off in* an airplane, *kick off* in football, *call up* on the telephone, and in each of these cases we convey a specific, often technical meaning, quite different from the sense that these expressions previously had.

A certain amount of experimenting with words is constantly going on, and at times the new use of a word may meet with opposition. Many people still object to the use of *contact as* a verb, and *impact* has drawn similar criticism (as in "The needs of industry have impacted the university's graduate program"). The shift in transitivity of verbs often meets with resistance: *transform* as intransitive ("He transformed into a hero") or *commit* as intransitive ("The player wouldn't commit to the team"). It is well to remember that Swift objected to *behave* without the reflexive pronoun. Time will decide the fate of these words, but whether or not the new uses establish themselves in the language, they must be considered as exemplifying a well-recognized phenomenon in the behavior of words.

The Influence of Journalism

In the introduction and popularizing of new words journalism has been a factor of steadily increasing importance. Newspapers and popular magazines not only play a large part in spreading new locutions among the people but are themselves fertile producers of new words. Reporters necessarily write under pressure and have not long to search for the right word. In the heat of the moment they are likely as not to strike off a new expression or wrench the language to fit their ideas. In their effort to be interesting and racy they adopt an informal and colloquial style, and many of the colloquialisms current in popular speech find their way into writing first in the magazine and the newspaper. In this way we have come to *back* a horse or a candidate, to *boost* our community, *comb* the woods for a criminal, *hop* the Atlantic, *oust* a politician, and *spike* a rumor, and we speak of a *probe*, a *cleanup*, a business *deal*, a *go-between*. Sportswriters are often hard pressed to avoid monotony in their descriptions of similar contests day after day, and in their desire to be picturesque they seldom feel any scruple about introducing the latest slang in their particular field of interest. Many an expression originating in the sports page has found its way into general use. We owe *neck and neck* and *out of the running*to the race track, and *sidestep, down and out, straight from the shoulder,* and many other expressions to boxing. In America we owe *caught napping* and *off base* to baseball. If some of these locutions are older than the newspaper, there can be no question but that today much similar slang is given currency through this medium. Several magazines make the use of verbal novelties a feature of their style with puns, rhymes, coinages *(nobelity* for winners of a Nobel prize, *jeerworthy),* strings of hyphenated words (from one short review: *zillion-dollar, double-dome, dimbulbed, dog-stealing, summer-stocked)*, and many other examples of the search for novelty.

Changes of Meaning

It is necessary to say something about the way in which words gradually change their meaning. That words do undergo such change is a fact readily perceived, and it can be illustrated from any period of the language. That we should choose to illustrate it by more or less recent examples is a matter merely of convenience. Differences of meaning are more readily perceived when they affect current use. It should be clearly recognized, however, that the tendencies here discussed are universal in their application and are not confined to the twentieth century or to the English language. They will be found at work in every language and at all times. The branch of linguistic study that concerns itself with the meanings of words and the way meanings develop is known as *semantics.*

It has been observed that in their sense development, words often pursue certain well-marked tendencies. Among the more common of these are *extension* of meaning, *narrowing* of meaning, *degeneration,* and *regeneration.* By *extension of meaning* is meant the widening of a word's signification until it covers much more than the idea originally conveyed. The tendency is sometimes called *generalization.* The word *lovely,* for example, means primarily worthy to be loved, and *great* means large in size, the opposite of *small.* But today *lovely* and *great* have no such meaning. A box of candy or a chair may be *lovely,* and anything from a ball game to the weather may be *great.* When a college student says that a certain book is *great,* it is more than likely that the statement has nothing to do with the value of the book judged as a work of art but simply means that he or she thoroughly enjoyed it. In everyday use these words have come to express only enthusiastic approval of a rather vague sort. The word *proposition* primarily means a statement set forth for purposes of discussion, or in mathematics, for demonstration. It was so used by Lincoln in his Gettysburg Address: "a new nation...dedicated to the proposition that all men are created equal." But in America during the last century it began to be used more loosely. Owen Wister says in *The Virginian,* "Proposition in the West does, in fact, mean whatever you at the moment please." "That's a different *proposition*" expresses an idea that in more formal English becomes "That's a different matter" (an equally general word). The word is often accompanied by an adjective: *a tough proposition; he was the coolest proposition I ever met.* All of these uses are distinctly colloquial and are not accepted in England, but they illustrate the principle of generalization. A more acceptable illustration is the word *dean.* It has, of course, its proper meanings, such as the head of the chapter in a cathedral church or the head of the faculty in a college. But it has come to be used as a designation for the senior or foremost person of any group or class, so that we may speak of the *dean* of American critics or, indeed, of sportswriters.

The opposite tendency is for a word gradually to acquire a more *restricted sense,* or to be chiefly used in one special connection. A classic example of this practice is the word *doctor.* There are doctors (i.e., learned men and women) in theology, law, and many other fields beside medicine, but nowadays when we send for *the* doctor we mean a member of only one profession. In some of the preceding paragraphs, especially that in which were presented examples of old words in new meanings, will be found a number of similar instances. The verb to *park* as applied to automobiles and the war word *tank* are cases in point. The use of a word in a restricted sense does not preclude its use also in other meanings. There was a time in the 1890s when the word *wheel* suggested to most people a bicycle, but it could still be used of the wheel of a cart or a carriage. Often the restricted sense of a word belongs to a special or class vocabulary. An *enlargement* means to a photographer a large print made from a small negative, and in educational circles a *senior* is a member of the graduating class. Consequently, it sometimes happens that the same word will acquire different restricted meanings for different people. The word *gas* is an inclusive term for the chemist, but it calls up a more restricted idea in the kitchen and a still different one in the garage. Narrowing of meaning may be confined to one locality under the influence of local conditions. *Nickel* in America means a coin, and for a number of years the word *prohibition* in this country generally suggested the prohibition of alcohol. In the same way the terms *democrat* and *republican* seldom have their broader significance to an American but rather imply adherence to one or the other of the two chief political parties in the United States.

Degeneration of meaning may take several forms. It may take the form of the gradual extension to so many senses that any particular meaning which a word may have had is completely lost. This is one form of generalization already illustrated in the words *lovely* and *great.3 Awful* and *terrible* have undergone a similar deterioration. In other cases a word has retained a very specific meaning but a less favorable one than it originally had. Phillips in his *New World of Words* (1658) defines *garble* as "to purifie, to sort out the bad from the good, an expression borrowed from Grocers, who are said to garble their Spices, i.e. to purifie them from the dross and dirt." The word was still used in this sense down through the eighteenth century and even beyond. But in the time of Johnson it occasionally carried the implication of selecting in an unfair or dishonest way, and as used today it always signifies the intentional or unintentional mutilation of a statement so that a different meaning is conveyed from that intended. *Smug* was originally a good word, meaning neat or trim; its present suggestion of objectionable self-satisfaction seems to have grown up during the nineteenth century. The same thing is true of *vulgar* in the meaning bordering on obscene, and of *pious* in its contemptuous sense. *Amateur* and *dilettante* now imply inexpertness or superficiality, although the former word still conveys a favorable idea when applied to athletics. In England one speaks only of *insects,* since the word *bug* has degenerated to the specialized meaning "bedbug." A very interesting form of degeneration often occurs in words associated with things that it is not considered polite to talk about. In 1790 the satirist Peter Pindar wrote:

> I've heard that breeches, petticoats and smock, Give to thy modest mind a grievous shock And that thy brain (so lucky its device) Christ'neth them *inexpressibles so* nice.[4]

Thus the common word for a woman's undergarment down to the eighteenth century was *smock.* It was then replaced by the more delicate word *shift.* In the nineteenth century the same motive led to the substitution of the word *chemise,* and in the late twentieth century, after various other euphemisms have come and gone, including *combinations* and *step-ins,* the usual words are *bra, panties,* and *slip* (the last of which referred to an outer garment in the eighteenth century and an undergarment as early as the mid-nineteenth). Changing attitudes toward this part of the vocabulary may halt the process of degeneration and give a longer life to those terms currently in use.

If words sometimes go downhill, they also undergo the opposite process, known as *regeneration.* Words like *budge, coax, nonplus, shabby, squabble, stingy, tiff, touchy, wobbfy,* which were recorded with proper disparagement by Dr. Johnson, have since passed into the standard speech. In the eighteenth century *snob* and *sham were* slang, but in the nineteenth they attained respectability, the former word partly through the influence of Thackeray. The word *sturdy* originally meant harsh, rough, or intractable. We now use it in a wholly complimentary sense. Even the word *smock,* which was mentioned above as losing caste in the eighteenth century, has now been rehabilitated as applied to an outer garment. We use it for a certain type of woman's dress and we speak of an artist's smock. The changes of meaning that words undergo are but another evidence of the constant state of flux that characterizes the living language.

Slang

All the types of semantic change discussed in the preceding paragraph could be illustrated from that part of the vocabulary which at any given time is considered slang. It is necessary to say "at any given time" not only because slang is fleeting and the life of a slang expression likely to be short, but also because what is slang today may have been in good use yesterday and may be accepted in the standard speech of tomorrow. Slang has been aptly described as "a peculiar kind of vagabond language, always hanging on the outskirts of legitimate speech, but continually straying or forcing its way into the most respectable company."[5] Yet it is a part of language and cannot be ignored. One of the developments that must certainly be credited to the nineteenth century is the growth of a more objective and scientific attitude toward this feature of language. The word *slang* does not occur in Johnson's *Dictionary.* It first occurs a few years later and in its early use always has a derogatory force. Webster in 1828 defines it as "low, vulgar, unmeaning language." But the definition in the *Oxford Dictionary,* expressing the attitude of 1911, is very different: "Language of a highly colloquial type, below the level of standard educated speech, and consisting either of new words, or of current words employed in some special sense." Here slang goes from being "unmeaning language" to having a "special sense," and it is treated frankly as a scientific fact.

One reason why slang cannot be ignored even by the strictest purist is that it has not infrequently furnished expressions that the purist uses without suspecting their origin. Even students of language are constantly surprised when they come across words that they use naturally and with entire propriety but find questioned or condemned by writers of a generation or a few generations before. The expression *what on earth* seems to us an idiomatic intensive and certainly would not be objected to in the speech of anyone today. But De Quincey condemned it as slang and expressed horror at hearing it used by a government official. The word *row* in the sense of a disturbance or commotion was slang in the eighteenth century and described by Todd (1818) as "a very low expression," but today we find it in the works of reputable writers as a word that fittingly suggests the qualities of a vulgar brawl. *Boom, slump, crank,* and *fad,* in becoming respectable, have acquired an exact and sometimes technical meaning. Even the harmless word *joke* was once slang.

In surveying contemporary English, not only do we have to consider the slang that has lifted itself into the level of educated speech but we must recognize the part played by slang in its own character. For there is hardly a person who does not make use of it upon occasion. Slang results from an instinctive desire for freshness and novelty of expression. Naturally the less a person is inclined to submit to the restraints imposed by a formal standard, the more ready he or she is to accept indiscriminately the newest slang locution. *To criticize* seems to the person in the street tame and colorless, if not stilted, so *to bad-mouth* is substituted. For the same reason a person who fails to keep an engagement with another person *stands him up.* Since novelty is a quality that soon wears off, slang has to be constantly renewed. *Vamoose, skedaddle, twenty-three skiddoo, beat it, scram, buzz off* have all had their periods of popularity in the twentieth century as expressions of roughly the same idea, usually in imperative form. It can hardly be denied that some slang expressions, while they are current, express an idea that it would be difftcult to convey by other means. *Nerd, geek, dweeb, dork, bimbo,* and *scumbag* undoubtedly owe their popularity to some merit that is recognized by a sure instinct among the people. It is sometimes difficult to define the precise quality that makes an expression slang. It is often not in the word itself, but in the sense in which it is used. *Put down* is proper enough if we speak of soldiers who put down a rebellion, but it is slang when we speak of a remark that *put someone down* or refer to the remark as a *put-down.*

It is dangerous to generalize about the relative prominence of slang in this and former times. But it would seem as though the role it plays today is greater than it has been at certain times in the past, say in the Elizabethan age or the eighteenth century, to judge by the conversation of plays and popular fiction. The cultivation of slang has become a feature of certain types of popular writing. We think of men like George Ade, who wrote *Fables in Slang,* or Ring Lardner or O.Henry. They are not only the creators of locutions that have become part of the slang of the day, but they have popularized this outer fringe of the colloquial and given it greater currency. It would certainly be an incomplete picture of the language of today that failed to include slang as a present feature and a source from which English will doubtless continue to be fed in the future.

Cultural Levels and Functional Varieties

The discussion of slang has clearly indicated that there is more than one type of speech. Within the limits of any linguistic unity there are as many language levels as there are groups of people thrown together by propinquity and common interests. Beyond the limits of the general language there are local and class dialects, technical and occupational vocabularies, slang, and other forms of speech. Even within the region of the common language from which these are diverging forms it is possible to distinguish at least three broad types.

Occupying a sort of middle ground is the *spoken standard.* It is the language heard in the conversation of educated people. It is marked by conformity to the rules of grammar and to certain considerations of taste that are not easily defined but are present in the minds of those who are conscious of their speech. Whatever its dialectal coloring or qualities varying with the particular circumstances involved, it is free from features that are regarded as substandard in the region. To one side of this spoken standard lies the domain of the *written standard.* This is the language of books, and it ranges from the somewhat elevated style of poetry to that of simple but cultivated prose. It may differ both in vocabulary and idiom from the spoken standard, although the two frequently overlap. When we say *big time* and write *to a superlative degree* we are making a conscious choice between these two functional varieties. In the other direction we pass from one cultural level to another, from the spoken standard to the region of *popular* or *illiterate speech*. This is the language of those who are ignorant of or indifferent to the ideals of correctness by which the educated are governed. It is especially sympathetic to all sorts of neologisms and generally is rich in slang.

While the three types—the literary standard, the spoken standard, and popular speech—are easily recognized, it is not possible to draw a sharp line of demarcation between them. To a certain extent they run into one another. The spoken standard itself covers a wide range of usage. In speech suitable to formal occasions the spoken standard approaches the written standard, whereas in easy and relaxed conversation it may tend in the direction of its more unconventional neighbor. Some interchange between one type and the next is constantly going on. The written and the spoken standards have been drawing appreciably closer, possibly because reading is such a widespread accomplishment today, possibly because we have come to feel that the simplest and best prose is that which most resembles the easy and natural tone of cultivated speech. In the same way words and locutions current among the masses sometimes find their way into the lower reaches of the spoken standard. This is particularly true of slang. One may reason that when slang is acceptable to those who in general conform to the spoken standard it should no longer be called slang. But such a conclusion is hardly justified. It is better to hold that there are different levels in slang, and that some use of slang is rhetorically effective in the conversation of most educated speakers.

It is necessary to recognize that from a linguistic point of view each of the varieties— whether of cultural level or degree of formality—has its own right to exist. If we judge them simply on their capacity to express ideas clearly and effectively, we must admit that one kind of English is seldom superior to another. I *seen it* and I *knowed it* may not conform to the standard of correctness demanded of cultivated speech, but these expressions convey their meaning just as clearly as the standard forms and historically are no worse than dozens of others now in accepted use. Likewise much could be said, historically and logically, for *ain 't* and the double negative. It is rather in their social implications that the varieties of English differ. The difference between the spoken standard and popular speech is in their association with broadly different classes. As Bernard Shaw once remarked, "People know very well that certain sorts of speech cut off a person for ever from getting more than three or four pounds a week all their life long—sorts of speech which make them entirely impossible in certain professions." Statements such as Shaw's reporting a bias against certain ways of speaking and the practical economic effect of that bias have been made by enlightened linguists who do not share the bias at all and who aim to remedy its practical effect. However, the topic is fraught with pitfalls for well-meaning observers and authorities, and the movement for bidialectalism during the 1960s was criticized on these grounds.[7] James Milroy cites ostensibly objective studies of linguistic variation and says of their treatment: "This has the effect of marginalizing non-standard vernaculars—appearing to present them as abnormal or pathological language states—when the majority of human beings throughout history must have used varieties that were, to a greater or lesser extent, nonstandard."[8] Thus, the tendency of the historical linguist is often to present the development of the language retrospectively as a uniform dialect proceeding in a straight line toward Received Standard English. The implicit ideology of the dispassionate and scientific study of the language may inadvertently reinforce the very bias that the linguists criticize as naïve and unfortunate. The irony is especially acute if the speaker of the standard variety happens to be pretentious or prolix. Listeners even of the same social class may find the speech of one who employs language of the literary variety in their conversation, who talks like a book, an obstacle to free intercourse, because they associate such language with stiff and pedantic qualities of mind or a lack of social ease. In this case what is objected to has clearly nothing to do with the question of correctness. It is a question merely of appropriateness to the occasion. As in numerous other linguistic matters, we have come in recent times to look upon the different types of speech more tolerantly, to recognize them as one of the phenomena of language. We do not expect (or wish) people to talk like Matthew Arnold, and we do not include in a sweeping condemnation all those who fail to conform to the spoken standard of the educated. In recent years a sometimes strident discussion among linguists and sociologists has dealt with the relations between the standard dialects of the middle classes and the nonstandard dialects of lower socioeconomic groups. African American Vernacular English in the United States presents especially vexed questions for the educational system and society as a whole (see § 250.8). The issues are finally economic, political, and psychological in a debate that seems far from arriving at a satisfactory resolution.

The Standard Speech

The spoken standard or, as it is called in Britain, *Received Pronunciation*, often abbreviated RP, is something that varies in different parts of the English-speaking world. In Britain it is a type of English perhaps best exemplified in the speech of those educated in the great public schools but spoken also with a fair degree of uniformity by cultivated people in all parts of the country. It is a class rather than a regional dialect. This is not the same as the spoken standard of the United States or Canada or Australia. The spread of English to many parts of the world has changed our conception of what constitutes Standard English. The growth of countries like the United States and Canada and the political independence of countries that were once British colonies force us to admit that the educated speech of these vast areas is just as "standard" as that of London or Oxford. It is perhaps inevitable that people will feel a preference for the pronunciation and forms of expression that they are accustomed to, but to criticize the British for omitting many of their *r's* or the Americans for pronouncing them betrays an equally unscientific provincialism irrespective of which side of the Atlantic indulges in the criticism. The hope is sometimes expressed that we might have a world standard to which all parts of the English-speaking world would try to conform. So far as the spoken language is concerned it is too much to expect that the marked differences of pronunciation that distinguish the speech of, let us say, Britain, Australia, India, and the United States will ever be reduced to one uniform mode. We must recognize that in the last 200 years English has become a cosmopolitan tongue and must cultivate a cosmopolitan attitude toward its various standard forms.[9]

English Dialects

In addition to the educated standard in each major division of the English-speaking world there are local forms of the language known as regional dialects. In the newer countries where English has spread in modern times these are not so numerous or so pronounced in their individuality as they are in the British Isles. The English introduced into the colonies was a mixture of dialects in which the peculiarities of each were fused in a common speech. Except perhaps in the United States, there has scarcely been time for new regional differences to grow up, and although one region is sometimes separated from another by the breadth of a continent, the improvements in transportation and communication have tended to keep down differences that might otherwise have arisen. But in Great Britain such differences are very great. They go back to the earliest period of the language and reflect conditions that prevailed at a time when travel was difficult and communication was limited between districts relatively close together. Even among the educated the speech of northern England differs considerably from that of the south. In words such as *butter, cut, gull,* and *some* the southern vowel [Ë] occurs in the north as [U], and in *chaff, grass,* and *path* the southern retracted vowel *[a:]* occurs as short [a] in northern dialects. In the great Midland district one distinguishes an eastern variety and a western, as well as a central type lying between. But such a classification of the English dialects is sufficient only for purposes of a broad grouping. Every county has its own peculiarities, and sometimes as many as three dialectal regions may be distinguished within the boundaries of a single shire. This wide diversity of dialects is well illustrated by the materials published since 1962 in the *Survey of English Dialects.* In the six northern counties at least seventeen different vowels or diphthongs occur in the word ***house,*** including the [u:] of Old English hûs.[10]

The dialect of southern Scotland has claims to special consideration on historical and literary grounds. In origin it is a variety of Northern English, but down to the sixteenth century it occupied a position both in speech and in writing on a plane with English. In the time of Shakespeare, however, it began to be strongly influenced by Southern English. This influence has been traced in part to the Reformation, which brought in the Bible and other religious works from the south, in part to the renaissance of English literature. The most important factor, however, was probably the growing importance of England and the role of London as the center of the English-speaking world. When in 1603 James VI of Scotland became the king of England as James I, and when by the Act of Union in 1707 Scotland was formally united to England, English was plainly felt to be standard, and Scots became definitely a dialect. During the eighteenth century it managed to maintain itself as a literary language through the work of Ramsay, Ferguson, and Robert Burns. Since then it has gradually lost ground. English is taught in the schools, and cultivation of English has, rightly or wrongly, been taken as the first test of culture. The ambitious have avoided the native dialect as a mark of lowly birth, and those who have a patriotic or sentimental regard for this fine old speech have long been apprehensive of its ultimate extinction.[11] Prompted in part by this concern, three major linguistic projects have focused on Scottish speech. *A Dictionary of the Older Scottish Tongue* records the language before 1700, *The Scottish National Dictionary* after that year. In addition, the Linguistic Survey of Scotland, which collected information since 1949 on both Scots and Gaelic, has published the three volumes of its *Atlas.*[12]

The characteristics of this dialect are known to most people through the poetry of Robert Burns:

O ye wha are sae guid yoursel,
Sae pious and sae holy,
Ye've nought to do but mark and tell
Your Neebour's fauts and folly!

Whase life is like a weel-gaun mill, [well-going]
Supply'd wi' store o' water,
The heapet happer's ebbing still, [heaped hopper]
And still the clap plays clatter.

Here we see some of the characteristic differences of pronunciation, *wha, whase, sae, weel, neebour, guid,* etc. These could easily be extended from others of his songs and poems, which all the world knows, and the list would include not only words differently pronounced but many an old word no longer in use south of the Tweed. Familiar examples are *ain* (own), *auld* (old), *lang* (long), *bairn* (child), *bonnie* (beautiful), *braw* (handsome), *dinna* (do not), *fash* (trouble oneself), *icker* (ear of grain), *maist* (almost), *muckle* (much, great), *syne* (since), *unco* (very).

Irish English, or Hiberno-English, has also left its mark on the literary tradition, although in different ways at different periods. In the eighteenth century, "stage Irish" was a familiar convention for representing and often ridiculing Irish characters in plays written by English authors whose use of stereotypical linguistic features was not always accurate. In the nineteenth and early twentieth centuries, Irish authors, especially Douglas Hyde (1860-1940), J.M.Synge (1871-1909), and W.B.Yeats (1865-1939), used selected features to give an Irish flavor to their works. In the twentieth century there has been a more realistic tradition, including the work of Sean O'Casey (1880-1964) and Brendan Behan (1923-1964) and the use by James Joyce (1882-1941) of carefully collected dialect phrases in *Ulysses* and *Finnegans Wake.1*[3] The distinctiveness of Irish English derives from a mixture of three sources: the influence of the Irish language; the influence of Scots, especially in the Northeast; and the nature of the original English that was brought to Ireland from western England in the seventeenth century and that has remained quite conservative compared with both RP and American English. For example, Irish English is firmly rhotic in contrast with RP. Except in the Scots-Irish district of Ulster, the English language in Ireland has not preserved so many old words as have survived in Scotland. But the language of the southern part of the island has an exuberance of vocabulary that recalls the lexical inventiveness of Elizabethan times, the period during which English began to spread rapidly in Ireland. The vocabulary has been influenced also by Irish *(blarney, galore, smithereens,* and many other examples of the diminutive ending *-een,* from the Irish diminutive ending *-in,* which may be added to any English word: *maneen, boyeen, girleen).* Although different varieties of Hiberno-English are distinguished, especially in the north and the south, certain peculiarities of pronunciation are fairly general. Dialect stories make use of spellings such as *tay* (tea), *desaive* (deceive), *foine* (fine), *projuce* (produce), *fisht* (fist), *butther* (butter), *thrue* (true), and the like. As an instance of *sh* for *s* before a long *u,* P.W.Joyce quotes the remark of one Dan Kiely "That he was now looking out for a wife that would *shoot* him."[14]

Syntactic structures in Hiberno-English often reflect the patterns of the Irish language.[15] The present perfect and past perfect tenses of English *(have got, had got),* which have no equivalents in Irish, can be expressed using *after,* the verb *to be,* and the present participle: *He said that he knew that I was after getting lost* (".. that I had got lost"). Irish also does not have the equivalent of indirect questions introduced by if and *whether;* instead of the declarative word order of Standard English, these sentences have the interrogative word order that is found in other varieties of English, including African American Vernacular English (see § 250): *He wanted to see would he get something to eat.* The influence of the Irish prepositional system upon Hiberno-English is evident in the use of *with* instead of *for* meaning "for the duration of": *He's dead now with many a year; He didn't come back with twenty-eight years.* The lack of an expression for *no one* in Irish, explains why *anyone* is used where *no one* is expected in Standard English: *Anyone doesn 't go to mass there.*

ENGLISH WORLD-WIDE

In the various parts of the former British Empire, as in the United States, the English language has developed differences that distinguish it from the language of England. In Australasia, Africa, South Asia, and Canada, peculiarities of pronunciation and vocabulary have grown up that mark off national and areal varieties from the dialect of the mother country and from one another. These peculiarities are partly such as arise in communities separated by time and space, and are partly due to the influence of a new environment. In some countries the most striking changes are the result of imperfect learning and systematic adaptations by speakers of other languages. Differences of nature and material civilization, and generally contact with some foreign tongue, are clearly reflected in the vocabulary.

Australia and New Zealand

In Australia it has been well said, "It is probably not too much to say that there never was an instance in history when so many new words were needed, and that there never will be again, for never did settlers come, nor can they ever come again, upon Flora and Fauna so completely different from anything seen by them before. An oak in America is still a *Quercus,* not as in Australia a *Casuarina.* But with the whole tropical region intervening it was to be expected that in the South Temperate Zone many things would be different, and such expectation was amply fulfilled."[16] Australian English uses many words that would not be understood in England or America. Some of these are old words that have acquired new meanings by being applied to new things. Thus the term *robin* is used for various birds not known in Europe. The word *jackass* (shortened from *laughing jackass)* means a bird whose cry is like a donkey's bray. Other words have been borrowed from the aboriginal languages of Australia and from Maori in New Zealand. *Kangaroo* and *boomerang* have become general English, but *wombat* is still chiefly Australian because it is the name of an Australian animal.[17] The Australian calls a rowdy street loafer a *larrikan.* A *swagman* is a man traveling through the *bush* (back country) carrying a *swag* (tramp's bundle). Where an American talks of a *ranch,* the Australian speaks of a *station* and, like us, distinguishes between a *sheep station* and a *cattle station.* A *boundary rider* is one who patrols an estate and keeps the owner informed concerning every part of it. The English of Australia not only is characterized by interesting differences of vocabulary but varies strikingly in pronunciation from the received standard of England. The accent of the majority of Australians has characteristics often associated with Cockney, especially in the quality of the vowels and diphthongs that occur in the words *say, so, beat, boot, high,* and *how.*[18] Because an Australian's pronunciation of *hay* may register on an American as *high,* or *basin* as *bison,* these systematic differences have been the source of misunderstandings between speakers of General Australian and speakers of other national varieties, though not among speakers of General Australian themselves. Within Australia there are possible difficulties in the different patterns of General Australian, the dialect of the great majority, and Cultivated Australian, a minority accent that approaches the received standard of England.[19] Social varieties such as these, and Broad Australian at the uncultivated extreme of the scale, are the only significant dialectal differences in a country where regional variations are negligible. The distinctive characteristics of General Australian pronunciation and the uniformity of the dialect throughout the continent are attributed to the circumstance that the early settlers were deported prisoners and adventurers often drawn from the lower classes of England. Although detailed information about the dialects spoken by these settlers is lacking, it is clear that the predominant varieties were lower-class urban dialects of southeastern England. In Australia the constant moving of convicts from place to place brought about the development of a mixed dialect that became homogeneous throughout the settled territory and distinct from any of the British dialects that contributed to the mixture. The English of Australia offers an interesting example of the changes that take place in a language transplanted to a remote and totally different environment.

South Africa

The same thing is true in a somewhat different way of Africa, the most multilingual continent on earth. The present Republic of South Africa had been occupied successively by the Bushmen, Hottentots, Bantus, Portuguese, and Dutch before the English settlers came. From all these sources, but especially from Dutch and its South African development, Afrikaans, the English language has acquired elements. A few words that occurred earlier in peculiarly South African contexts have passed into the general English vocabulary. In addition to *apartheid* and *veldt* (or *veld),* which retain their original associations, British and American speakers use *commando, commandeer,* and *trek* in contexts that no longer reflect their South African history. The great majority of Afrikanerisms (i.e., words and expressions borrowed from Dutch and Afrikaans) would still be generally meaningless in other parts of the English-speaking world yet are quite common in the daily life of South Africans. A recently compiled list of words and phrases that South Africans themselves consider to be characteristic of their variety of English includes *biltong* (strips of dried meat), *braaivleis* (a barbecue), *donga* (ravine), *gogga* (insect), *koeksisters* (a confection), *kopje* (hill), *lekker* (nice), *mealies* (Indian corn), *ou* (fellow, U.S. *guy), spruit* (gully), *stoep* (verandah, U.S. *stoop),* and *veldskoen* (hide-shoes).[20] As in Australian English, a number of good English words are used in quite new senses. South African racial policies gave a new meaning to *location* as an area in which black Africans are required to live. *Lands* in South Africa are just those portions of a farm that can be used for cultivation of crops, *camp* refers to the fenced-in portion of a farm, and the *leopard* (Afrikaans *tier,* from *tyger)* is sometimes called a *tiger.*[21] *Cookies* (small cakes) is the same as our word, which we also learned from the Dutch. *Divide* (watershed) is said to be borrowed from American use, and *upcountry* is used much as we use it in the eastern states. The use of *with* without an object *(Can I come with?)* can be found dialectally in this country, but we do not say "He threw me over the hedge with a rock" (i.e., "He threw a stone over the hedge and hit me"), a syntactic pattern that occurs in the English speech of Afrikaners and in the spoken language of relatively uneducated English speakers. Occasionally an old word now lost to Standard English in Britain has been preserved in South Africa, although this does not seem to have happened so often as in America. *Dispense* or *spens,* meaning a pantry or kitchen cupboard, is found in Chaucer (Al vinolent as botel in the spence: *Summoner's Tale).* It was doubtless carried to South Africa from one of the English dialects. The variations of the English vocabulary in different parts of the former British Empire are so fascinating that one is tempted to pursue them at too great a length. Enough has probably been said to illustrate the individual character of many expressions in South African use. In pronunciation the English of South Africa has been much influenced by the pronunciation of Afrikaans and to a lesser extent by the speech of many Scottish schoolmasters.[22] To Afrikaans it apparently owes not only the peculiar modification of certain vowels (e.g., [pen] for *pin;* [kåb] for *cab,* etc.), but also its higher pitch and the tendency to omit one of two or more consonants at the end of a word (e.g., tex for *text).* South African shares with American English the general disposition to pronounce the *r* when it appears in the spelling and to give full value to unaccented syllables *(extraordinary,* rather than the English *extraord'n'ry).*

West and East Africa

In other parts of sub-Saharan Africa that were once British colonies and are now independent countries, the English language has a complex relationship to the many African languages. Ghana, Nigeria, Sierra Leone, Kenya, Uganda, and other former colonies have a choice of retaining their colonial linguistic inheritance or rejecting it. In Nigeria three main African languages—Hausa, Yoruba, and Igbo—and scores of languages spoken by smaller groups exist alongside English. Although only a tiny minority of the population speaks English, almost always as a second language, it is the official language of the country. Ethnic jealousies that would arise from the selection of one of the African languages, and the advantages of English for communication both internally and internationally, are sufficient to overcome the reluctance toward using a colonial language. Swahili is the official language in Tanzania, but government business is routinely transacted in English. Some nations have deferred making the choice of an official language and continue to use English simultaneously with one or more of the African languages. Even more complex than the choice of an official language is the question of a standard. Among speakers who learn English as a second language there will inevitably be a wide range of varieties, from pidgin at one extreme to a written standard of international acceptability at the other. Because many speakers know no English and many know only the patois of the marketplace, West African English is remarkable for its varieties. With as yet no identifiable West African standard, graders of examinations often have difficulty drawing the line between an incorrect answer and a local variant. Such practicalities illustrate the larger philosophical problem of correctness and acceptability in varieties of English that diverge markedly from the international Standard English of educated speakers in Great Britain, the United States, Canada, Australia, New Zealand, South Africa, and many speakers in the West African countries. The question of whether a West African standard will emerge, and if so, whether such a standard is desirable and should be taught, evoke a wide range of answers that reflect a bewildering diversity of opinion concerning language and its use.[23]

Examples from Nigerian English illustrate the distinctions that must be made in describing a regional or national standard. We have seen differences in pronunciation among standard British dialects, and in Chapter 11 we shall see an even more basic set of differences between British English and American English. It is to be expected that the standard dialects of English throughout the world will vary according to settlement history and the local linguistic influences that are at work. In Nigeria the phonological systems of the languages spoken as first languages by the great majority of people— Yoruba and Igbo and in the South and Hausa in the North—have contributed to the distinctive Nigerian accent. Vowel harmony in Igbo, for example, causes *follow* to be pronounced with the same back vowel in both syllables: I- -IHausa speakers tend to break up consonant clusters by inserting a vowel, so that *screw* becomes [sukuru]. The smaller number of vowel contrasts in the African languages carries over into Nigerian English, where *beat* and *bit* have the same tense vowel, distinguished if at all by length: [bit] *beat* and [bit] *bit*. The absence of the tense-lax distinction, which J.C.Wells calls "one of the most characteristic features of African English," produces a large number of homophones in Nigerian English and in other African varieties: *leave—live, seen—sin,* and *Don't sleep on the floor—Don't slip on the floor,* all with the tense vowel.[24] The rarity of the central vowel [ə] and of syllabic consonants accounts for the full value of vowels in the final syllables of words—for example, *smoother* [smuèa], [smuda] (where Nigerian English, like Southern British

English, is nonrhotic), *bottle* (bətɛ) lesson (lɛsən) The rarity of reduced vowels and weak forms is typical of syllable-timed languages such as those of West Africa, in contrast with the stress-timed rhythms of English—thus, the difference between the Received Pronunciation and the West African pronunciation of the following sentence:

RP	[aIv sín hIm təde]
West African	[aI hav si-n him tude][25]

Notice also the lack of a diphthong in *today,* which has the simple vowel [e] instead, a feature that is common in African English.

The usual processes that allow for expansion of vocabulary and for new meanings of words operate with especially interesting effect in countries where English is mainly a second language. Typical lexical items in Nigerian English, which often reflects aspects of the cultural background by way of borrowings or calques from the local languages, include *head-tie* (woman's headdress), juju *music* (a type of dance music), *bush meat* (game), *tie-dye cloth* (cloth into which patterns are made by tying up parts of it before dyeing), *akara balls* (bean cakes), *white-cap chiefs* (senior chiefs in Lagos whose rank is shown by the white caps they wear). Extensions and narrowing of meanings of words occur in *corner* (a bend in a road), *globe* (a lightbulb), *wet* (to water [flowers]), *environment* (neighborhood), *gallops* (potholes), and *bluff* (to give an air of importance).[26] It is sometimes difftcult to distinguish general West African usage from a national variety—Nigerian English, Ghanaian English, Cameroon English; the following words and expressions occur in West African English, some with quite widespread currency: *balance* (change, "You did not give me any balance"), *bata* (sandals, shoes), *move with* (court, go out with), *wedding bells* (invitation to a wedding), *take in* (become pregnant), *be in state* (be pregnant), *give kola* (offer a bribe), *have long legs* (have influence), *cry die* (wake, funeral rites).

The morphology and syntax of English in Africa have generally the same structures as those of the international varieties of standard English, although one may note formations with the plural suffix of words that are not ordinarily count nouns *(equipments, aircrafts, deadwoods, offsprings).* Also, some standard English transitive verbs gain particles and become phrasal verbs, as in *voice out* instead of "voice" ("I am going to voice out my opinion"); *discuss about instead* of "discuss" ("We shall discuss about that later"); and *cope up with* instead of "cope with." After some verbs the *to* is dropped from the following infinitive ("enable him do it"). As in other second-language varieties and pidgins, certain tag questions are common: "He loves you, isn't it?" or "He loves you, not so?"

In East Africa, including Kenya, Tanzania, Uganda, Zambia, Malawi, Ethiopia, Somalia, and Seychelles, the syntactic and lexical patterns of English that differ from varieties spoken elsewhere in the world often do so in ways that parallel the West African divergencies. For example, verbs that are phrasal in standard English lose the adverbial particle but keep the meaning of the phrasal verb ("Her name *cropped* in the conversation" for "cropped up"; "I *picked him* outside his house and he *dropped at* work" for "picked him up" and "dropped him off"). Some nouns in Kenyan and Tanzanian colloquial speech have a plural form but are treated as singulars: *behaviours, bottoms, laps, minds, nighties, noses, popcorns.* Hancock and Angogo point out that in "My noses are stuffed up," the influence of Bantu is clearly apparent since there is no single word for nostril in Bantu.[27] The Bantu language Kiswahili is the most important African language throughout East Africa, and from its influence the East African variety of English has acquired some of its characteristic phonological patterns (for example, the lack of *[ð]/[è]* as in [zis siK] *this thing).* From Kiswahili also have come loanwords that have passed into international currency: *safari, simba* (lion), *bwana* (master), *jambo* (hello).

South Asia

The issues concerning English in India, Bangladesh, Pakistan, Sri Lanka, and Nepal are similar in many respects to those in Africa except that a clearly identifiable South Asian variety of English has emerged over the years. The problems and prospects of Indian English were summarized by Raja Rao more than half a century ago: "The telling has not been easy. One has to convey in a language that is not one's own the spirit that is one's own. One has to convey the various shades and omissions of a certain thought-movement that looks maltreated in an alien language. I use the word 'alien,' yet English is not really an alien language to us. It is the language of our intellectual make-up...but not of our emotional make-up. We are all instinctively bilingual, many of us writing in our own language and in English. We cannot write like the English. We should not. We cannot write only as Indians. We have grown to look at the large world as part of us. Our method of expression therefore has to be a dialect which will some day prove to be as distinctive and colorful as the Irish or the American. Time alone will justify it."[28] Peculiarly Indian features of pronunciation, vocabulary, and syntax, which the British regarded with condescension during the days of the Empire, have in recent years received more appropriately neutral descriptions from linguists. Certain pronunciations result from the systematic influence of Indian languages. For speakers of the variety of Hindi that does not permit *sk, st,* and *sp* at the beginning of words, English *station* is regularly pronounced with an initial vowel [Iste: šYn][29] In some varieties of Indian English [v] and [w] are not distinguished, and [t], [d], [l], and [r] are pronounced with retroflection. Dozens of words and phrases that strike British and American speakers as strange are the natural expressions of cultural contexts that are absent in Western society. Indian English is characterized by greetings such as *bow my forehead, Ml at your feet, blessed my hovel with the good dust of your feet;* abuses and curses such as *you eater of your masters, you of the evil stars, the incestuous sister sleeper;* blessings and flattery such as *thou shalt write from an inkwell of your shoe and my head;* and modes of address such as *cherisher of the poor, king of pearls, policewala, mother of my daughter.*[30] The future of English in India and the rest of South Asia will be determined by a complex set of social, political, and linguistic forces. The Indian Constitution of 1950 recognized fourteen Indian languages, of which Hindi was to be the first national language. English was to serve as a transitional language with Hindi until 1965, but it has continued to be used as an official language. Whatever the stated policies may be in the future, it is certain that the English language will be spoken and written by a small but influential minority of the Indian population, including leaders in government, education, and the press. It is also certain that the variety of English recognized as standard in India—and in Bangladesh and in Pakistan—will be a distinctively South Asian variety in its pronunciation, syntax, and vocabulary. It will continue to be affected by the culture and native languages of South Asia, and in turn it will affect those languages and serve as the medium for Western influences on the culture.

Singapore, Malaysia, Hong Kong

The development of English as a second language in the Pacific rim is especially interesting because of the influence of background languages (the Chinese dialects Hokkien, Cantonese, and Mandarin; Malay; the southern Indian Tamil) and because of the effects of different language policies instituted by the various governments. Historically, the Malay peninsula has been among the most important trading areas of the world, the site of a productive if sometimes uneasy cultural mix of Chinese, Malays, Indians, and, since the sixteenth century, Europeans. The state of Malacca on the Malay peninsula was ruled by the Portuguese from 1511 to 1640, then by the Dutch, and, after 1824, by the British. In 1819 Sir Stamford Raffles founded Singapore at the tip of the Malay peninsula, which together with Malacca and Penang became a British crown colony, the Straits Settlements. From the very beginning, Singapore prospered economically, and throughout the rest of the nineteenth and twentieth centuries, English was an important language of government, business, and education.

When independence came to the British colony in 1957 Singapore was originally federated with the Malaysian mainland and islands that surrounded it. The separation of the states two years later resulted partly from ethnic and cultural tensions between the Malays, who formed a majority of the population outside of Singapore, and the Chinese, who formed a majority of the population within Singapore. These different cultural settings are reflected in the subsequent history of the English language in the region. During the 1970s a national fervor in Malaysia brought about a policy of promoting Bahasa Malay as the official language, and the use of English declined rapidly. By the mid-1980s, however, it was clear that the advantages that had been gained in unifying the country's diverse ethnic populations under a national language had been offset by the growing inability of Malaysians to read English, including scientific publications, and to compete internationally in commerce. A former vicechancellor of the University of Malaya described the situation: "You should sit among the students in the library. You see these people open the book and they don't move the pages. And they're looking awfully concerned."[31] Recently, the Malaysian government has quietly begun to reemphasize English.

In Singapore the changing relationship between English and the Asian languages has been in a sense the reverse of that in Malaysia. With English as one of the four official languages and the main medium for administration, commerce, industry, and education, the country has prospered in international trade and in its domestic economy. However, key government leaders, including the founder of the independent state, Lee Kuan Yew, have expressed concern over the loss of Asian values and have begun to promote the use of Mandarin. As the director of the Confucian Ethics Project Team expressed it: "English is for getting on in life, for practical use. But for moral behavior we must learn Chinese, our own language."[32] Thus, Malaysia and Singapore in their separate ways illustrate the tensions between the international language and the languages of ethnic and cultural identity. Bilingualism and multilingualism will be essential in both countries for years to come.

Hong Kong, although more than a thousand miles across the South China Sea from Singapore, has similarities in the use of English because of its British colonial history. The main difference is in the relatively homogeneous population, which is 97 percent Chinese. English is much less frequently used for oral communication among Hong Kong's Cantonese-speaking Chinese than among the Chinese in Singapore.

Some of the specific features of English in Malaysia and Singapore are shared by English-based creoles in other parts of the world and by African American Vernacular English in the United States: the lack of an ending to mark the third person singular present tense of the verb; the omission of *be* both as a copula ("This coffee house—very cheap," in contrast with standard British and American English "This coffee house is very cheap") and also as an auxiliary ("My brother—working" instead of "My brother is working").[33] These structures reflect corresponding structures in the background languages. Among the differences in syntax is the word order of indirect questions ("May I ask where is the stamp counter?" or "I'd like to know what are the procedures"). In phonology, the pronunciation of both British and American English is with a "stress-timed rhythm." Stressed syllables recur at equal intervals, but unstressed syllables are unequally spaced in time. In Singaporean English, however, the rhythm is "syllable-timed." Syllables tend to recur at equal intervals of time, stressed or unstressed.

The Caribbean

The countries of the Caribbean face multilingual situations that in certain respects of their history and present status resemble those of the Pacific. Paradoxically, however, the solutions to social problems involving languages in contact appear to become more difficult as the varieties of the languages are more similar. The very question of whether Jamaican Creole is a separate language or a point on a continuum that includes Jamaican English is a charged political question with implications for educational policy, the legal system, and the mass media.

A determination of these questions requires a consideration of the complex history of the region, which, for the English language, goes back to the arrival of settlers in Jamestown, Virginia, in 1607 and in Bermuda two years later. A full history would take into account the Spanish presence in the Caribbean during the sixteenth century, a heritage that is clearly seen in Puerto Rico, where both Spanish and English survive side by side, as well as in Belize, Panama, and Guyana.[34] For most of the anglophone Caribbean islands, however, including Jamaica, Barbados, Trinidad and Tobago, the Leeward Islands, and the Windward Islands, the most relevant languages in contact are those of the west coast of Africa. Ewe, Twi, Efik, Yoruba, Ibo, Hausa, and other African languages were spoken by slaves who were brought to the islands during the seventeenth, eighteenth, and nineteenth centuries. In addition to the syllable-timed rhythm that we have seen in other varieties of world English, final syllables in Jamaican Creole frequently have rising tone, reflecting the West African tone language spoken by the slaves, who carried their own phonology into their reinterpretation of a Germanic language with light and heavy stresses.

Despite gaps in the written records of both the early forms of Caribbean English and of the African source languages, continuing lexicographical efforts have revealed much about the complex history of English in this part of the world. A large number of words can be traced clearly to African languages. Forms of *nyam* (to eat) occur as verbs in Wolof and Fula and as nouns referring to food in Hausa *na:ma* (flesh, meat), Efik *unam* (flesh), Twi *ånãm* (flesh, meat of any animal). In Jamaican Creole, *nyam* is generally the verb, *ninyam* a noun (food), and *nyaams* a specific food (yam). One of the most characteristic Jamaicanisms, *juk* (to prick, poke, spur, jab, stab), has been traced to several possible sources, the most plausible of which is perhaps F.G.Cassidy's suggestion of Fula *jukka* (to spur, poke, knock down).[35] *Obeah* (the practice of malignant magic) has roots in Efik *ubio* (a charm) and Twi ᵓ*-bayifő* (witch, wizard). Part of the vitality of Caribbean English is in the formation of compounds that are loan-translations of African metaphors: *door-mouth* (a doorway, or the place just outside the doorway of a small house or hut) can be compared with Yoruba *iloro enu* (threshold; literally porch mouth) and Hausa *baki* (a mouth, an opening, an entrance); and *strong-eye* (firm, determined) is possibly a loan-translation from Twi *n'ani yɛ de ŋ* (strong-eye, insolent, self-willed). It is often difficult to be certain about etymologies in Caribbean creoles. Cassidy points out that *kakanabu* (foolishness, nonsense) at first appears African, with the initial reduplication and the final vowel [u], but it turns out to be quite regularly derived from *cock-and-a-bull,* as in "a cock-and-bull story." Conversely, *dutty* (earth, soil; excrement) at first appears to be a regular Jamaican development of Standard English *dirt, dirty;* however, the main source turns out to be Twi d ᵓ t é (soil, earth), with some influence from the English words. More recent developments are recorded fully in print and especially as regards music in the electronic media. The speech of the Rastafari (a religious and social movement that arose during the 1940s among the Jamaican poor and was energized by a sense of identification with Africa, and specifically Ethiopia) has given new forms to pronouns: *you* is eliminated for being divisive and *I and*

I is used instead, as well as for I and for *me*. From popular culture Jamaican English and the world at large have received the words *reggae* and *ska*.

The variety of creoles in the Caribbean can be illustrated by versions of sentences in as many as thirty-three different languages.[36] The Standard English sentence "The dog of the man who lives in that house is named King" becomes in Jamaican Creole [di ma:n wa lIb i:na da hɔus da:g njåm kIη]; in Trinidad Creole [didɔg dat bɪlɔŋ tu di man dat IIvεn In dat hɔus ne:m kIη]; in Caymans Creole [da man hu lrv In dahɔus, i dag ne:m kIη]. Comparisons can be made with African creoles. In Nigerian Creole the sentence takes the form [di dɔg we na di man we lif fɔ da haõs gåt am, i nem kiK] and in Krio, the creole language of Sierra Leone, [di man we tap na da osdɔg nεm kiη]. Phonetic transcription is useful for those who have studied it, though not for the general public, and the question of the written representation of creole languages is part of the unresolved complex of political, social, and psychological issues surrounding the linguistic question. A modified standard orthography with markings for tone is another way of representing speech on paper, as in these examples of Jamaican English:

mi granma chier

"my grandmother's chair"

Him did go down Hope Ruod

"He/she went down Hope Road"

Canada

Canadian English, as would be expected, has much in common with that of the United States while retaining a few features of British pronunciation and spelling. Where alternative forms exist the likelihood for a particular choice to be British or American varies with region, education, and age. British items such as *chips*, *serviette*, and *copse* tend to occur more frequently in the West, while the more common American choices *French fries*, *napkin*, and *grove* tend to occur in the East. British spellings such as *colour* and pronunciations such as *schedule* with an initial [š] occur most frequently throughout Canada among more highly educated and older speakers.[37] In addition there are a number of words with meanings that are neither British nor American but peculiarly Canadian. Thus one finds *aboiteau* (dam), *Blue nose* (Nova Scotian), *Cre litiste* (member of the Social Credit party), *Digby chicken* (smoke-cured herring), *mukluk* (Inuit boot), *reeve* (chairman of a municipal council), *salt-chuck* (ocean), and *skookum* (powerful, brave). The *Dictionary of Canadianisms*, published in Canada's Centennial Year, allows historical linguists to establish in detail the sources of Canadian English.[38] Many of the earlier settlers in Canada came from the United States, and the influence of the United States has always been very strong. A writer in the *Canadian Journal* in 1857 complained of the new words "imported by travellers, daily circulated by American newspapers, and eagerly incorporated into the language of our Provincial press." Needless to say, he considered the influence wholly bad, and his words are still echoed by Canadians who deplore the wide circulation of American books and magazines in Canada and in recent years the further influence of movies and television. Nevertheless a linguistically informed opinion would have to concede that in language as in other activities "it is difftcult to differentiate what belongs to Canada from what belongs to the United States, let alone either from what might be called General North American."[39]

PIDGINS AND CREOLES

Of the varieties of English discussed in the preceding section, those of West and East Africa, the Caribbean, and the Pacific Rim coexist and interact with well-established English-based pidgins and creoles.[40] The linguistic and sociological issues that are raised by these varieties of language in daily contact have already been suggested with respect to Jamaican English. The theoretical interest to linguists, however, goes even deeper, because the study of pidgin and creole languages may give clues to a better understanding of a number of interrelated problems: the analyticsynthetic distinction, which we have considered in the development of Middle English; the idea of a "continuum" among varieties of a single language and between closely related languages; the acquisition of language by children; the language-processing abilities of the human brain; and the origin of language. Because English-based creoles are so numerous and so widespread, the study of present-day English in all its worldwide varieties is useful not only in itself but also in the illumination that it gives to some of these most basic issues in language and cognition. Of the approximately 125 pidgin and creole languages throughout the world, spoken by more than nine million people, about thirty-five are English-based.[41] Historical settlement and colonization produced two major groups of English-based creoles, an Atlantic group and a Pacific group. The Atlantic creoles were established in West Africa and the Caribbean area mainly during the seventeenth and eighteenth centuries and include varieties in Sierra Leone (Krio), Liberia, Suriname (formerly Dutch Guiana in northern South America), Barbados, Trinidad and Tobago, Guyana, Jamaica, and other West African countries and Caribbean islands. The Pacific group, established largely during the nineteenth century, includes varieties in Hawaii, Papua New Guinea (Tok Pisin), and other islands.

The lexical impoverishment of pidgin and creole language often results in periphrastic and metaphorical expressions to designate things and events which in established language are signified by unrelated morphemes. The single word *hum* in English is expressed in Tok Pisin (literally 'talk pidgin') by the circumlocution, *singsing long taim maus i pas* ('to sing when the mouth is closed'). English 'grass' in Tok Pisin is *gras;* 'moustache' is *mausgras;* 'beard' is *gras bilong fes* ('grass on face'); 'hair' is *gras bilong hed;* 'eyebrow' is *gras antap longai* ('grass on top along eye'); 'weed' is *gras nogut.* In these pidgin expressions, prepositions and word order rather than inflectional endings signal the grammatical and semantic relationships.[42] The preposition *bilong* (from the verb 'belong') serves a number of functions in

Tok Pisin that in English would be assigned to varying case forms, including possession: 'my mother' is *mama bilong mi;* 'John's house' is *haus bilong John.* With a greatly reduced system of inflections and a correspondingly greater reliance on function words and word order, pidgin and creole languages show clearly the analytic structure that we noted when we observed the development from Old English to Middle English.

The other side of lexical impoverishment is the visibility and richness of certain aspectual distinctions, some never explicitly marked in the verb phrase of historical English. For example, habitual or continuing action is indicated in Hawaiian Creole by including the particle *stay* in the verb phrase, and other creoles have similar markers: I *stay run in Kapiolani Park every evening* indicates habitual or repetitive action rather than action completed at a certain point. Similarly, the accomplishment of purpose is made explicit in creole languages around the world. The English sentence "John went to Honolulu to see Mary" does not specify whether John actually saw Mary. Such ambiguity must be resolved in Hawaiian Creole. If the speaker knows that John saw Mary, the appropriate sentence is *John bin go Honolulu go see Mary.* If John did not see Mary or if the speaker does not know whether John saw Mary, the appropriate verb form expresses intention without expressing completion: *John bin go Honolulu for see Mary.*[13]

Another important factor of language in general which the study of pidgins and creoles clarifies is the idea of a linguistic continuum. Whereas earlier observations noted only a binary distinction between the standard language and the "patois," research during the past quarter century has made it clear that there are multiple, overlapping grammars between the *basilect* (the most extreme form of pidgin or creole) and the *acrolect* (the standard language). These intermediate grammars are known as *mesolects.* There is often an observable hierarchy of linguistic features associated with various points on the continuum (for example, different past tense formations of verbs, some closer than others to the standard). If a speaker has a nonstandard feature located near the basilectal extreme, it is likely that the speaker will also have all of the other nonstandard features that are increasingly closer to the standard language. This technique of analysis is known as an "implicational scale."[44] The regularity of such scales in pidgin and creole languages world-wide leads to yet another interesting problem: the order of acquisition of the scaled features in the process of learning a language. Typically the standard features near the basilectal end of the implicational scale are learned first, and those near the acrolectal end are learned later if at all. The study of language acquisition leads finally to a convergence in the concerns of creolists and generative grammarians. In what Noam Chomsky has called "Plato's problem," generative grammarians have aimed to explain how language can be acquired at all, given the poverty of the stimulus.[45] "How can we know so much on the basis of so little experience?" they ask. Their answer is that a knowledge of linguistic universals is part of the innate structure of the human brain. Similarly, on the basis of evidence such as we have seen, Derek Bickerton has developed a theory of a "bioprogram" for the acquisition of language.[46] Although these theories often differ on the details of their specific analysis, as indeed all theories do, they both see the study of language as ultimately rooted in the biology of the speaking animal.

SPELLING REFORM

In the latter part of the nineteenth century renewed interest was manifested in the problem of English spelling, and the question of reform was vigorously agitated. For nearly 400 years the English have struggled with their spelling. It was one of the chief problems that seemed to confront the language in the time of Shakespeare, and it continued to be an issue throughout the seventeenth and to some extent in the eighteenth century. The publication in 1837 of a system of shorthand by Isaac Pitman led to his proposal of several plans of phonetic spelling for general use. In these schemes Pitman was assisted by Alexander J.Ellis, a much greater scholar. They were promoted during the 1840s by the publication of a periodical called the *Phonotypic Journal,* later changed to the *Phonetic Journal.* The Bible and numerous classic works were printed in the new spelling, and the movement aroused considerable public interest. By 1870 the English Philological Society had taken up the question, and the *Transactions* contain numerous discussions of it. Prominent members who took part in the debate included Ellis, Morris, Payne, Sweet, Furnivall, Skeat, and Murray. The discussion spread into the columns of the *Academy* and the *Athenaeum.* America became interested in the question, and in 1883 the American Philological Association recommended the adoption of a long list of new spellings approved jointly by it and the English society. Spelling Reform Associations were formed in both countries. In America men like March, Lounsbury, Grandgent, William Dean Howells, and Brander Matthews lent their support to the movement. In 1898 the National Education Association formally adopted for use in its publications twelve simplified spellings—*tho, altho, thoro, thorofare, thru, thruout, program, catalog, prolog, decalog, demagog,* and *pedagog.* Some of these have come into general use, but on the whole the public remained indifferent. In 1906 there was organized in the United States a Simplified Spelling Board, supported by a contribution from Andrew Carnegie. Their first practical step was to publish a list of 300 words for which different spellings were in use *(judgement—judgment, mediaeval—medieval,* etc.) and to recommend the simpler form. This was a very moderate proposal and met with some favor. Theodore Roosevelt endorsed it. But it also met with opposition, and subsequent lists that went further were not well received. Newspapers, magazines, and book publishers continued to use the traditional orthography, and though the Simplified Spelling Board continued to issue from time to time its publication, *Spelling,* until 1931, its accomplishment was slight, and it eventually went out of existence.

The efforts that have been described produced only slender results, but they did succeed in stimulating public interest for a time and gained the support of various people whose names carried weight. This interest, however, was far from universal. Advocates of reform had to contend with the apathy of the public and face at the same time a certain amount of active opposition. Innate conservatism was responsible for some of it, and there are always those who feel that the etymological value of the old spelling is an asset not to be lightly relinquished.[47] An influential opinion was expressed by Henry Bradley in his paper "On the Relation of Spoken and Written Language" (1919). He held that it was a mistake to think that the sole function of writing was to represent sounds. For many people nowadays the written word is as important as the spoken word, and as we read, many words convey their meaning directly without the intermediate process of pronunciation, even mental pronunciation. To change the symbol that long practice enables us instantaneously to translate into an idea would be a handicap to many people, even though a temporary one. Besides, there are the numerous words that are distinguished in writing, though pronounced alike. For these and other reasons Bradley was opposed to any radical change in English spelling. The history of spelling reform makes it clear that in opposing radical change he was expressing the attitude of the majority of people. It is probably safe to say that if our spelling is ever to be reformed, it must be reformed gradually and with as little disruption to the existing system as is consistent with the attainment of a reasonable end.

PURIST EFFORTS

Conservatives in matters of language, as in politics, are hardy perennials. We have seen many examples of the type in the course of this history. They flourished especially during the eighteenth century, but their descendants are fairly numerous in the nineteenth and scarcely less common today. They generally look upon change with suspicion and are inclined to view all changes in language as corruptions. In retrospect they seem often melancholy figures, fighting a losing fight, many times living to see the usages against which they fought so valiantly become universally accepted. Thomas De Quincey argued at length against the use of *implicit* in such expressions as *implicit faith* or *confidence,* wishing to restrict the word to a sense the opposite of *explicit.* The American philologist George P.Marsh spoke against "the vulgarism of the phrase *in our midst*" and objected to a certain adjectival use of the participle. "There is at present," he says, "an inclination in England to increase the number of active, in America, of passive participles, employed with the syntax of the adjective. Thus, in England it is common to hear: 'such a thing is *very damaging,*' and the phrase has been recently introduced into this country. Trench says: 'Words which had become unintelligible or *misleading,*' and 'the phrase could not have been other than more or less *misleading*'; 'these are the most serious and most *recurring.*' Now, though *pleasing, gratifying, encouraging,* and many other words have long been established as adjectives, yet the cases cited from Trench strike us as unpleasant novelties."[48] Dean Alford, the author of *The Queen's English* (1864), a curious composite of platitude and prejudice with occasional flashes of unexpected liberality, a book that was reprinted many times, finds much to object to, especially in the English of journalism. "No man ever *shows* any feeling, but always *evinces* it.... Again, we never *begin* anything in the newspapers now, but always *commence*.... Another horrible word, which is fast getting into our language through the provincial press, is to *eventuate*... *Avocation* is another monster patronised by these writers.. *Desirability* is a terrible word.... *Reliable* is hardly legitimate..." and so with many others. The battle over *reliable* was still being waged at the end of the nineteenth century, as over *lengthy* and *standpoint.* Often the American was accused of introducing these supposed outrages against good English, and just as often accused unjustly. It is unnecessary to multiply examples that could be useful only to the future historian of human error. If we might venture a moral, it would be to point out the danger and the futility of trying to prevent the natural development of language.

An effort that gave promise of being saved from some of the pitfalls that beset the reformers of language took the form of a *Society for Pure English (S.P.E.).* If it were to escape the common fate of such efforts, it would have been because of the moderateness of its aims and the fuller knowledge of the ways of language that some of its members possessed. The society was founded in 1913, but World War I delayed its plans and it was not until after the Armistice that it began its activities. The original committee was composed of Henry Bradley, the distinguished philologist, Robert Bridges, the poet laureate, Sir Walter Raleigh, Oxford Professor of English Literature, and Logan Pearsall Smith, a well-known literary man. The moving spirit was Bridges. In their proposals they stated their aim to be "to agree upon a modest and practical scheme for informing popular taste on sound principles, for guiding educational authorities, and for introducing into practice certain slight modifications and advantageous changes." They specifically disavowed any intention "of foolish interference with living developments." Their hope of directing the development of the vocabulary seems, in the light of history, perhaps overoptimistic, but their recognition of the popular voice inspired confidence. "Now, believing that language is or should be democratic both in character and origin, and that its best word-makers are the uneducated classes, we would prefer vivid popular terms to the artificial creations of scientists." This at least is sound doctrine. One must likewise applaud the recognition given to local dialects, from which the standard speech has so often been enriched in the past. But most praiseworthy of all was the intention to achieve its ends not by authoritative pronouncement but by the dissemination of fact and enlightened opinion. For this purpose it proposed to issue from time to time short *Tracts* on various linguistic topics and promote the discussion of pertinent questions. In this respect the *S.P.E.* recalls the proposal of the anonymous writer of 1724 (cf. § 196). The difference lies in the fact that this society actually issued more than three score of its *Tracts* before becoming inactive.

Almost from the beginning some skepticism was expressed. Dissent appeared as early as 1926. "The 'Society for Pure English,' recently formed by the Poet Laureate, is getting a great deal of support at this moment, and is the literary equivalent of political Fascism. But at no period have the cultured classes been able to force the habit of tidiness on the nation as a whole.... The imaginative genius of the uneducated and half-educated masses will not be denied expression."[49] Nevertheless the movement appealed to many on both sides of the Atlantic. In 1922 a group of Americans proposed that some plan of cooperation between England and America be devised, and a committee was appointed in England to consider the question. A few years later, at a meeting of the Royal Society of Literature held in London, a number of English and American writers and scholars agreed to form an "International Council for English" to consider the problems of the common language of the English-speaking countries.[50] Such movements indicate that even if the idea of a formal academy was no longer entertained, not all hope had been given up of exercising some control over the development of the language.

Gender Issues and Linguistic Change

The course of the history of English since the Renaissance has seen numerous conscious attempts to reform the language in one way or another: to prohibit or encourage borrowings, to prescribe matters of grammatical usage, to change the established spellings of words, to found an academy with goals like these. More often than not the reforms have failed and the language has developed in a seemingly inexorable way, especially in the later periods when the efforts of any one person or group of persons appear powerless against the language's very vastness in geographical extent and number of speakers. Since the 1970s the efforts to eliminate sexism from English, though having met with resistance, have been more successful than most attempts at reform. Published works from just a few years earlier now seem oddly dated in their use of what is now seen as sexist language. Among the most obvious instances of the earlier usage are the noun *man* and the masculine pronoun *he*, sometimes with *man* as the antecedent, both words referring to men and women. Such usage was normal in the English language for two centuries, although one interesting result of recent research is the demonstration that grammarians since the eighteenth century, mostly male, have helped to bring about and reinforce a usage that is socially biased and grammatically illogical.

Writers at the end of the twentieth and the beginning of the twenty-first century have generally found it easy to substitute *people, person,* or *human beings* for *man* and *mankind,* though the problem of the pronoun has proved thornier. In the sentence, "Everybody should button their coat," males and females are treated equally, but the plural pronoun *their* has as its antecedent the singular noun *everybody.* English does not have a gender-neutral, or epicene, pronoun for persons. For more than a century proposals have been suggested to remedy this lack including *thon; e, es, em; heshe, hes. hem; shey, shem, sheir,* and many others. None of these has gained general acceptance, and it is clear that none will. The closed class of personal pronouns is much more resistant to additions and substitutions than the open classes of nouns and adjectives. We have seen during the late medieval period the plural pronouns in *h- (hie, hem, hir)* replaced by borrowings from Old Norse (Present-day *they, them, their)* and the rise of analogical *its* during the Renaissance. However, most of the changes in pronouns have simply been losses in number and case, and it would be unprecedented for a consciously constructed pronoun to come into general use.

There is precedence, however, for the simplest solution to the problem of pronoun agreement in gender, and that is lack of agreement in number, as in the sentence with which we began: "Everybody should button their coat." English, which once distinguished between singular *thou, thee, thy* and plural *ye, you, your* in the second person, has had plural *you, your* as the standard form for the past four centuries. An extension of the plural *they, their* to certain singular contexts would cause no more disruption in syntax than the change in the second person, and of course it already shows up in informal usage, as in the sentence quoted.[51]

Other nouns, adjectives, and forms of address have supplanted sexist language so naturally that it is sometimes hard to imagine the resistance with which they originally met. *Ms* is a happy replacement in many contexts for the uncertainties that often attend a choice of *Miss* or *Mrs.,* putting the female form of address on the same footing as *Mr.,* for which indications of marital status have always been considered irrelevant. *Flight attendant* has given *stewardess* a dated ring, somewhat like a 1950s movie, where one might also hear *girl for woman* in a way that now jars, especially if there is no question of referring to the *man* as a *boy. Poetess, authoress;* and *sculptress* were out or on their way out before the feminist writings of the 1970s, while *actress* has had more resilience, possibly in part because of distinctions in awards for performance that would not apply to *poets, authors,* and *sculptors.* Job titles ending in *-man,* such as *chairman* and *Congressman,* sometimes substitute *-person,* though there is variation according to personal preference. A familiar choice in recent years is the shorter form *chair,* a word that the *Oxford English Dictionary*records with this meaning as early as 1658.

REFERENCES

1. More than 520,000 other examples have been collected in *Acronyms, Initialisms, and Abbreviations Dictionary,* ed. Jennifer Mossman (16th ed., Detroit, 1992).
2. See Louise Pound, *Blends: Their Relation to English Word Formation* (Heidelberg, 1914) and Garland Cannon, "Blends in English Word Formation," *Linguistics,* 24 (1986), 725-53.
3. Chesterfield has an interesting comment on this development in the word *vast* in his time: "Not contented with enriching our language by words absolutely new, my fair countrywomen have gone still farther, and improved it by the application and extension of old ones to various and very different significations. They take a word and change it, like a guinea into shillings for pocket-money, to be employed in the several occasional purposes of the day. For instance, the adjective *vast,* and its adverb *vastly,* mean anything, and are the fashionable words of the most fashionable people. A fine woman, under this head I comprehend all fine gentlemen too, not knowing in truth where to place them properly, is *vastly* obliged, or *vastly* offended, *vastly*glad, or *vastly sorry.* Large objects are *vastly great,* small ones are *vastly* little; and I had lately the pleasure to hear a fine woman pronounce, by a happy metonymy, a very small gold snuff-box that was produced in company to be *vastly pretty,* because it was *vastly* little." *(The World,* No. 101, December 5, 1754.)
4. *Roland for Oliver.*
5. Greenough and Kittredge, *Words and Their Ways in English Speech* (New York, 1901),S p.55.

6. For the distinction, see John S.Kenyon, "Cultural Levels and Functional Varieties of English," *College English,* 10 (1948), 1-6. For a criticism of the distinction, see William Labov, *The Study of Nonstandard English* (Champaign, IL, 1970), pp. 22-28.
7. See James Sledd, "Bi-dialectalism: The Linguistics of White Supremacy," *English Journal,* 58 (1969), 1307-15; and Rosina Lippi-Green, *English with an Accent: Language, Ideology, and Discrimination in the United States* (London, 1997).
8. *Linguistic Variation and Change* (Oxford, UK, 1992), p. 52.
9. The issues are clearly presented and debated by Randolph Quirk, "Language Varieties and Standard Language," *English Today,* 21 (1990), 3-10, and Braj B.Kachru, "Liberation Linguistics and the 'Quirk Concern,'" *English Today,* 25 (1991), 3-13.
10. Orton and Dieth, eds., *Survey of English Dialects,* 1, part 2, 459. See also two studies deriving from the *Survey:* Eduard Kolb, *Phonological Atlas of the Northern Region* (Bern, Switzerland, 1966), and Harold Orton and Nathalia Wright, *A Word Geography of England* (London, 1974).
11. See an interesting address by the philologist most responsible for Scottish lexicography in the twentieth century, Sir William Craigie, "The Present State of the Scottish Tongue," in *The Scottish Tongue* (London, 1924), pp. 1-46. The survival of the dialect now appears unlikely. Cf. David Murison, "The Scots Tongue—the Folk-Speech," *Folklore,* 75 (1964), 37-47.
12. See Angus McIntosh, *An Introduction to a Survey of Scottish Dialects* (Edinburgh, 19521 and T.Y Mather and H H Sneitel eds *The Linmiistic Atlas of Scotland* London
13. See Alan Bliss, *Spoken English in Ireland 1600-1740* (Dublin, 1979), pp. 312-26, and Michael V.Barry, "The English Language in Ireland," in *English as a World Language,* ed. R.W.Bailey and M.Görlach (Ann Arbor, MI, 1982), pp. 92-93.
14. *English as We Speak It in Ireland* (Dublin, 1910), p. 96.
15. An illuminating treatment of Hiberno-English syntax, from which the following examples are taken, is A. Lunny, "Linguistic Interaction: English and Irish in Ballyvourney, West Cork," in *Aspects of English Dialects in Ireland, 1,* ed. Michael V.Barry (Belfast, 1981), pp. 118-41. See also P.L.Henry, *An Anglo-Irish Dialect of North Roscommon* (Dublin, 1957).

16. E.E.Morris, *Austral English: A Dictionary of Australasian Words, Phrases and Usages* (London, 1898), p. xii.

17. Of course, this has not prevented *kangaroo* from gaining general currency.

18. For important differences with Cockney, see A.G.Mitchell, *The Pronunciation of English in Australia*, rev. ed. with Arthur Delbridge (Sydney, 1965), pp. 7-8.

19. See A.G.Mitchell and Arthur Delbridge, *The Speech of Australian Adolescents: A Survey* (Sydney, 1965), pp. 37, 83.

20. William Branford, "Aardvark to Zwarthout: Social and Historical Aspects of the South African English Vocabulary," in *Seven Studies in English*, ed. Gildas Roberts (Cape Town and London, 1971), p. 134.

21. See also Charles Pettman, *Africanderisms: A Glossary of South African Colloquial Words and Phrases and Place and Other Names* (London, 1913), and W.S.Mackie, "Afrikanerisms," in *Standard Encydopedia of South Africa*, 1 (Cape Town, 1970), 188.

22. See David Hopwood, *South African English Pronunciation* (Cape Town and Johannesburg, 1928), and L.W.Lanham, *The Pronunciation of South African English* (Cape Town, 1967).

23. Cf. the contrasting views in M.A.K. Halliday, Angus McIntosh, and Peter Strevens, *The Linguistic Sciences and Language Teaching* (London, 1964), pp. 203-4 et passim; C.H.Prator, "The British Heresy in TEFL," in *Language Problems of Developing Nations*, ed. Joshua A. Fishman *et al.* (New York, 1968), pp. 459-76; J.H.Sledd, "Un-American English Reconsidered," *American Speech*, 48 (1973), 46-53; and K.A.Sey, *Ghanaian English: An Exploratory Survey* (London, 1973).

24. J.C.Wells, *Accents of English* (3 vols., Cambridge, UK, 1982), III, 637.

25. This example and several other examples in this section are from Loreto Todd, "The English Language in West Africa," in Bailey and Görlach, pp. 281-305.

26. See Ayo bangbose, *Language and Society in Nigeria* (Stanford, 1973), pp. 106-7.

27. Ian F.Hancock and Rachel Angogo, "English in East Africa," in Bailey and Görlach, p. 316.

28. *Kanthapura* (1938; reprinted New York, 1963), p. vii. Cf. Noah Webster on American English.

29. Braj B.Kachru, "South Asian English," in Bailey and Görlach, p. 359.
30. Further examples are given in Braj B.Kachru, "The *Indianness* in Indian English," *Word,* 21 (1965), 391-410.
31. Margot Cohen, "Malaysian Students Struggle to Cope with Language Shift," *Chronicle of Higher Education* (June 8, 1988), p. A29.
32. Ian Buruma, "Singapore," *New York Times Magazine* (June 12, 1988), p. 58.
33. John Platt and Heidi Weber, *English in Singapore and Malaysia: Status, Features, Functions* (Kuala Lumpur, Malaysia, 1980), pp. 63-64.
34. See John Holm, "The Spread of English in the Caribbean Area," in *Focus on the Caribbean,* ed. Manfred Görlach and J.A.Holm (Amsterdam, 1986), pp. 1-22.
35. See F.G.Cassidy, *Jamaica Talk: Three Hundred Years of the English Language in Jamaica,* (2nd ed., London, 1971), p. 146. For other examples cited here, see also F.G.Cassidy, "Etymology in Caribbean Creoles," in Görlach and Holm, pp. 133-39.
36. See Ian Hancock, "A Preliminary Classification of the Anglophone Atlantic Creoles with Syntactic Data from Thirty-three Representative Dialects," in *Pidgin and Creole Languages: Essays in Memory of John E.Reinecke,* ed. Glenn G.Gilbert (Honolulu, 1987), pp. 264-333.
37. See H.J.Warkentyne, "Contemporary Canadian English: A Report of the Survey of Canadian English," *American Speech,* 46 (1971; pub. 1975), 193-99.
38. Walter S.Avis *et al., Dictionary of Canadianisms on Historical Principles* (Toronto, 1967).
39. Raven I.McDavid, Jr., "Canadian English," *American Speech,* 46 (1971), 287.
40. A creole, like a pidgin, is based on two or more languages, but unlike a pidgin it is learned as a native language, and it contains fuller syntax and vocabulary.
41. For helpful surveys of pidgins and creoles, see Ian F. Hancock, "Appendix: Repertory of Pidgin and Creole Languages," in *Pidgin and Creole Linguistics,* ed. Albert Valdman (Bloomington, IN, 1977), pp. 362-91; and John Holm, *Pidgins and Creoles,* 2 vols. (Cambridge, UK, 1988-1989), especially, for English-based creoles, 11.405-551.
42. See Suzanne Romaine, *Pidgin and Creole Languages* (London, 1988), pp. 26-36.

43. These examples are from Derek Bickerton, "Creole Languages," *Scientific American* (July 1983); rpt. in *Language. Writing and the Computer* (New York, 1986), pp. 24-30.

44. On the theory underlying the creole continuum, see Derek Bickerton, *Dynamics of a Creole System* (Cambridge, UK, 1975).

45. Among many writings by Chomsky on this subject, see *Knowledge of Language: Its Nature, Origin, and Use* (New York, 1986).

46. Languageand Species (Chicago, 1990).

47. The case against spelling reform is stated by Sir William Craigie, *Problems of Spelling Reform* (Oxford, 1944; *S.P.E. Tract No. 63).* More recently it has been argued that predictable morphophonemic alternations (e.g., *divine~divinity)* make conventional orthography "a near optimal system for the lexical representation of English words." See Noam Chomsky and Morris Halle, *The Sound Pattern of English* (New York, 1968), p. 49.

48. *Lectures,* I, 657.

49. Robert Graves, *Impenetrability, or The Proper Habit of English* (London, 1926), pp. 30-31. Cf. Basil de Selincourt: "The best and most English instinct is still that of resistance to change, and above all to any plan or method of change, any committee or academy or association to school and enlighten us." *(Pomona, or The Future of English,* London, n.d., p. 69.)

50. See J.H.G.Grattan, "On Anglo-American Cultivation of Standard English," *Review of English Studies,* 3 (1927), 430-41, and Kemp Malone, "The International Council for English," *American Speech,* 3 (1928), 261-75. Nothing came of the proposal.

51. See Ann Bodine, "Androcentrism in Prescriptive Grammar: Singular 'they', Sex-indefinite 'he', and 'he or she,'"*Language in Society,* 4 (1975), 129-46.

Bibliography

Arnold, J. (ed) 1999. *Affect in Language Learning.* Cambridge: CUP *An interesting and somewhat controversial collection of papers on the affective and humanistic dimensions of language learning. Contributors include Earl Stevick, Rebecca Oxford, Gertrude Moskowitz, Adrian Underhill, and Herbert Puchta (Rod)*

Barks, D. & Watts, P. (2001). In D. Belcher & A. Hirvela (Eds.), *Linking literacies: Perspectives on L2 reading-writing connections* (pp. 246-267). Ann Arbor: The University of Michigan Press.

Bee, F. and R. Bee, 1998. *Facilitation Skills.* London: Institute of Personnel and development.

Bentley, T. 1994. *Facilitation: Providing opportunities for learning.* Maidenhead: McGraw-Hill.

Biber, D., Leech, G. , Johansson, S. Conrad, S. & Finegan, E. (2000) *Longman Grammar of Spoken and Written English.* Longman Publications Group.

Bloch, J. (2001). Plagiarism and the ESL student: From printed to electronic text. In

Bloch, J., & Chi, L. (1995). A comparison of the use of citations in Chinese and English

Bohm, D. 1996. *On Dialogue.* London: Routledge.

Brinton, D., Frodesen, J., Holten, C, Jensen, L. & Repath-Martos, L (1997/ *Insights: A content-based approach to academic preparation.* White Plains, NY: Longman.

Byrd, P. & Reid, J. (1998). *Grammar in the composition classroom: Essays on teaching ESL for college bound students.* Boston: Heinle & Heinle.

Campbell, C. (1990). Writing with others'words: Using background reading text in academic compositions. In B. Kroll (Ed.), *Second language writing: Research insights for the classroom* (pp. 211-30). Cambridge, UK: Cambridge University Press.

Carter, M. & M. McCarthy. (2006).*Cambridge Grammar of English: A Comprehensive Guide. Spoken and Written Grammar and Usage.* New York: Cambridge University Press.

Carter, R. (1987). *Vocabulary: Applied linguistics perspectives.* London: Allen and Unwin.

Casanave, C.P. (2004). *Controversies in second language writing: Dilemmas and Decisions in Research and Instruction.* Ann Arbor: The University of Michigan Press.

Celce-Murcia, M. & Larsen-Freeman, D. (1999). *The grammar book: An ESL/EFL teacher's course,* 2nd Ed. Boston: Heinle & Heinle.

Celce-Murcia, M. & Olshtain, E. (2000). *Discourse and context in language teaching: A guide for language teachers.* Cambridge: Cambridge University Press.

Chambers, R. 2004. *Participatory workshops: a sourcebook of 21 sets of ideas and activities.* London: Earthscan.

Collins COBUILD Advanced Learner's English Dictionary of American English with interactive CD ROM. (2007). Boston: Thomson Heinle.

combining: A rhetorical perspective (pp. 334-50). Carbondale: Southern Illinois University Press.

Connors, R. (2000). The erasure of the sentence. *College Composition and Communication 2:* 96-128.

Currie, P. (1998). Staying out of trouble: Apparent plagiarism and academic survival. *Journal of Second Language Writing* 7: 1-18.

D. Belcher & A. Hirvela (Eds.), *Linking literacies: Perspectives on L2 reading-writing connections* (pp. 209-228). Ann Arbor: The University of Michigan Press.

De Carrico, J. (2005). Lexical phrases and discourse contexts: Questions of form and

DeCarrico, J. (2001). Vocabulary learning and teaching. In M. Celce-Murcia (Ed.), *Teaching English as a second or foreign language,* 3rd Ed. (pp. 285-299). Boston: Heinle & Heinle.

Dillon, J.T. 1988. *Questioning and Teaching.* London: Croom Helm.

Dillon, J.T. 1994. *Using Discussion in Classrooms.* Buckingham: Open University Press.

document to see typical words that combine with it (collocations). Look up a word's meanings in the Oxford Advanced Learner's Dictionary by clicking on the word.

Dörnyei, Z. & Murphey, T. 2003. *Group Dynamics in the Language Classroom.* Cambridge: Cambridge University Press

Doughty, C. & Williams, J. (1998). *Focus on form in classroom second language acquisition.* Cambridge: Cambridge University Press.

Douglas, T. 1995. *Survival in Groups.* Buckingham: Open University Press.

Ellis, R. (1998). Teaching and research: Options in grammar teaching. *TESOL Quarterly* I32: 39-60.

Ferris, D.R. (2005). *Treatment of error in second language student writing.* Ann Arbor: The University of Michigan Press.

Forsyth, Donelson R. 1999 *Group dynamics.* Belmont Ca.: Brooks/Cole. *Very good section on group formation and group stages. (Meg)*

Francis, E. (ed) 1986. *Learning to discuss.* Edinburgh: Scottish Curriculum Development Service.

Frodesen, J. & Eyring, J. (2007). *Grammar Dimensions, Form, Meaning and Use, Book 4,* 4th Ed.. Boston: Thomson Heinle.

Frodesen, J. & Holten, C. (2003). Grammar in the ESL writing class. In B. Kroll (Ed.) *Exploring the dynamics of second language writing* (pp. 141-161). Cambridge: Cambridge University Press.

Frodesen, J. (2001). Grammar in writing. In M. Celce-Murcia (Ed.), *Teaching English as a second or foreign language,* 3rd Ed. (pp. 233-248). Boston: Heinle & Heinle.

function. In J. Frodesen & C. Holten (Eds.) *The power of context in language teaching and learning* (pp. 107-114.). Boston: Heinle & Heinle.

Graf, G. & Birkenstein, C. (2006). *They say: I say: The moves that matter in academic writing.* New York: W. W. Norton and Company.

Hadfield, J. 1992. *Classroom Dynamics.* Oxford: OUP.

Haswell, R.H. (2005). NCTE/CCCC's recent war on scholarship. *Written Communication,* 22.2: 198-223.

Hillocks Jr., G. (1986). *Research on written composition: New directions for teaching.* Urbana: NCTE.

Hillocks Jr., G. (2005). At last: The focus on form vs. content in teaching writing. *Research in the Teaching of English* 40 (2): 238-248.

Hinkel, E. (2004). *Teaching academic ESL Writing: Practical techniques in vocabulary and grammar.* Mahwah, NJ: Lawrence Erlbaum Associates.

Hinkel, E. & Fotos., S. (Eds.). (2002). *New perspectives on grammar teaching in second language classrooms.* Mahwah, NJ: Lawrence Erlbaum.

Hinkel, E. (2002a). *Second language writers' text: Linguistic and rhetorical features.* Mahwah, NJ: Lawrence Erlbaum Associates.

Hinkel, E. (2002b). Grammar teaching in writing classes: Tenses and cohesion. In E. Hinkel & S. Fotos (Eds.). (2002). *New perspectives on grammar teaching in second language classrooms* (pp. 181-198. Mahwah, NJ: Lawrence Erlbaum.

Hogan, C. 2002. *Understanding Facilitation: Theory and Principle.* 2nd edition. London: Kogan Page.

Hogan, C. 2003 *Practical facilitation: A tool kit of techniques.* London.

Holten, C. & Mikesell, L. (forthcoming). Using discourse-based strategies to address the lexico-grammatical development of generation 1.5 ESL writers. *CATESOL Journal* special issue on grammar teaching: 129-152.

Holten, C. (2002). Charting new territory: Creating an interdepartmental course for generation 1.5 writers. *CATESOL Journal* 14.1: 173-189.

Holten, C. and Marasco, J. (1998). *Looking ahead: Mastering academic writing: Book 4:* J. Reid and P. Byrd, Series Editors. Boston: Heinle & Heinle.

Howard, R.M. (1995). Plagiarisms, authorships and the academic death penalty. *College English 57(7):* 788-806.

Hughes, R. and McCarthy, M. (1998). From sentence to discourse: Discourse grammar and English language teaching. TESOL Quarterly 32.2: 263-287.

Hunter, D., Bailey, A. Taylor, B. 1992. *The Zen of Groups. A Handbook for People Meeting with a Purpose.* Aldershot: Gower Publishing

Hyland, K. & Milton, H. (1997). Qualification and certainty in L1 and L2 students'writing. *Journal of Second Language Writing* 6(2): 183-205.

Hyland, K. (2000). *Disciplinary discourses: Social interactions in academic writing.* London: Longman Publishing.

Hyland, K. (2005). Stance and engagement: A model of interaction in academic discourse. *Discourse Studies* 7(2): 173-192.

Hyland, K. and Tse, P. (2005). Hooking the reader: A corpus study of evaluative *that* in abstracts. *English for Specific Purposes* 24:123-139.

Jabbour, G. (2001). Lexis and grammar in second language reading and writing. In D. Belcher & A. Hirvela (Eds.), *Linking literacies: Perspectives on L2 reading-writing connections* (pp. 291-308). Ann Arbor: The University of Michigan Press.

Jaques, D. 1992. *Learning in Groups.* London: Kogan Page.

Johns, A. (Ed.) (2002). *Genre in the classroom.* Mahwah, NJ: Lawrence Erlbaum. Halliday, M.A.K, & Hasan, R. (1976). *Cohesion in English.* London: Longman.

Johns, A.M. (1985). Summary protocols of "underprepared" and "adept" university students: Replications and distortions of the original. *Language Learning* 35: 495-517.

Johns, A.M., & Mayes, P. (1990). An analysis of summary protocols of university ESL students. *Applied Linguistics* 11: 253-271.

Johnson, K.E. (1992). Cognitive strategies and second language writers: A re-evaluation of sentence combining. *Journal of Second Language Writing* 1.1: 61-75.

Keck, C. (2006). The use of paraphrase in summary writing: A comparison of L1 and L2 writers. *Journal of Second Language Writing,* 15.4: 261-278.

Kogan Page.

Kolln, M. (2006). Rhetorical Grammar: Grammatical Choices, Rhetorical Effects. New York: Longman.

Lane, J. & Lange, E. (1999). *Writing Clearly: An Editing Guide,* 2nd Ed. Boston: Heinle & Heinle.

Larsen-Freeman, D. (2001). Teaching grammar. In M. Celce-Murcia (Ed.), *Teaching English as a second or foreign language,* 3rd Ed. (pp. 251-266). Boston: Heinle & Heinle.

Larsen-Freeman, D. (2003). *From Grammar to Grammaring.* Boston: Heinle & Heinle.

Le Baron, M. 2003. Bridging Cultural Conflicts: A New Approach for a Changing World. *San Francisco: Jossey Bass*

Leki, I., Carson, J. (1997). "Completely different worlds": EAP and the writing experiences of ESL students in university courses. *TESOL Quarterly 31*: 39-69.

Longman Language Activator: 2e. (2001). Essex: Longman.

Luft, J. 1984. *Group Processes: an introduction to group dynamics.* Pal Alto, California: Mayfield.

MacDonald, S. P. (2007). The erasure of language. *College Composition and Communication,* 58 (4): 585-625.

Martin, J.R. (2002). Meaning beyond the clause: SFL perspectives. *Annual Review of Applied Linguistics* 22: 52-74.

meaning making. In M.J. Schleppegrell & M.C. Columbi (Eds.), *Developing advanced literacy in first and second languages: Meaning with* power(pp. 119-142). Mahwah, NJ: Lawrence Erlbaum Associates.

Micciche, L.R. (2004). Making a case for rhetorical grammar. *College Composition and Communication* 55 (4): 567-93.

Michaelsen, L. K., A. Bauman Knight, &, L. Dee Fink (eds) 2004 *Team-Based Learning: A Transformative Use of Small Groups in College Teaching.* Sterling, Va.: Stylus Publishing

Michigan Press.

Miller, T. (Ed.) (1997). *Functional Approaches to Written Text: Classroom Applications.* Washington, D.C.: USIA.

Morenberg, M., & Sommers, J. with Daiker, D. and Kerek, A. (2003). *The writer's options: Lessons in style and arrangement.* New York: Longman.

Morgan, N. and J. Saxton 1991. *Teaching, Questioning and Learning.* London: Routledge.

Myers, S. (2003). Re-Membering the sentence. *College Composition and Communication* 54 (4): 610-628.

Nation, I.S.P. (2001). *Learning Vocabulary in Another Language.* Cambridge: Cambridge University Press.

Oxford Collocations Dictionary for Students of English (2002). New York: Oxford UP.

Oxford Phrasebuilder Genie (2003) New York: Oxford UP. Software: Point at a word in a

Pecorari, D. (2003). Good and original: Plagiarism and patchwriting in academic second language writing. *Journal of Second Language Writing* 12: 317-345.

Pecorari, D. (2004). Plagiarism and international students: How the English-speaking

Pennycook, A. (1996). Borrowing others'words: Text, ownership, memory, and plagiarism. *TESOL Quarterly* 30: 210-230.

Porter, P. & vanDommelen, D. (2005) *Read, write, edit: Grammar for college writers.* Boston: Houghton Mifflin Company.

Porter, P. (2005). Focusing on form: Seven habits of highly skillful teachers. In J. Frodesen & C. Holten (Eds.) *The power of context in language teaching and learning* (pp. 187-198). Boston: Heinle & Heinle.

Reid, J. (2001). Advanced EAP writing and curriculum design: What do we need to know? In T. Silva & P.K. Matsuda (Eds.), *On second language writing* (pp. 143-156). Mahwah, NJ: Lawrence Erlbaum Associates.

Reynolds, M. 1994. *Groupwork in Education and Training.* London: Kogan Page.

Richardson, V. (ed.). 2003 *Constructivist Teacher Education: Building a World of New Understandings.* London. Routledge Falmer.

Santos, T. (2005). The role of grammar in TESL and composition. In J. Frodesen & C. Holten (Eds.) *The power of context in language teaching and learning* (pp. 153-162). Boston: Heinle & Heinle.

Scannell, E. E. & J.W. Newstrom 1998 *Games Trainers Play* Columbus, Ohio: McGraw-Hill

Scarcella, R. (1996). Secondary education in California and second language research: Instructing ESL students in the 1990s. *CATESOL Journal 9* (1): 129-152.

Schleppegrell, M. J. (2004). *The language of schooling.* Mahwah, NJ: Lawrence Erlbaum Associates.

Schleppegrell, M. J. (2007). The meaning in grammar. *Research in the Teaching of English* 42 (1): 121-128.

Schleppegrell, M.J. & Columbi, M.C. (Eds.). (2002). *Developing advanced literacy in first and second languages: Meaning with power.* Mahwah, NJ: Lawrence Erlbaum Associates.

Schleppegrell, M.J. (2002). Challenges of the science register for ESL students: Errors and

Shaughnessy, M. (1977). *Errors and Expectations: A Guide for Teachers of Basic Writing.* New York: Oxford University Press.

Sherrard, C. (1986). Summary writing: A topographical study. *Written Communication* 3: 324-343.

Shi, L. (2004). Textual borrowing in second-language writing. *Written Communication 21(2):* 171-200.

Smith, W. (2005). What can pragmatics tell us about developing writers? In J. Frodesen & C. Holten (Eds.) *The power of context in language teaching and learning* (pp. 163-172). Boston: Heinle & Heinle.

Stanfield, B.R. (ed) 2001. The Art of Focused Conversation: 100 Ways to Access Group Wisdom in the Workplace. *Gabriola Island, BC, Canada: New Society Publishers.*

Stangor, C. 2004. *Social Groups in Action and Interaction* New York: Psychology Press.

Steer, J. & Carlisi, K. (1998). *The advanced grammar book.* 2nd Ed. Boston: Heinle & Heinle.

Strong, W. (1973). How sentence combining works. In Daiker et al (Eds.).

Swales, J. (1990). *Genre analysis: English in academic and research settings.* Cambridge: Cambridge University Press.

Swales, J. M. & Feak, C. B. (2004). *Academic writing for graduate students: Essential tasks and skills.* Ann Arbor: University of Michigan Press.

Taylor, K.K. (1984). The different summary skills of inexperienced and professional writers. *Journal of Reading* 27: 691-699.

university responds. In D. Belcher & A. Hirvela (Eds.), *Linking literacies: Perspectives on L2 reading-writing connections* (pp. 229-245). Ann Arbor: The University of Michigan Press.

Vella, J. 2002. *Learning to Listen, Learning to Teach: The power of dialogue in educating adults* San Francisco: Jossey Bass

Vennix, J.A.M. 1996. *Group Model Building* San Francisco: Wiley

Webne-Behrman, H. 1998. *The Practice of Facilitation.* Westport ,CT: Quorum Books

Wells, G. (2003) *Dialogic inquiry: toward a sociocultural practice and theory of education.* Cambridge: CUP.

Wheelan, S. A. 1990. *Facilitating Training Groups. A Guide to Leadership and Verbal Intervention Skills* Westport, CT. Praeger Publishers.

Williams, J. (2002). *Ten lessons in clarity and grace.* 7th ed. New York: Longman.

Williams, M. & Burden, R. 1997. *Psychology for language teachers.* Cambridge: Cambridge University Press.

Yamada, K. (2003). What prevents ESL/EFL writers from avoiding plagiarism? Analyses of 10 North-American college websites. *System* 31: 247-258.

Zwier, L. & Bennet, G. (2006). *Teaching a lexis-based academic writing course.* Ann Arbor: University of Michigan Press.